HOW THE WORD IS PASSED

A Reckoning with the History of Slavery Across America

CLINT SMITH

LITTLE, BROWN AND COMPANY

LARGE PRINT EDITION

Little, Brown and Company
Hachette Book Group
1290 Avenue of the Americas, New York, NY 10104
littlebrown.com

First Edition: June 2021

Little, Brown and Company is a division of Hachette Book Group, Inc. The Little, Brown name and logo are trademarks of Hachette Book Group, Inc.

The publisher is not responsible for websites (or their content) that are not owned by the publisher.

The Hachette Speakers Bureau provides a wide range of authors for speaking events. To find out more, go to hachettespeakersbureau.com or call (866) 376-6591.

ISBN 978-0-316-49293-5 (hardcover) / 978-0-316-26947-6 (signed edition) / 978-0-316-27874-4 (large print)
LCCN 2020949144

Printing 1, 2021

LSC-C

Printed in the United States of America

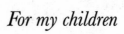
For my children

Our past was slavery. We cannot recur to it with any sense of complacency or composure. The history of it is a record of stripes, a revelation of agony. It is written in characters of blood. Its breath is a sigh, its voice a groan, and we turn from it with a shudder. The duty of to-day is to meet the questions that confront us with intelligence and courage.

—Frederick Douglass,
"The Nation's Problem"

You know, they straightened out the Mississippi River in places, to make room for houses and livable acreage. Occasionally the river floods these places. "Floods" is the word they use, but in fact it is not flooding; it is remembering. Remembering where it used to be.

—Toni Morrison,
"The Site of Memory"

CONTENTS

Contents

AUTHOR'S NOTE

The visits I describe in this book took place between October 2017 and February 2020. I visited some places on multiple occasions, others only once. All quotations were captured with a digital recorder. Some names have been changed to protect the privacy of individuals.

I would like to note that while this book is focused on the places where the story of slavery in America lives on, the land upon which many of these historical sites sit belonged to Indigenous communities before it belonged to anyone else. Of the eight US-based sites I visited for this book, New Orleans sits on Chitimacha and Choctaw land; Monticello sits on Monacan land; the Whitney Plantation sits on Choctaw land; Angola prison sits on Choctaw land; Blandford Cemetery sits on Appomattoc and Nottoway land; Galveston, Texas, sits on Akokisa, Karankawa, and Atakapa land; New York City sits on Munsee Lenape land; the National Museum

Author's Note

of African American History and Culture sits on Nacotchtank (Anacostan) and Piscataway land. It should be noted that Native territories often overlapped and had malleable borders that shifted over time. This list is not definitive but is one attempt to acknowledge those who first traversed this land, and to do so as accurately as possible.

HOW THE WORD IS PASSED

"The whole city is a memorial to slavery"

PROLOGUE

THE SKY ABOVE THE MISSISSIPPI River stretched out like a song. The river was still in the windless afternoon, its water a yellowish-brown from the sediment it carried across thousands of miles of farmland, cities, and suburbs on its way south. At dusk, the lights of the Crescent City Connection, a pair of steel cantilever bridges that cross the river and connect the east and west banks of New Orleans, flickered on. Luminous bulbs ornamented the bridges' steel beams like a congregation of fireflies settling onto the backs of two massive, unbothered creatures. A tugboat made its way downriver, pulling an enormous ship in its wake. The sounds of the French Quarter, just behind me, pulsed through the brick sidewalk underfoot. A pop-up brass band blared into the early-evening air, its trumpets, tubas, and trombones commingling with the delight of a congregating crowd; a young man drummed on a pair of upturned plastic buckets, the drumsticks in his hands moving with speed and dexterity; people gathered for photos along the river's edge, hoping to capture an image of themselves surrounded by a recognizable piece of quintessential New Orleans iconography.

After the transatlantic slave trade was outlawed in 1808, about a million people were transported from the upper South to the lower South. More than one hundred thousand of them were brought down the Mississippi River and sold in New Orleans.

Leon A. Waters came and stood next to me on the riverfront, hands in pockets, lips compressed, overlooking the Mississippi's slow bend between the two shores of the city. I had been introduced to Waters by a group of young Black activists in New Orleans who were part of the organization Take 'Em Down NOLA, whose self-espoused mission is "the removal of ALL symbols of white supremacy in New Orleans as a part of a broader push for racial & economic justice." Waters has served as a mentor to many members of the group—they see him as an elder statesman of their movement and credit him for being a central part of their political education.

Waters—in his late sixties with a greying mustache sitting over his lips—wore a black sports coat over a grey-and-white-striped shirt with the top button undone. A navy-blue tie hung loosely below his unfastened collar and swung over the waistband of his faded blue jeans. A pair of thin-framed, rectangular-shaped glasses sat high on the bridge of his nose, the left lens with a slight smudge in its bottom corner. His voice was low and un-varying in its tone. Waters might be mistaken for surly, but his disposition is simply a reflection of the seriousness with which he takes the subject matter he often is discussing, the subject of slavery.

We were standing in front of a plaque, recently put up by the New Orleans Committee to Erect Markers on the Slave Trade, outlining Louisiana's relationship to the transatlantic slave trade. "It's doing its job," Waters said of the plaque. "All through the day people come in, they stop, they read, take pictures... It's another way of educating people to this."

In recent years, markers like this began to go up throughout the city, each documenting a specific area's relationship to enslavement—part of a broader reckoning. After years of Black people being killed by police and having their deaths broadcast in videos streamed across the world, after a white supremacist went into a Black church in Charleston, South Carolina, and killed nine people as they prayed, after neo-Nazis marched in Charlottesville, Virginia, to protect a Confederate statue and reclaim a history born of a lie, after George Floyd was killed by a police officer's knee on his neck, cities across the country have begun to more fully reckon with the history that made such moments possible—a history that many had previously been unwilling to acknowledge. Waters, who identifies as a local historian and revolutionary, was not new to this. He and others like him have, for years, been working to illuminate the city's legacy—and by extension the country's legacy—of oppression.

Only recently, after decades of pushing by activists, amid the larger groundswell of national pressure, have city officials begun to listen, or perhaps feel like they finally have the political capital to act. In 2017, New Orleans removed four statues and monuments that, it had determined, paid tribute to the legacy of white supremacy. The city removed memorials to Robert E. Lee, the general who led the Confederacy's most successful army during the Civil War, a slaveholder; Jefferson Davis, the first and only president of the Confederacy, a slaveholder; P. G. T. Beauregard, a general in the Confederate Army who ordered the first shots of the Civil War, a slaveholder; and a monument dedicated to the Battle of Liberty Place, an 1874 insurrection in which white supremacists attempted to overthrow the integrated Reconstruction-era state government of Louisiana. These monuments are gone now, but at least a hundred streets, statues, parks, and schools named after Confederate figures, slaveholders, and defenders of slavery remain. On a cool February afternoon, Waters, the founder of Hidden History Tours of New Orleans, promised to show me where some of these vestiges of the past remain.

Waters drove me past two schools named after John McDonogh, a wealthy slave-owning merchant after whom dozens of schools, filled largely with Black children, were named until the 1990s; we drove past shops and restaurants and hotels where there once had been the offices, showrooms, and slave pens of more than a dozen slave-trading firms that made New Orleans the largest slave market in antebellum America—like the Omni Royal Orleans Hotel, built on the site of the St. Louis Hotel, where men, women, and children were bought, sold, and separated from one another; we drove past Jackson Square, in the heart of the tourist-filled French Quarter, where rebellious enslaved people were executed.

Even the street on which Waters dropped me off at the end of our tour, where my parents now live, is named after Bernard de Marigny, a man who owned more than 150 enslaved people over the course of his lifetime. The echo of enslavement is everywhere. It is in the levees, originally built by enslaved labor. It is in the detailed architecture of some of the city's oldest buildings, sculpted by enslaved hands. It is in the roads, first paved by enslaved people. As historian Walter Johnson has said about New Orleans, "The whole city is a memorial to slavery."

New Orleans is my home. It is where I was born and raised. It is a part of me in ways I continue to discover. But I came to realize that I knew relatively little about my hometown's relationship to the centuries of bondage rooted in the city's soft earth, in the statues I had walked past daily, the names of the streets I had lived on, the schools I had attended, and the buildings that had once been nothing more to me than the remnants of colonial architecture. It was all right in front of me, even when I didn't know to look for it.

It was in May 2017—after the statue of Robert E. Lee near downtown New Orleans had been taken down from its sixty-foot pedestal—that I became obsessed with how slavery is remembered and reckoned with, with teaching myself all of the things I wish someone had taught me long ago. Our country is in a moment, at an inflection point, in which there is a willingness to more fully grapple with the legacy of slavery and how it shaped the world we live in today. But it seems that the more purposefully some places have attempted to tell the truth about their proximity to slavery and its aftermath, the more staunchly other places have refused. I wanted to visit some of these places—those telling the truth, those running from it, and those doing something in between—in order to understand this reckoning.

In *How the Word Is Passed* I travel to eight places in the United States as well as one abroad to understand how each reckons with its relationship to the history of American slavery. I visit a mix of plantations, prisons, cemeteries, museums, memorials, houses, historical landmarks, and cities. The majority of these sites are in the South, as this is where slavery was most saturated over the course of its nearly two-hundred-fifty-year existence on these shores, but I also travel to New York City and Dakar, Senegal. Each chapter is a portrait of a place but also of the people in that place—those who live there, work there, and are the descendants of the land and of the families who once lived on it. They are people who have tasked themselves with telling the story of that place outside traditional classrooms and beyond the pages of textbooks. They are, formally or informally, public historians who carry with them a piece of this country's collective memory. They have dedicated their lives to sharing this history with others. And for this book, many of them have generously shared that history with me.

"There's a difference between history and nostalgia"

MONTICELLO PLANTATION

HEADING OUT FROM MY HOME in Washington, DC, in the morning, I drove against traffic, moving from the new condos of an increasingly gentrifying DC, through the single-family-home suburban land-scape of Northern Virginia, and into the vast green expanse surrounding I-95 South. As I drove to Monticello, I observed how Virginia is largely a tale of two states. Northern Virginia, those incorporated municipalities that serve as suburbs to the District of Columbia, has always felt somewhat distant from "the South" in the ways I grew up understanding it. But beyond the suburbs, once I started driving past the diners and gas stations with Dixie flags hanging in their windows, I was reminded that this state was once the bastion of the Confederacy.

As I made my way down the highway, finding myself on cruise control—both in the car and in my mind—I saw a sign in my peripheral vision indicating the entrance to a plantation. Assuming it to be Monticello, I put my blinker on and began to turn, only to jerk the car back onto the highway when I realized this was not Thomas Jefferson's plantation but that of James Madison—Jefferson's dear friend, confidant, fellow Virginian, and successor to his presidency.

Madison's Montpelier plantation, less than thirty miles northeast of Jefferson's, is almost a prelude to Monticello. Not simply as a result of their relative proximity, but because the two men share similarly contradictory relationships to the aspirational documents they ushered into existence while enslaved people worked on their plantations. The Madison family held more than three hundred enslaved people over the course of their time on that property. Both of the men inscribed words that promoted equality and freedom in the founding documents of the United States while owning other human beings. Both men built a nation while making possible the plunder of millions of people. What they gave our country, and all they stole from it, must be understood together. I did not turn into Montpelier, but there was something about driving past it on the way to Monticello that reminded me that Jefferson was not singular in his moral inconsistencies; rather he was one of the founding fathers who fought for their own freedom while keeping their boots on the necks of hundreds of others.

How the Word Is Passed

Within a few miles of Monticello, the highway transitions into a one-way road lined with white pines and hemlocks. I pulled into the dirt parking lot and made my way up the concrete stairs to see if tour tickets were still available.

One of the first things I noticed about Monticello was how the vast majority of its visitors seemed to be white. It's not so much unexpected as it is markedly conspicuous, to see a plantation that has had its ratios reversed. There were a few tourist groups from different Asian countries, but they were the small exception. Two hundred years ago Monticello, like most plantations, was populated largely by the enslaved descendants of Africans, while white laborers and Jefferson's family were a much smaller proportion of its inhabitants. At any given time at Monticello there were approximately 130 enslaved people, far outnumbering Jefferson, his family, and the paid white workers.

I walked toward the stately mansion, which sat just a couple hundred feet ahead of me. Waves of heat rose from the dirt path, and mulberry trees spread themselves out across the land, creating intermittent pockets of cool respite for visitors. Underneath a lush sugar maple on one side of the house was a group of about a dozen people all sharing what city they had come from. The group ranged in age and geography, spanning generations and state borders.

"And what about you, sir?" the guide said as I scurried under the tree where the rest of the group was standing. I had chosen the tour that began ten minutes after I arrived, one that focused specifically on Jefferson's relationship to slavery.

"From DC," I said.

"Right down the road!" he responded, nodding his head and giving a smile that was as courteous as it was practiced.

Before I was able to gather myself and bring my full attention to the group, I was struck by what lay behind us, in the distance. The entire plantation sat at the top of a mountain ringed by a thick cascade of sundry trees, so tightly packed together that I could not tell where one began and the next ended. Behind the first string of trees were rolling hills that went off in every direction, as the silhouette of outlying mountains kissed the clouds resting over their peaks.

David Thorson, our guide, wore a blue-and-white-striped oxford shirt, short sleeved but a size too big, leaving his sleeves fluttering along his elbows when a light mountain breeze passed by. His crisply ironed khaki pants sat high on his waist, impressive creases moving down the front of his pant legs from his belt buckle to his shoes. David's peach face, reddened from all the hours spent standing in the sun, was clean-shaven and sunk gently into itself around his cheeks. Ridges and wrinkles made their way down his jawbone and onto his neck. He wore large, thick-rimmed glasses and a brown wide-brimmed hat that cast a slight shadow over his eyes. He spoke with a calm evenhandedness that invited people into discussion, like a professor.

I found out later that prior to becoming a tour guide at Monticello, David served for more than thirty years in the US Navy. He had no experience as a teacher and no exposure to anything resembling museum studies before taking his job as a guide. Both of his children had enrolled in the University of Virginia, and he and his wife had fallen in love with Charlottesville during their frequent visits over the years. They loved it so much that they decided to relocate after David retired from the military, even though his children had graduated from the university long before.

"I didn't want to sit around talking back to the TV set," he would tell me. "It gets you out where you are interacting with the public, with a broad international audience of people who have an interest in American history, an interest in Thomas Jefferson. So I was interested in sharing the story because I really do believe that you can't understand the United States without going back and understanding Jefferson."

While the shadow over David's eyes gave him a sense of mystery, when he began speaking to the tour group, there was nothing enigmatic about what he was saying. "Slavery's an institution. In Jefferson's lifetime it becomes a system. So what is this slave system? It is a system of exploitation, a system of inequality and exclusion, a system where people are owned as property and held down by physical and psychological force, a system being justified even by people who know slavery is morally wrong. By doing what? Denying the very humanity of those who are enslaved solely on the basis of the color of their skin."

People in the group began to murmur to one another, some with their hands over their mouths.

In just a few sentences, David had captured the essence of chattel slavery in a way that few of my own teachers ever had. It's not that this information was new, it's that I had not expected to hear it in *this* place, in this way, with this group of almost exclusively white visitors staring back at him.

David paused and then said, "There's a struggle going on here." He continued discussing how Jefferson's relationship to slavery was in plain sight because Jefferson maintained extensive records, the best known of which is his Farm Book. In these documents he kept track of the name, birth date, location, and sale of each person he held in bondage. He also kept track of the rations distributed to the enslaved. A typical week's worth of rations, said David, included "a pack of cornmeal, half a pound of meat, usually pork, occasionally half a dozen salted fish."

David discussed how Jefferson's records showed who was bought and sold over the course of decades. Jefferson sold, leased, and mortgaged enslaved people—often in an effort to pay off debts he owed, as well as to preserve his standard of living. (The people Jefferson sold while he was alive were mostly from Poplar Forest, his plantation in Bedford County, but also from Monticello and a smaller plantation in Goochland County called Elkhill.) Having enslaved workers, David explained, helped Jefferson maintain his lifestyle, by giving him the time and space to do what he cared about most: reading, writing, and hosting guests who came to visit.

"Jefferson also gave presents to his kids and grandkids," he said in a pivot. A moment of respite for those who, within just a few minutes, had begun to see their prior conceptions of Jefferson evaporate away. I felt disappointed, wanting David to continue exposing the parts of Jefferson's legacy that so frequently remain buried. This was the purpose of the tour, I thought: to excavate unsavory stories and wrestle with them, outwardly, honestly, without pause. But as soon as the thought came, David began the second half of his statement. "Those presents were human beings among the enslaved community."

Monticello Plantation

David knew what he was doing: the pedagogical equivalent of a crossover in basketball, lulling your opponent in one direction—inducing them into a momentary assurance that they know in which direction things are moving—before promptly switching hands right underneath their outstretched arms, leaving them frozen in place behind you as you drive to the basket.

David continued to refer to the enslaved Black people living on Monticello as "human beings." The decision to use "human" as the primary descriptor rather than "slave" was a small yet intentional move. He described the games the children played on warm Sunday afternoons (the only day of the week they did not have to work), the songs enslaved workers sang late into the evenings, the celebrations they took part in when someone was married. What reverberated throughout was the humanity of the enslaved people—their unceasing desire to live a full life, one that would not be defined simply by their forced labor.

David, and every other tour guide on the plantation, had to convey this sense of personhood with limited access to stories of the enslaved themselves. Historian Lucia Stanton, who worked as a historian at Monticello for over three decades, has wrestled with this. "To reconstruct the world of Monticello's African Americans is a challenging task. Only six images of men and women who lived there in slavery are known, and their own words are preserved in just four reminiscences and a handful of letters," she wrote. "Without the direct testimony of most of the African American residents of Monticello, we must try to hear their voices in the sparse records of Jefferson's Farm Book and the often biased accounts and letters dealing with labor management and through the inherited memories of those who left Monticello for lives of freedom."

Even with limited resources, David brought these stories to life. He finished his preamble to the tour: "You know, if you take it all together, those documents, like Jefferson's Farm Book, the memories from people who call Monticello home, and then the archeology, the story does begin to unfold. Despite the horror and oppression of slavery, those families who once lived here, what are they doing? They're trying to carve out some kind of a normal life. They are passing on tradition. They are giving their kids a chance to learn, and a chance to play. Maybe they're even trying to shield those children from the reality."

I looked around the lawn and imagined what Monticello would have been like two centuries ago. It belonged to Jefferson, yes, but it was not his home alone. It was the home of hundreds of enslaved people, including several large families. Some families were enslaved at Monticello for three generations or more. There were the

Gillettes, the Herns, the Fossetts, the Grangers, the Hubbards, and the Hemingses.

I scanned the landscape and imagined the Gillette children running between horses as the animals were groomed and fed, their adolescent voices swirling in the mountain air. I thought of David and Isabel Hern, how, despite marriage between enslaved people being illegal in Virginia, they were wed and remained so until Isabel's death. I imagined how they might have taken breaks from work under the shade of mulberry trees, whispering and laughing and holding each other in their arms. I thought of Joseph Fossett, who remained at Monticello while his wife was taken to Washington, DC, to train as a cook in the White House kitchen during Jefferson's presidency. How three of their children were born in the White House. How in 1806 Jefferson thought Joseph had run away, when he had in fact gone to see his wife in Washington.

I thought too of how in 1827, after Jefferson's death, Edward and Jane Gillette along with nine of their children and twelve of their grandchildren were sold. How David Hern along with his thirty-four surviving children and grandchildren were sold. How Joseph Fossett was freed in Jefferson's will, but his wife, Edith, and seven of their children were sold. How these families were separated to posthumously pay off Jefferson's debts.

I thought of all the love that had been present at this plantation, and I thought too of all the pain.

David waved his hand for us to follow him, and we walked from the area adjacent to Jefferson's home down Mulberry Row, where some of the enslaved families had lived. David found a cluster of benches under a grove of mulberry trees and motioned for us all to take a seat. As he positioned himself between us and the garden behind him, he told the story of an enslaved worker named Cary, a teenage boy who was part of the plantation's nail-making operation. The enslaved adolescent boys were directed to make close to one thousand nails a day, and they could be beaten if they fell too far behind.

One day Cary's friend Brown Colbert hid one of Cary's tools as a joke. Cary knew there was nothing funny about not being able to find his tools. Cary became so angry—an anger likely stemming from a profound sense of fear—that he hit his friend over the head with a hammer, temporarily putting him in a coma. Although Brown Colbert recovered, Jefferson found him-self in a difficult position. What was Jefferson to do with someone who had almost killed another member of the Monticello community? Should he be whipped? What did the community of other enslaved people want? What would Brown's family want? What were the implications of letting Cary stay? What were the implications of sending him away? Ultimately, Jefferson gave orders to sell Cary, as David put it, "to a place so far away he'll never be heard from again, so that it will appear to the other nail makers as though he had been put away by death." Soon after, slave traders came to Monticello and paid three hundred dollars for Cary. No one at Monticello would ever see or hear from him again.

While largely the same families remained on the Monticello plantation throughout their lives, Cary's story made me think of the larger practice of family separation during slavery, beyond Monticello. The splitting of families was not peripheral to the practice of slavery; it was central. In *Soul by Soul,* historian Walter Johnson writes, "Of the two thirds of a million interstate sales made by the traders in the decades before the Civil War, twenty-five percent involved the destruction of a first marriage and fifty percent destroyed a nuclear family—many of these separating children under the age of thirteen from their parents. Nearly all of them involved the dissolution of a previously existing community. And those are only the interstate sales." Historian Edward Bonekemper estimates that over the course of chattel slavery's existence about one million enslaved people were separated from their families.

Scenes and descriptions of family separation are

central to the narratives enslaved people wrote and published throughout the eighteenth and nineteenth centuries. One of the most harrowing comes from a man named Henry Bibb, in his *Narrative of the Life and Adventures of Henry Bibb, An American Slave, Written by Himself,* which was published in 1849 (four years after the publication of Frederick Douglass's book with a similar title). Bibb escaped slavery in Kentucky and fled to Canada, where he became a well-known abolitionist, starting a newspaper called *Voice of the Fugitive.*

In his book, there is an astonishing illustration of a man in a suit standing atop a table in the middle of a room, looking down at the people beneath him. In his left hand is a gavel, his fingers wrapped around its neck, and in his right hand is a Black infant, the small child dangling by the wrist. A woman—who looks to be the child's mother—is beneath the man, on her knees, arms outstretched in desperation, pleading for mercy from men who have sought to render themselves gods. There are several other white men in the frame, all wearing suits and brimmed hats. The one to whom the mother seems to be directing her pleas stands to the left of the table, with what looks like a cigarette between his lips. Another, at the edge of the frame, holds a whip above his head, its lash cracking in the air. Along the lower half of the frame are the enslaved. Some of them are in chains, and two of them are holding each other. One has his head buried in his hands.

Next to the illustration, Bibb writes in devastating detail:

After the men were all sold they then sold the women and children. They ordered the first woman to lay down her child and mount the auction block; she refused to give up her little one and clung to it as long as she could, while the cruel lash was applied to her back for disobedience. She pleaded for mercy in the name of God. But the child was torn from the arms of its mother amid the most heart rending-shrieks [*sic*] from the mother and child on the one hand, and bitter oaths and cruel lashes from the tyrants on the other. Finally the poor little child was torn from the mother while she was sacrificed to the highest bidder. In this way the sale was carried on from begining [*sic*] to end.

There was each speculator with his handcuffs to bind his victims after the sale; and while they were doing their writings, the Christian portion of the slaves asked permission to kneel in prayer on the ground before they separated, which was granted. And while bathing each other with tears of sorrow on the verge of their final separation, their eloquent appeals in prayer to the Most High seemed to cause an unpleasant sensation upon the ears of their tyrants, who ordered them to rise and make ready their limbs for the caffles. And as they happened not to bound at the first sound, they were soon raised from their knees by the sound of the lash, and the rattle of the chains, in which they were soon taken off by their respective masters,—husbands from wives, and children from parents, never expecting to meet until the judgement of the great day.

Though Jefferson was acutely aware of the impact that selling an enslaved person to another plantation could have on the rest of the enslaved population, he still sold more than one hundred over the course of his life. Lucia Stanton writes that Jefferson, like other antebellum Virginians who considered themselves enlightened, preferred that his enslaved property be sold in family units. Typically, he only sold individuals when he was hard-pressed financially. In 1820, he wrote that he had "scruples about selling negroes but for delinquency, or on their own request." And it is true that there were occasions in which Jefferson would sell or buy an enslaved person to reunite them with a spouse "where it can be done reasonably." According to Jefferson, he wanted a scenario in which neither husbands and wives nor children and parents would be split apart.

But Jefferson did allow families to be separated under his watch. He separated children as young as thirteen from their parents by sale, bought children as young as eleven, and separated children under ten from their families by transferring them between his own properties or giving them to family members as gifts. Jefferson believed himself to be a benevolent slave owner, but his moral ideals came second to, and were always entangled with, his own economic interests and the interests of his family. Jefferson understood, as well, the particular economic benefits of keeping husbands and wives together, noting that "a child raised every 2 years is of more profit than the crop of the best laboring man."

Jefferson believed that he might absolve himself of some of the barbarism of slavery by reducing the extent to which he employed its most brutal tactics. The whippings of his slaves, for example, "must not be resorted to but in extremities." He wanted the best of both worlds, looking for overseers who might be less brutal than was typical for late-eighteenth-century Virginia and who could do so without compromising the yield and efficiency of the plantation. When Robert Hemings—the mixed-race enslaved workman who was the child of Elizabeth Hemings and Jefferson's father-in-law, John Wayles—found a wife and requested to buy his freedom, Jefferson grew angry because he "expected loyalty for the 'indulgences' he had granted Hemings and could not understand that a slave might choose freedom and family over fidelity to the master."

But absolution, in Jefferson's case, could never be attained by simply refusing to participate in the most heinous aspects of slavery. To own an enslaved person was to perpetuate the barbarism of the institution. And when he felt it necessary to maintain the order that made his life possible, Jefferson engaged in some of the very practices he claimed to so deeply abhor.

Around 1810, James Hubbard, an enslaved man who worked in Monticello's nail factory, ran away. He had done so once before, about five years prior, and was caught shortly after his escape. This time he was caught about a year later. When Hubbard was returned, Jefferson wrote, "I had him severely flogged in the presence of his old companions." Although he attempted to create distance between himself and the abuse by assigning the task to an overseer, Jefferson knew, just as slaveholders throughout the South knew, that the spectacle of public assault was a means of both asserting authority over, and maintaining order among, enslaved workers.

Over the course of David's hour-long tour, I found myself watching two women in particular. Each time he presented a new story, fact, or piece of historical evidence about Jefferson as an enslaver, their faces would contort in astonishment, their mouths would sit agape, and they would shake their heads, almost as if they were being told on authority that the earth was flat after all.

After David completed his tour, and people dispersed to visit the rest of the plantation, I approached the two women and asked them if they were open to sharing their reactions to what they had just heard.

Donna folded her brochure and used it to fan the back of her neck. Her silver hair took on a yellowish hue under the midsummer sun and was tied in a ponytail that fell past her shoulders. She rocked from side to side as we spoke, shifting her weight from one leg to the other, her black flip-flops squeaking softly under the changing pressure. Her voice was imbued with a gentle Texas lilt that stretched out her *i*'s and melted her *l*'s into the breeze. Grace's voice, on the other hand, was higher and more hurried. Her short salt-and-pepper hair was only a few inches long and hugged her scalp. Her skin had become sun blotched from years spent living in Florida, even though, she told me, she was originally from Vermont.

Both were warm and welcoming when I approached them, as a cool wind passed and gave us a moment of relief from the summer heat.

I asked them if, before coming on this tour, they had been aware of Jefferson's relationship to slavery, how he had flogged his enslaved workers, how he had separated loved ones, how he had kept generations of families in bondage. Their answers were swift and sincere.

"No."

"No."

They both shook their heads, as if still perplexed by what they had just learned. There was a discernible sense of disappointment—perhaps in themselves, perhaps in Jefferson, perhaps in both.

"You grow up and it's basic American history from fourth grade...He's a great man, and he did all this," Donna said, gesticulating with her hands and almost retroactively mocking the things she had previously been taught about Jefferson. "And granted he achieved things. But we were just saying, this really took the shine off the guy."

"Yes...That's a good word," said Grace, nodding her head.

Grace had been married to Donna's brother before he passed away. They were already close, but since his passing, they had found comfort in each other's companionship, traveling together to different places across the country, particularly sites of historical significance. They explained that they had been drawn to Monticello because they were fascinated by architecture that was created without the aid of modern-day tools and machinery. Donna, in particular, admired the artisans who constructed such intimately detailed designs on structures that were still standing today.

"I am kind of a history nut," she said, "and I just wanted to see the house because I love going to towns, because they built things back in a time without all the fancy tools."

Jefferson's house, which took more than forty years to complete, was the embodiment of so much of what they admired. Historian Annette Gordon-Reed has written of how before the home could even be built, enslaved workers had to shave off the top of the mountain in the dead of winter, at a time when there was no mechanical technology to assist them beyond a shovel in their hands. Additionally, because there was no available water supply at the peak of the mountain, enslaved workers had to dig sixty-five feet into the earth—twice as deep as was typically required—over the course of forty-six days before they found water.

The home itself is an eleven-thousand-square-foot, forty-three-room manor. Its iconic West Front has four Doric-style columns, constructed using more than four thousand curved bricks that were then plastered to resemble stone. The columns support a roof that extends from the front of the house, forming a portico where Jefferson would sit and entertain his guests—statesmen, philosophers, tradesmen, and old friends. Hundreds of thousands of cinnamon-red bricks provide texture to the home's facade, with green shutters hugging white-framed windows that glittered in the sunlight. Much of the house's design was inspired by Jefferson's time in Europe, and by ancient Roman and Renaissance architecture. He used both free white laborers and his own enslaved workers to move his vision toward reality.

"That's why I like to go to these," Donna said, again referring to the impressive aesthetics of the house. "[Jefferson] was just a sideline. But boy, this... this..." She was looking down, shaking her head.

"This man here," Grace interjected, looking in the direction of David, who was chatting with two visitors who had lingered behind after the tour, "just opened a whole new avenue to me."

"It just took his shine off," Donna repeated. "He might have done great things, but boy, did he have a big flaw."

What's fascinating about Jefferson is that this is a flaw of which he was wholly cognizant. In *Notes on the State of Virginia*, he wrote, "There must doubtless be an unhappy influence on the manners of our people produced by the existence of slavery among us. The whole commerce between master and slave is a perpetual exercise of the most boisterous passions, the most unremitting despotism on the one part, and degrading submissions on the other. Our children see this, and learn to imitate it; for man is an imitative animal...The parent storms, the child looks on, catches the lineaments of wrath, puts on the same airs in the circle of smaller slaves, gives a loose to his worst of passions, and thus nursed, educated, and daily exercised in tyranny, cannot but be stamped by it with odious peculiarities. The man must be a prodigy who can retain his manners and morals undepraved by such circumstances."

Despite this apparent self-awareness, Jefferson considered his enslaved workers a valuable asset that might help reduce the debts that plagued him. "The torment of mind I endure till the moment shall arrive when I shall not owe a shilling on earth is such really as to render life of little value," he wrote in a letter to a friend in July 1787. "I cannot decide to sell my lands. I have sold too much of them already, and they are the only sure provision for my children. Nor would I willingly sell the slaves as long as there remains any prospect of paying my debts with their labour." Jefferson hoped to put his enslaved workers "on an easier footing" once his finances were stable, but he remained in debt for the rest of his life. Nearly all of his enslaved workers—about two hundred people at the time, at Monticello and another property—were auctioned after his death in 1826 to pay his debts.

Jefferson knew that slavery degraded the humanity of those who perpetuated its existence because it necessitated the subjugation of another human being; at the same time, he believed that Black people were an inferior class. This is where Jefferson's logic falls apart, historian Winthrop D. Jordan wrote in 1968. If Jefferson truly believed that Black people were inferior, then he must have "suspected that the Creator might have in fact created men unequal; and he could not say this without giving his assertion exactly the same logical force as his famous statement to the contrary."

Jefferson believed that it was impossible for Blacks and whites to live peacefully alongside one another after the emancipation of the enslaved, stating in his 1821 autobiography, "The two races, equally free, cannot live in the same government. Nature, habit, opinion has drawn indelible lines of distinction between them."

In a letter written to his friend Jared Sparks on February 4, 1824, Jefferson reflected on the possibility of the expatriation of Black people through "the establishment of a colony on the coast of Africa." But he had already discarded African colonization as unfeasible because of the expense. "I do not say this to induce an inference that the getting rid of them is for ever impossible. For that is neither my opinion, nor my hope," he wrote to Sparks. "But only that it cannot be done in this way. There is, I think, a way in which it can be done," he continued, "that is, by emancipating the after-born, leaving them, on due compensation, with their mothers, until their services are worth their maintenance, and then putting them to industrious occupations, until a proper age for deportation."

He had come to believe that the Caribbean was a promising destination. "St. Domingo is become independant [*sic*], and with a population of that colour only; and, if the public papers are to be credited, their Chief offers to pay their passage, to recieve [*sic*] them as free citizens, and to provide them employment." What Jefferson was proposing was that the government purchase newborn slaves from their enslaver, have them stay with their mothers until they were ready to separate, and then send them off to Santo Domingo—modern-day Haiti.

He expressed similar views in an 1814 letter to Edward Coles, then James Madison's private secretary and a man who would go on to become the second governor of Illinois. "I have seen no proposition so expedient," Jefferson wrote, "as that of emancipation of those [slaves] born after a given day, and of their education and expatriation at a proper age."

In 1807, during the second term of his presidency, Jefferson signed an act prohibiting the importation of slaves to the United States. If Jefferson believed slavery would slowly die out after the transatlantic slave trade was abolished, however, it was a hypothesis that ran counter to the evidence available on his own farm. Per his Farm Book, there were at least twenty-two births and twelve deaths among his enslaved population between 1774 and 1778. According to the scholar Michael Tadman, "Among North American slaves, births greatly exceeded deaths, so that the slave population expanded rapidly...Indeed, the North American pattern was probably, with a few local and sometimes short-term exceptions, unique in the history of slavery." As historian C. Vann Woodward wrote: "So far as history reveals, no other slave society, whether of antiquity or modern times, has so much as sustained, much less greatly multiplied, its slave population by relying on natural increase."

After the invention of the cotton gin in 1793, the cotton industry exploded, and with it the need for slave labor. According to the National Archives, the yield of raw cotton doubled every decade following 1800. In 1790, there were eight slave states, and in 1860 there were fifteen.* Jefferson

---

* While there were eight slave states in 1790, twelve states had slave populations. Pennsylvania, Connecticut, and Rhode Island typically are not counted as slave states because they

saw the beginning of this expansion, but he would not live to see how all-encompassing the "peculiar institution" became. By 1860, about one in three Southerners was an enslaved person.

As much as he said he detested slavery, Jefferson did not spend a large portion of his life attempting to limit it in the United States. His original Ordinance of 1784 would have barred slavery in the northwestern territories after 1800 (although it would have allowed enslavement during a sixteen-year grace period in between), but that proposal was rejected. Afterward, Jefferson largely left the issue of the domestic abolition of slavery untouched beyond private conversations and correspondence. Jefferson, it seems, was above all a statesman. And upon recognition of how increasingly steadfast opposition to any semblance of abolition was in Virginia and throughout the South, he largely backed away from public admonishment of the system. Privately, he both condemned slavery and expressed ambivalence about freeing enslaved

---

passed gradual abolition laws in the 1780s—but all three states still had slaves in 1790, according to the census. (Pennsylvania had 3,737; Connecticut had 2,764; and Rhode Island had 948.) Slavery also still existed on a small scale in New Hampshire, where the 1790 census counted 158 slaves. (United States Census Bureau, *Heads of Families at the First Census: 1790*, accessed October 23, 2020, https://www2.census.gov/prod2/decennial/documents/1790m-02.pdf.)

people. "To give liberty," he wrote in a letter in 1789, "or rather, to abandon persons whose habits have been formed in slavery is like abandoning children."

Gordon-Reed notes that in the latter half of his life, Jefferson resigned himself to the fact that slavery would not be abolished in his lifetime, and certainly not through any endeavor led by him. He believed that the project of emancipation would be carried out by another generation, and that he and his revolutionary colleagues had done their part by emancipating the colonies from Great Britain and creating the world's first constitutional republic, a place where these questions would even be able to be grappled with in the first place.

The sun now was hidden behind a thin layer of clouds that temporarily eased the heat on our necks. I asked both Donna and Grace what they had previously been taught about all of this.

"You know, we studied Jefferson," Grace said. "The slavery part was not part of it."

"Well, it wasn't detailed," Donna shared. "It didn't put any heart and thought into it. In high school and college, you didn't think, *These are families. These are moms and dads being separated from each other.* So that wasn't part of the education."

David had spent time in the early part of the tour talking about how the children on the plantation made marbles out of the clay from the road, playing with one another under the shadow of their shacks as the sun set each evening. He had talked about how the enslaved celebrated weddings, birthdays, and funerals; how they used writing slates they hid from overseers in order to learn how to read and write.

Donna and Grace and so many people—specifically white people—often have understood slavery, and those held in its grip, only in abstract terms. They do not see the faces. They cannot picture the hands. They do not hear the fear, or the laughter. They do not consider that these were children like their own, or that these were people who had birthdays and weddings and funerals; who loved and celebrated one another just as they loved and celebrated their loved ones.

Donna seemed particularly appalled by how the institution of slavery had affected the children. "I mean, splitting families," she said. "Oh my God, how can you split a family?"

"It's happening now," said Grace.

As the three of us held our conversation in July 2018, the Trump administration had already separated roughly three thousand children from their parents at the southern border of the United States, invoking the outrage of millions in the US and abroad. We had heard about mothers and fathers being told that their children were simply going to be given showers, only to have them learn, after hours had passed, that their children had been taken somewhere else—someplace they did not know.

These two women, self-proclaimed Southern Republicans, found themselves identifying the parallels between families separated during slavery and those separated while seeking asylum in the United States from violence in Central America.

Donna came from a family in which she said her mother had "extreme" views. When I asked her what she meant by "extreme," Donna described her mother's stance using a phrase that was not uncommon in the discourse of many white Southerners: "The only good one is a dead one."

The "one" here is, of course, a genteel metonym. It was a phrase I had heard from my grandparents as they spoke of the way white people had talked to them, growing up in the mid-twentieth-century Jim Crow South, where the law did not protect you from the terror of white supremacy but instead abetted it. The uncensored version of the phrase goes "The only good nigger is a dead nigger."

Here I was, on a plantation that enslaved hundreds of people who had skin like mine, having a conversation with a white, conservative, Fox News –consuming woman from Texas, whose mother had conveyed to her throughout her life that people like me were—that perhaps I was—better off dead than alive. A woman with whom, surprisingly even to me, I was sharing photos of my fourteen-month-old son.

We spoke for a few more minutes but soon felt the temperature of the air shift. We looked down and saw small droplets of rain begin to freckle the clay road.

At one point, Grace, repeating for herself more than for anyone else, summed up what she, only an hour before, had never been forced to wrestle with.

"Here he uses all of these people and then he marries a lady and then they have children," she said, letting out a heavy sigh. (A reference to Sally Hemings, an enslaved woman who bore at least six of Jefferson's children. The two were never married.) "Jefferson is not the man I thought he was."

The truth is that it was not until much later in my life that I too realized Jefferson was not the man I had been taught he was. It wasn't until 2014, in my first year of graduate school, when I read *Notes on the State of Virginia,* that I was presented with a more complicated, or rather a more accurate, version of Jefferson. I had cautiously flipped toward the sections that specifically considered Jefferson's relationship to slavery and encountered a passage in which he theorized that Black people "are inferior to the whites in the endowments both of body and mind."

I had also read the passage where he said of Phillis Wheatley—widely understood to be the first published Black woman poet in the history of the United States—that "the compositions published under her name are below the dignity of criticism." Jefferson believed that Black people, as a rule, were not capable of poetic expression. "Misery is often the parent of the most affecting touches in poetry," he wrote. "Among the blacks is misery enough, God knows, but no poetry. Love is the peculiar oestrum of the poet. Their love is ardent, but it kindles the senses only, not the imagination."

At the time I encountered this passage I was finishing what would be my first collection of poetry. I was writing in the aftermath of the Ferguson uprising, using poetry to process the incessant state-sanctioned violence happening to Black people all around me, attempting to put my life in conversation with this political moment and the history that birthed it. I spent hours poring over both the voice and the form of my poems, revising, rearranging, adding, and deleting, until there were dozens of iterations of every stanza, every line. I thought of how seriously I took the craft. I thought of how all of my work, even in response to violence, stemmed from a place of love—a love of my community, a love of my family, a love of my partner, a love of those hoping to build a better world than the one we live in.

When I read Jefferson's disparagement of Wheatley, it felt like he had been disparaging the entire lineage of Black poets who would follow her, myself included, and I saw a man who had not had a clear understanding of what love is.

When Robert Hayden gave us the ballads to remember how captured Africans survived the Middle Passage and arrived on these shores, it was an act of love.

When Gwendolyn Brooks wrote about the children on the South Side of Chicago playing with one another in neighborhoods left neglected by the city, it was an act of love.

When Audre Lorde fractured this language and then built us a new one, giving us a fresh way to make sense of who we are in the world, it was an act of love.

When Sonia Sanchez makes lightning of her tongue, moving from Southern colloquialisms to stanzas shaped by Swahili, traversing an ocean in one breath, it is an act of love.

Jefferson's conceptions of love seem to have been so distorted by his own prejudices that he was unable to recognize the endless examples of love that pervaded plantations across the country: mothers who huddled over their children and took the lash so their little ones wouldn't have to; surrogate mothers, fathers, and grandparents who took in children and raised them as their own when their biological parents were disappeared in the middle of the night; the people who loved and married and committed to one another despite the omnipresent threat that they might be separated at any moment. What is love if not this?

There is no story of Monticello—there is no story of Thomas Jefferson—without understanding Sally Hemings. We have no letters or documentation written by Sally (birth name likely Sarah) Hemings and nothing written by Jefferson about her. There are no photographs of her. Almost all of what we know of her physical appearance comes from Isaac Jefferson, who was enslaved at Monticello at the same time as Hemings and described her as "mighty near white...Sally was very handsome, long straight hair down her back." Other than that, all portraits that depict her likeness are rendered from the imagination of the artists. She is a shadow without a body. A constellation for whom there are no stars. And yet the story of Sally Hemings sits at the center of Monticello. For two centuries Jefferson scholars, as well as Jefferson's *acknowledged* descendants, rejected the idea—despite evidence to the contrary—that Jefferson had either a romantic or a sexual relationship with Sally. They most certainly rejected the idea that he fathered all six of her children.

Sally Hemings's mother, Elizabeth, was a mixed-race enslaved woman owned by Jefferson's father-in-law, John Wayles. Elizabeth, often called Betty, likely gave birth to six of Wayles's children while in bondage. Sally Hemings was the youngest. This meant that Sally and Jefferson's wife, Martha, were half sisters. Before Martha passed away at age thirty-three, she made Jefferson promise not to marry again. Jefferson, who deeply loved his wife, abided by that promise. This did not prevent him, however, from beginning a nearly four-decade sexual involvement with Sally, one that started when she was around sixteen and Jefferson was in his mid-forties. Jefferson's relationship with Sally—to the extent that an association animated by ownership of one person over another can be classified as such—was seemingly an open secret during Jefferson's lifetime. In 1802, journalist James Callender wrote a series of salacious articles in the *Richmond Recorder* in which he claimed that Jefferson had fathered several illegitimate children by his slave "concubine": "It is well known that the man, whom it delighteth the people to honor, keeps, and for many years past has kept, as his concubine, one of his own slaves," one story began. "Her name is SALLY."

Callender had not always been an antagonist of

Jefferson. In fact, after Callender was fired from his job at the *Philadelphia Gazette* and found himself drowning in debt, Jefferson, aware of the political importance of having strong relationships with newspapers, assisted Callender in finding a new newspaper job and even paid him directly, off and on, for several years. After being imprisoned under the Alien and Sedition Acts for his anti-Federalist writing, Callender returned to a world in which Jefferson was president of the United States. Callender, in light of his friend's newfound power, expected some expression of material gratitude for the years of pro-Jefferson writings. Callender wanted to be Richmond postmaster; Jefferson did not appoint him to this position. In fact, he did not appoint Callender to any job. Callender, feeling particularly aggrieved, used his new position at the *Richmond Recorder* to circulate the Jefferson-Hemings story, hoping to sabotage Jefferson's political career.

Word spread as the story was reprinted in newspapers across the country. Jefferson never outwardly denied the allegation. He didn't have to. As Gordon-Reed writes, most people either did not believe the Jefferson-Hemings story or did not consider it significant enough to alter their vote for Jefferson's second term. Further, though it may have been taboo, it was not at all uncommon for white male enslavers to have sex with the Black women enslaved on their plantations. Jefferson went on to win reelection.

A new exhibit about Sally Hemings was one of the reasons I decided to visit Monticello. The exhibit promised to capture her story in its fullness and complexity. It is a story that Monticello had been figuring out how to tell for a long time, a story that perhaps took them too long to tell.

A blade of light cut through the open doorframe of what may have been Hemings's living quarters—a small, plaster-walled room with a red brick floor. Inside, a five-minute video played, telling the story of Sally Hemings and her involvement with Jefferson. The video was projected onto the wall, and Sally, because we don't know what she looked like, appears as a silhouette, first with a pregnant belly, then alongside silhouettes of her four children who survived into adulthood: Beverly, Harriet, Madison, and Eston—three sons and one daughter. She is seen braiding her daughter's hair while the child's brothers practice violin, the instrument Jefferson played, just a few feet away. The shadows of the children fade away, reappear, and then fade away again, almost as if to resemble their fleeting presence in the discourse around their father. On the projection, their names appear in Jefferson's Farm Book on a page entitled "Roll of Negroes," their cursive monikers easily lost amid the other names. "He was not in the habit of showing partiality or fatherly affections to us children," said Jefferson's formerly enslaved son, Madison Hemings, to an interviewer in 1873.* "We were the only children of his by a slave woman."

Jefferson's association with Hemings was not an aberration of the time, and it was also reflective of the insidious, tangled relationships between white men and enslaved women. In eighteenth-century Virginia, white male enslavers had full dominion over their enslaved human beings, and full sexual dominion over enslaved women. The relationships were inherently corrupted by the power dynamics embedded within them. These women were in no position to refuse the advances of their owners, or of any other white man who wanted them. There was no legal recourse, and both parties knew this. In fact, one of Jefferson's dear friends, John Hartwell Cocke, wrote in his diary that it was not at all uncommon for "bachelor and widowed slave owners" to have an enslaved woman serve as a "substitute for a wife." For Jefferson, after promising Martha that he would not marry again, being involved with an enslaved woman like Sally

---

* Almost fifty years earlier, Madison was one of the only enslaved people freed in Jefferson's will.

would have, in its own unsettling way, allowed him to keep his promise.

I stepped out of the room after the short film was complete and began reading the signage on the outside walls of the living quarters. To my left was a woman with a badge that indicated she worked for Monticello. She looked in my direction, seeming to anticipate a question, so I asked her what had been on my mind since my conversation with Donna and Grace: whether she thought the people who visited this plantation, and more recently this exhibit, left thinking of Jefferson differently. I knew what Donna and Grace had experienced, but I wanted to know if that was somehow atypical.

Theresa, a white woman with reddish-blond hair and soft eyes, stood adjacent to the Sally Hemings exhibit. She explained that she *did* think the majority of people left the plantation changed. She said that between the slavery tour and the new Sally Hemings exhibit, Monticello was pushing its visitors to see the more complex and holistic version of Jefferson. She did say, however, that some visitors thought the museum was trying to be too politically correct and, by portraying Jefferson more holistically, trying to change history.

"We're not changing history," Theresa said, unfazed. "We're telling history by telling the full story, more of the story of everyone who lived here, not just certain people who were *able* to tell their stories."

She continued by saying that there were those who derided her and the rest of the staff at the plantation for trying to "tear Jefferson down.

"But to me, I think they put him up on a pedestal and they deny the fact that he was human. He had things about his life that were flaws, and you've gotta look at his life. From the moment he got up in the morning till the moment he went to bed at night, he's relying on slave labor for every aspect."

Theresa's own journey to understand Jefferson in totality was also one that required unlearning so much of what she had been taught. She had lived her entire life one county over from the grandeur of Jefferson's mountaintop plantation, but when I asked her if she knew about Jefferson's relationship to slavery or to Hemings before she started working at Monticello, she responded, "Oh gosh, no." She told me she had known him only as the man who wrote the Declaration of Independence.

For Theresa, her years of working at Monticello have been a journey of learning and unlearning. Before giving a tour at Monticello, guides go through weeks of training. There are also regular development sessions in which guides converse about what they've learned and share the questions guests may have raised on their respective tours.

Training gives staff the tools to deal with people like Donna and Grace, who, while shocked, accepted what they had heard, as well as those who might push back a little bit harder on what they perceive to be an unwarranted tarnishing of Jefferson's legacy. The training has also helped Theresa put the history of Jefferson in conversation with what she sees happening in the broader landscape of US politics. "Those rallies they've been having in Charlottesville..." She sighed, alluding to the white supremacist rallies that had taken place in the summer of 2017. "We need to make sure we know our history. I don't know if I wanna go so far as to say embrace it, but learn from it."

Behind Theresa was Mulberry Row, which served as the hub of the plantation. Workshops and homes had once lined the road, including several slave cabins. Today, there stood a single replica, meant to serve as an example of the homes where people enslaved at Monticello would live. The cabin sat away from the main residence but within its proximity, like a moon still caught in the orbit of a planet it could not escape.

I stepped inside the cabin and stared at the cracked, uneven planks lining the walls. I looked up at the roof and observed the whisper of sunlight squeezing through one small opening. Soft beads of light rested on my shoulder; it was a crack that let in these glimmers of sunlight on clear days but would just as easily admit streaks of rain on others. Even knowing this was just a replica of what the slave quarters looked like, I was overwhelmed by how little shelter this structure offered.

I stood with three other people inside the space mirroring what someone once called a home, and felt the four of us tussle around one another in order to move about, the fabric of our clothes emitting static electricity as we rubbed against one another. The cabin was a quarter the size of the entrance hall to Jefferson's mansion.

I walked out of the cabin and into the afternoon light. As I stepped back onto the road, a white woman walked past with two small girls I presumed were her daughters, their blond and brunette ponytails bouncing against the backs of their respective necks as they trotted by. The mother looked at the cabin and said to the girls, "How would you like that to be your home?"

The little girls didn't even turn around before they started running away from the cabin, shouting, "Nuh-uh!" the red gravel spitting up into the air behind them.

I left Monticello that day wanting to get a better sense of who David was and how he understood his role as a guide at Monticello. So a couple of months after my initial visit, I drove back down to Charlottesville to meet him and get one of the tours I had missed, one focused entirely on the Hemings family.

It had been raining for hours when I arrived; undulations of rain and wind pulsed in the shadow of a grey afternoon. The plantation was far less crowded than it had been during my previous trip. Intermittent bodies carrying umbrellas splashed through the puddles that were scattered across the visitor center's courtyard.

Before I met with David, I sat down with Brandon Dillard and Linnea Grim. At the time of my visit, Brandon was the manager of special programs in the education and visitor programs department at Monticello. (He is now the department's manager of historic interpretation.) Linnea is the department's director.

Brandon was wearing a checkered brown oxford shirt with the sleeves rolled up to just below his elbows. His black hair was thin and receding to the top of his head, and he had a thick black goatee that swallowed his mouth, except when he laughed, which he did often. He was, in some ways, an unlikely candidate for his position. He had been a philosophy major in college and worked as a bartender in Charlottesville for years after graduating. One day he saw an ad in the local newspaper that Monticello was looking for tour guides. Eight years later, he was still here, having been promoted to his new position after years of leading tours.

Linnea wore a black pantsuit, her brown hair cut just above her shoulders. She often paused for just a moment before speaking. The practice reflected a thoughtfulness that I imagined had been cultivated from years of managing the public work of an institution grappling with its relationship to one of the most heinous periods in our nation's history.

Brandon and Linnea had been at Monticello long enough to see the public discourse around Jefferson, and more broadly the conversation around slavery and racism, evolve in profound ways. Both said Monticello had a responsibility to respond to, and in many ways lead, that change. "One of the things that I've been trying to work with guides to do, and I think successfully this has changed," Brandon said, "is that we talk a great deal more about the transatlantic slave trade, how it is inextricably entwined with race, the development of that notion over time, and because of that it helps us set up a conversation more for understanding race and what that means, which allows us to have more of this conversation on legacy."

Generally, Monticello leaves a significant amount of agency to the individual tour guides, almost all of whom are paid employees. The rigorous training process does not include tour scripts; each guide writes a narrative draft that their manager reviews, and new guides shadow the tours of veteran guides. Even in recruiting, the education teams attempt to get a sense of a guide's ability to convey difficult, honest truths that force visitors to reckon with the brutality of the slave trade and also to understand that such a reckoning looks different based on each visitor's own set of experiences. "So if you have...guests who came in and are like, 'I had no idea there was slavery,' if you just come out and hit them over the head with it, they wouldn't listen," Linnea said.

Although Monticello has been open to the public since the Thomas Jefferson Memorial Foundation purchased the property in 1923, the plantation's public wrestling with Jefferson's relationship to slavery began in 1993, as part of the foundation's Getting Word oral history project, in which the foundation interviewed the descendants of enslaved people from Monticello in an effort to preserve those histories. The oral histories represented an attempt to get the descendants to share stories their elders might have shared with them. The stories that arose from Getting Word became part of the tours Monticello created based on the lives of the enslaved population there. "This is how the word is passed down," remarked one of the descendants in an interview for the project.

Not long after, in 1997, Annette Gordon-Reed published *Thomas Jefferson and Sally Hemings: An American Controversy*. Gordon-Reed pushed back against centuries of claims suggesting that Jefferson had never had a sexual relationship with Sally Hemings. "It really goes through the historiography," Brandon said, "and shows how Madison Hemings's words are really externally verifiable, and all of the arguments against them are pretty easily refuted."

The most detailed information we have about the relationship between Sally Hemings and Jefferson comes from Madison Hemings, their second surviving son, who gave an extended interview with the *Pike County Republican* newspaper's editor, S. F. Wetmore, published on March 13, 1873. Most historians rejected these claims. Many of Jefferson's recognized descendants suggested instead that the Hemings children had been fathered by one or both of Jefferson's nephews Peter and Samuel Carr, a theory originally propagated by two of Jefferson's grandchildren. Some historians also claimed that the *Pike County Republican* could not be trusted because, as historian Julian Boyd once noted, the publisher of the newspaper "must surely have been a fanatical abolitionist," a blatant effort to dismiss Madison as a tool of abolitionist propaganda. As Gordon-Reed puts it, "The stereotype employed here is the feebleminded black person as pawn to a white man." She goes on: "One of the striking features of the writing about the Jefferson-Hemings controversy is the easy manner with which historians make the black people in the story whatever they want or need them to be, on the basis of no stated evidence." Gordon-Reed cross-checked claims made at the time by both Madison Hemings and Israel Jefferson—another formerly enslaved person from Monticello—against primary source evidence she uncovered that Madison could not have been cognizant of at the time he made the claim. Additionally, Gordon-Reed cross-checked the stories of the Hemings family against Jefferson's own records from Monticello. The result was a book that is now understood to have vindicated Madison Hemings's testimony and has made clear that historians long ignored compelling evidence of the relationship between Sally and Thomas.

Then, in 1998, a DNA test ruled out the Carr brothers and established that the father of Sally Hemings's youngest child was a Jefferson. Researchers analyzed DNA samples from several people, including the descendants of Field Jefferson, who was Thomas Jefferson's paternal uncle. They also tested a man named John Weeks Jefferson, who was a descendant of Sally's son Eston Hemings—and most importantly, the only available member of the Hemings family who was part of an unbroken line of male descendants, meaning that he would have had a direct Y chromosome match. At the time of the DNA test, researchers didn't think Madison or any of his male descendants were options. Even when the grave of Madison's son was found a couple of years later, his descendants didn't want to exhume the body. "My family doesn't need to prove themselves," said Shay Banks-Young, one of Madison Hemings's great-great-great-granddaughters. "If they want to dig up Thomas Jefferson at the same time, maybe I'll reconsider."

The combination of Gordon-Reed's book and the DNA test forced the Thomas Jefferson Memorial Foundation (now named simply the Thomas Jefferson Foundation), which owns and operates Monticello, to reexamine its stance on Sally Hemings. After the DNA revelation, which received national attention and even an extended PBS program, the foundation began their own internal investigation. Two years later, they publicly confirmed that they believed Jefferson was indeed the father of Hemings's children. After their announcement, they began to say so on their tours. "So almost twenty years now we've been saying on tours—every house tour—it's a rule that we say, 'We believe Jefferson was the father of Hemings's children.' But in recent years with the opening of the new exhibit, the equivocation is gone," Brandon said, his face becoming more sober. "It's just 'Jefferson's the father of Hemings's children.'"

Not everyone is a fan of the changes the Thomas Jefferson Foundation has made over the past two decades, and some Jefferson loyalists explicitly oppose the contemporary project of Monticello. For example, the Thomas Jefferson Heritage Society claims that, among other things, Monticello is misrepresenting the nature of Jefferson's relationship with Hemings. Vivienne Kelley, vice president of the organization, has written that the Thomas Jefferson Memorial Foundation "is using Jefferson's Monticello to make a political statement about the evils of slavery" and "seems to have taken things too far."*

At the time of my visit, of the eighty-nine tour guides, only four of them were Black, and three of the four were a part of the incoming class that had yet to officially begin their jobs. Over the past dozen years, Brandon and Linnea told me, there have been only about ten in total. Both Brandon and Linnea admit that this is a place where Monticello falls short but said that it is not for lack of effort. They point out a number of barriers,

---

* When I followed up with Linnea via email about this contention, which appeared in an essay coauthored by Kelley, she responded, "We're committed to being honest interpreters of history. The historical content we share with guests, including information on the humanity of the enslaved community and the realities of slavery, is informed by decades of archaeology, documentary research, and oral history."

including the way Black guides are treated by visitors. "Many African American interpreters who have worked here...it's been challenging, because people say some pretty insensitive and unbelievable things," said Brandon.

Linnea told the story of a younger Black woman guide who worked at Monticello for about two years and experienced a range of challenges, including harassment from visitors, people asking her on dates, and even people coming up and asking, "Oh, are you related to Sally Hemings?" Another staff member was sitting in the café when a white woman who had just completed a tour came up from behind, hugged her, weeping, and said, "I'm sorry for slavery."

My tour guide, David, when I met with him later, expressed his own surprise at the extent to which people respond differently to him than they do to some of his counterparts. "One of the things I have learned here at Monticello is that I have a certain style and I am who I am, but there are colleagues of mine, who are brilliant, who have problems being taken seriously or who are spoken to by visitors in unpleasant ways because they're not an old white guy, because they're a thirty-five-year-old woman." He paused. "I'm almost embarrassed to say it today, but I never thought about that until I saw it happening to my colleagues."

I thought of how this might extend beyond the

guides at Monticello, and to the visitors as well. What would motivate a Black family to come spend the day at a plantation if they were concerned about how the story of that land would be told, what kind of people would be standing alongside them as it was told, and who was telling it?

After I finished speaking with Brandon and Linnea, I made my way up to the top of the mountain, where I met David for the Hemings family tour of Monticello, the tour I had missed on my initial visit. The thunderstorm had just finished making its way across the mountain, and rivulets of rainwater slid down the roof of the replica cabin and dripped onto the ground. Just as he did during the Slavery at Monticello tour, David did not mince words. "There's a chapter in *Notes on the State of Virginia*," he said to the five of us, standing in front of the east wing of Jefferson's manor, "that has some of the most racist things you might ever read, written by anyone, anywhere, anytime, in it. So sometimes I stop and ask myself, "If Gettysburg had gone the wrong way, would people be quoting the Declaration of Independence or *Notes on the State of Virginia*?" It's the same guy writing."

After the tour, David led me past the other tour groups into Jefferson's home, up a narrow stairwell onto the second floor and into a room with an empty table, three chairs, and misty windows overlooking the lawn.

David sees it as essential that a guide be able to find the balance between telling the truth and not pushing people so much that they shut down. He told me that when you challenge people, specifically white people's conception of Jefferson, you're in fact challenging their conception of themselves. "I've come to realize that there's a difference between history and nostalgia, and somewhere between those two is memory," he said. "I think that history is the story of the past, using all the available facts, and that nostalgia is a fantasy about the past using no facts, and somewhere in between is memory, which is kind of this blend of history and a little bit of emotion...I mean, history is kind of about what you need to know...but nostalgia is what you want to hear."

David knows that some visitors to Monticello arrive with an understanding of history that is not only misguided but also harmful. He has a difficult time disentangling this from the current political moment. "That's not the story of who we are," he said, referencing the language of Make America Great Again, "but some people really, for whatever reason, they want to believe that and they want to go back there, right? They want to go back to something that never existed."

As David spoke, I thought about the tours I took during my first visit to Monticello. I had done the Slavery at Monticello tour with David but had also participated in the main house tour, the one that nearly each person who buys a ticket to Monticello goes on. I took that tour after David's and was astonished by the difference. The house tour takes guests on a visit through Jefferson's home, explains the architecture, shares his family history, and outlines the role the house played in shaping Jefferson's life of ideas, exploration, and public service. What struck me was how little slavery was mentioned on this tour as compared to the one I had taken right before it. It is true that while Jefferson's life was always animated by slavery, it was not singularly tied to it. I understand there is much to be shared and explored about his life. It makes sense that people should know about the range of his scientific work, his political work, and his family life. I wonder, however, if we can understand any of these things without understanding Jefferson as a slave owner.

Of the approximately 400,000 people who tour Monticello every year, only about 80,000, roughly a fifth, take the Slavery at Monticello tour or participate in a program for students that uses content from Slavery at Monticello.

Before I left, I wanted to understand how much David's role as a former military officer—responsible for protecting and promoting this country's foreign policy agenda at home and abroad—was something that felt, if at all, in tension with his role now. "I was born in the United States of America. I served the country for thirty years, so I actually believe in the idea of America," he said, straightening up in his chair. "Are we exceptional? No. Have we had unique advantages based on geography, based on a whole host of factors? Yes. Did a group of people come together in 1776 and conceive of an idea that was pretty radical in its time and then create a system of government, through the Constitution and its amendments, that was pretty radical and pretty novel? Yeah. Have other countries found their own way? Sure. So I believe in the idea of America. I don't believe that this country *was* perfect. I don't believe it *is* perfect. I don't believe it's going to *be* perfect. I believe that the journey to make this a better place is worth the effort and that the United States, if you conceive it not so much as a place to be in but an idea to believe in, it is worth fighting for."

The office of Monticello's public historian is about half a mile down the road from the plantation and in a building that sits adjacent to the Jefferson Library. Niya Bates, then Monticello's director of African American history and director of the Getting Word oral history project, was at once erudite and wholly accessible. Her desk was covered in annotated books—some scattered, some stacked, but all examining the entanglement of slavery, Jefferson, and Monticello. "These are my bibles," she said as I picked each one up and flipped through its pages.

As director of the oral history project, she has been responsible for engaging with the descendants of the enslaved community at Monticello. The project began in 1993 (prior to the publication of Gordon-Reed's book), the 250th anniversary of Jefferson's birth. Researchers traveled over 40,000 miles around the country, seeking out the families of descendants. At the time of our conversation, more than 200 people had been interviewed.

Part of Niya's job is to cultivate and maintain relationships with the descendants. "I'm looking for more surnames," she said. "Jefferson owned 607 people, and so far we've only identified twelve to fifteen different surnames, which says a lot about the type of community that was here. A lot of these families were related to each other by marriage, or unofficial marriage."

I asked her how she goes about even beginning to look for these descendants, specifically for descendants of Jefferson and Hemings, in a country of more than 325 million people. She explained that her team uses both traditional, records-based genealogical tracing and DNA test results to identify descendants of enslaved people, including those of Madison and Eston Hemings. Little is known about Beverly and Harriet Hemings, the two oldest children of Sally Hemings and Jefferson, who passed as white after leaving Monticello.* Finding their descendants is far more challenging. "It's tricky," she said, leaning back in her chair. "Right now our only way of doing that is DNA testing. We're hoping that as more people are getting tested, that someone will pop up as a match."

"So just across Ancestry and 23andMe?" I asked. "You're hoping that someone will pop up with a match to—"

"To other known Hemings descendants," she said, finishing my sentence, "which would be a pretty phenomenal discovery. We've tried the paper-trail method of looking them up and have not been successful. We're not sure if they changed their names when they passed. We don't know what their married names would be, or at least for Harriet. For Beverly, we don't know anything. That trail went pretty cold quickly. We're hoping that through DNA research we'll find some more people." She emphasized that her team isn't looking just for descendants of the Hemings family

---

* Jefferson never officially freed Beverly and Harriet, as he did Eston and Madison, but in the early 1820s he allowed them to leave Monticello without being pursued.

but descendants of a number of other enslaved families who lived and worked at Monticello.

Niya said they've also had people who claim to be descendants of enslaved families at Monticello reach out to them directly. When this happens, Monticello goes through a series of interviews to trace the person's lineage in order to determine the legitimacy of their claim.

"Another example," she said, "is we had a family whose mother had passed, and very late in her life she started revealing secrets about their family. They'd gone on a family trip to Buckingham County, which is the next county over, or south of here. They drove past the church, and their mom said, 'That's my home church.' And they said, 'No, Mom. That's the Hemings's family church.' And she was like, 'Yeah, I know.' So she was revealing sort of these secrets at the end of her life. We get a lot of people who are putting together pieces that way."

In her capacity as public historian, Niya uses the information gathered from the oral history interviews as well as her own research to inform the training for the guides, the exhibits, the website, and how Monticello publicly reckons with and talks about its relationship to this history.

As much as Niya's work centers on historiography and research, her relationship to Monticello is not merely intellectual; it's personal. She grew up right down the road in Charlottesville, and as she told me, "I don't remember a year where I didn't come to Monticello on a field trip."

As she was growing up, her town was the center of the ever-evolving debate around Thomas Jefferson's legacy, a debate that was happening both in the community and across the country. When she was around eight years old, she said, the Sally Hemings DNA results were released, and she remembered hearing people argue about them in the grocery store. "I just remember being a kid and being like, 'Who's Sally Hemings, and why is everybody so upset?' I do remember the field trip I took after that, where we came here, and I asked about Sally Hemings, and the guide at the time told me, 'We don't talk about that.'"

This unwillingness of people, particularly the guides at the plantation, to talk about something so relevant to the history of the town and the mountaintop plantation above it stayed with Niya for years. But it was when Niya was a junior at the University of Virginia that she realized reshaping public history was the work she wanted to do. She was enrolled in a class called Art and Culture of the Slave South, and as part of the course they took field trips to local historical sites. One of those sites was a plantation called Cloverfields, a place Niya had driven past almost every day of her life but had never actually visited.

"We walked around the outside of the plantation,

and then we looked at all the outbuildings, and they were telling us about the people who built the buildings, the material culture of slavery," she said, leaning forward on the desk as she recalled the story. "They're going on and on, then we finally went into the big house. We came into the big house from the basement, and in the basement there was a kitchen. The whole class squeezed into this kitchen, and the woman who was leading the tour, who's a descendant of the owners of the plantation, reached behind her to close the door. When she closed the door, there were photographs of all the people who had worked at this plantation on the back of the door. I caught a glimpse of the door, and the first picture I saw was my grandma. I was like, 'Oh my God, that's my grandma.' Next to my grandmother was my aunt. There were other members of my family on that, and I started thinking about, like, I've always had an awareness that they worked at these places, but I hadn't connected it to this academic history of plantations. I was like, *Do people in my community know this is here? Are they aware of how they helped shape this history that is often talked about without them?*"

Niya soon learned that her family had been central to maintaining Cloverfields in the decades following emancipation. She'd had no idea. This led her to write her master's thesis on the historical district that Cloverfields was part of and its exclusion of post-emancipation Black communities in historic preservation efforts. She discovered that in the early twentieth century her grandfather had been a stonemason, her aunt had been a cook, and her grandmother had been a maid.

"This kind of started my path of thinking about public history," she said. "That is, public history, historic districts, historic landmarks, the signs that people see along the road. *How do I make sure that our history is part of it, or that my people are represented?*" She paused. "Very literally, my people."

Following the 2017 attack in Charlottesville and the rise in white-nationalist terrorism over the past few years, Niya sees her work not just as an extension of her personal and intellectual commitments but also as a political commitment. She thinks Monticello has an important role in helping people reckon with who they are in relation to this country's history. "I think people come to us because they're grappling with their own identity," she said. "And Monticello in particular is a place that is so intimately connected to who we are, or who we believe we are, as Americans with freedom and democracy. Yet it's also a place of bondage, and now people are really, really grappling with that question. I think it makes our work here that much more important, that we are able, maybe, to navigate people through the conversation."

I told Niya that my experience on the Slavery

at Monticello tour had been significantly different from my experience on the primary tour of
Jefferson's home.

"We've been giving essentially the same main
tour since the mid-fifties. You go in through the
front door, you walk in a circle, and then you come
out the other side. That's the tour. There's some
interesting history there too. In the first thirty
years that Monticello was a museum, most of the
guides were Black. Black men—they were dressed
in livery." She paused, because she must have been
able to tell I wasn't familiar with that word. She
leaned forward and spoke with the same measured
conviction she had used throughout our conversation. "They were dressed as enslaved people."

I almost choked on my own tongue. I uncrossed
my legs and sat back in my chair. "For the first
thirty years of its existence," I said, repeating what
she had just told me so I could make sure I had
heard correctly, "tours of the house were given by
Black men dressed as enslaved people?"

Niya nodded. "Let me show you some pictures."
She turned to her computer. In a sepia-toned
photo, taken in the 1930s or 1940s, two Black men
stood in front of Monticello's west-facing portico
columns with the entrance open behind them.
They each wore three-piece tuxedo suits with two
rows of buttons ornamenting their outer jackets.
They each had thin bow ties and striped vests

underneath. They looked toward the camera with expressions difficult to interpret. "Some of them were descendants of people who were enslaved here," Niya said. Sometimes the stories the men told about the plantation had been passed on to them by family members.

While losing myself in the photo, it was easy to forget that this was not actually a photograph of two enslaved people but people tasked with playing the role of enslaved people. In *Memoirs of a Monticello Hostess*, Terry Tilman, who worked as a hostess in the 1940s and 1950s and who became Monticello's head tour guide, writes, "[T]he transition from colored guides to [white] hostesses in 1951 was not too well received, visitors resented our becoming more factual and less entertaining."

"It's like your *Gone with the Wind* plantation story," Niya said.

I mentioned my conversation with Grace and Donna. "They came here—they bought a ticket, made a reservation, got on a plane, rented a car, self-identified as history buffs, and showed up, and were like, 'I had no idea that Jefferson owned slaves,'" I said. "And it was such a fascinating moment for me because I'm like, 'You're clearly not an uncurious person. You literally said, "I'm a history buff. I wanted to come see where Thomas Jefferson lived. I wanted to see Jefferson's house," but had no conception—'"

"Of who he really was, right?" Niya said.

Not just who he was, I said. But even that Monticello was a plantation.

Niya nodded. "So many people come here without an understanding of the primary cause of the Civil War. Some people think Jefferson wrote the Constitution. I mean there are just so many ways that our public education is failing people by just not giving them the context to understand that Monticello is a plantation, and that slavery was a system that created the economic prosperity that enabled our country to exist. That is not something most people understand. I don't really blame them, because they're not taught to engage that history, and most people are not out here reading all these books that are piled on my desk."

She continued: "So we try to be very gentle. We try to give people a number of disclaimers, like 'What you're going to hear today might be difficult. This may be the first time you've thought about it since seventh grade, and that's okay. You're gonna have a lot of questions. No question is a stupid question.' We just try to make it as easy as possible, acknowledging the fact that those women may have been here on vacation. That many people are stopping here after they stopped at a vineyard. That they're bringing their kids, who are curious and doing a unit on slavery at school but are otherwise not engaged in the visit at all. There are just so many different reasons that people come to these places that we try not to judge them based on their understanding, especially being the only American plantation on the UNESCO World Heritage List. There are a number of international visitors that actually have no understanding of American slavery or the transatlantic slave trade...So we just get so many people with no background."

Niya added, however, that she has "zero patience" for those who, when confronted with that history, contend that Monticello is attempting to tear down Jefferson's legacy. "It's telling the full truth of who he was," she said. "Yes, he contributed great things. Yes, he gave us the Declaration of Independence, and the university where I got my degree, but he also owned people. He owned ancestors of people I know. That's reality. I think in order to really understand him, and to fully understand him, you have to grapple with slavery. You have to grapple with [physical] violence and psychological violence, and family separation. We would not be doing the story justice if we don't tell those stories."

To get to Jefferson's grave you walk for about a third of a mile along a winding uphill path. The gravel, a thin membrane scattered atop the red clay of this Virginia mountainside, crunches under your feet with each step.

As you walk along the serpentine path to the cemetery, bending branches and thick pockets of leaves provide shadowy respite from the mid-summer heat. Splashes of light sneak between the leaves and onto the ground, the tree branches reaching up to slice open the sky. Lining the auburn road leading up to the graveyard are rows of golden willow trees that sit among white oaks. In the Monticello graveyard, Jefferson is buried alongside his descendants. At the center of the graveyard sits a large tulip poplar tree, its thick trunk a discolored medley of browns.

The grave site—its iron gates, majestic tomb-stones, and gold ornamentation—stands in stark contrast to the grave site farther down the hill, where over forty of Thomas Jefferson's enslaved workers are buried. That space is enclosed by wooden fencing that has weathered over time. Dull emerald algae grows along much of the un-evenly cut timber. The ground is an unremarkable coalescence of soil and wood chips and indis-criminate patches of foliage dotting the graveyard with small streaks of green. While the Jefferson cemetery is filled with tombstones heralding the names of roughly two hundred of Jefferson's de-scendants and their spouses, the burial ground of the enslaved has no ornamentation or personal designation. There are a few scattered headstones, though no visible names or inscriptions. The trees around the graves hold court for a congregation of unmarked ruins. No one knows the names of the people buried here.

In the hours just before Jefferson died, when no one else could understand his mumbled, near life-less words, it was another of his enslaved attendants who, knowing that he was asking to have his pillow repositioned, raised Jefferson's head. Only a short time after, Jefferson passed away. Throughout his life, Jefferson valued the company of cosmopolitan guests, the time to read and write and think, the elegance of fine architecture, the flavor of savory food, and the fragrance of the natural world—a life in which he could nurture his mind and satisfy his tastes. This life was only possible because of the enslaved men and women he held, sold, and separated; because of the people he allowed to be threatened, manipulated, flogged, assaulted, de-ceived, and terrorized. Jefferson's vacillation from moral repugnance to hollow justification reflects how he largely succumbed to that which he knew was indefensible. He still held hostage the men and women and children enslaved on his plantation, he still separated them, he still refused to provide freedom to more than a handful of people.

But Monticello is not singularly defined by

Jefferson. It could not have existed without the enslaved people who lived there, who had families there, who built a community there that spanned generations. As a public servant, Jefferson spent more than half his life away from his plantation, while many of the hundreds of people enslaved at Monticello stayed on that land for the entirety of their lives. As much as this land illuminates the contradictions of Jefferson's legacy, it also serves as a reminder of the hundreds of Black people who made a home there. Their lives are also worthy of remembrance, and commemoration.

One of the last things David said before I left my second tour at Monticello spoke to this duality: "You're here. [Sally's brother James] Hemings got beat here. Not in a book, right? Right here is where that happened." When one hundred enslaved people at Monticello were auctioned after Jefferson's death, it was "right there in the west lawn behind us," David continued. "It happened right there. And Jefferson's ideas about the Declaration of Independence, even though he wrote that document in Philadelphia, his whole idea of where he was going, was formulated right here on this mountaintop."

"An open book, up under the sky"

THE WHITNEY PLANTATION

BETWEEN THE WOODEN WHITE FENCE and the red brick path where I stood, there was a plot of earth where the dark heads of fifty-five black men sat on metal stakes. Their heads were balanced on robust silver rods that pushed their necks toward the sky. Their eyes were shut and some of their faces were contorted, as if frozen in a permanent state of anguish. Each jawbone was chiseled, as much by indignation as by a tool in someone's hand. Many had thin white bandanas wrapped around their foreheads, the small knots lying against their temples. Sunlight glinted from the ceramic statues and created a soft glow. It almost seemed as if their gleaming cheeks were covered in both blood and sweat.

These heads, renderings of a violent past, are an exhibit at the Whitney Plantation in Wallace, Louisiana—located an hour west of New Orleans, past the brackish estuary of Lake Pontchartrain, through the residue of sugarcane that still sings to the land. From a distance, the human likeness of these statues is so unsettling that I get closer, just to be sure. In the warmer months, gnats and flies swarm, while wasps begin nesting on the undersides of open necks, their collective buzzing around the heads sounding like an army of small drones. Each of the faces is nameless, with the exception of the ten that sit at the front. *Mathurin. Cook. Gilbert. Amar. Lindor. Joseph. Dagobert. Komina. Hippolite. Charles.* These were the leaders of the largest slave rebellion in US history. These were the people who decided that enough was enough.

On a rainy southern Louisiana evening in January 1811, Charles Deslondes, a mixed-race slave driver, led this massive armed rebellion. Composed of hundreds of people, Deslondes's army advanced along the serpentine path of southern Louisiana's River Road to New Orleans with a military discipline that surprised many of their adversaries. It is remarkable to consider that hundreds of enslaved people, who came from different countries, with different native languages and different tribal affiliations, were able to organize themselves as effectively as they did.

On the German Coast of Louisiana, where the rebellion took place—named as such for the German immigrants who settled there—roughly 60 percent of the total population was enslaved.

The fear of armed insurrection had long been in the air.

That fear had escalated over the course of the Haitian Revolution, in which the enslaved population in Haiti rose up against the French and in 1804 founded what became the first Black-led republic in the world. The French army was so beleaguered from battle and disease—by the end of the war, more than 80 percent of the soldiers sent to the island had died—that Napoleon Bonaparte, looking to cut his losses and refocus his attention on his military battles in Europe, sold the entire territory of Louisiana to Thomas Jefferson's negotiators for a paltry fifteen million dollars—about four cents an acre. Without the Haitian Revolution, it is unlikely that Napoleon would have sold a landmass that doubled the size of the then United States, especially as Jefferson had intended to approach the French simply looking to purchase New Orleans in order to have access to the heart of the Mississippi River. For enslaved people throughout the rest of the "New World," the victory in Haiti—the story of which had spread through plantations across the South, at the edges of cotton fields and in the quiet corners of loud kitchens—served as inspiration for what was possible.

Even William C. C. Claiborne, the governor of the territory that would become the state of Louisiana in 1812, wanted the territory to stop importing enslaved people from Haiti, fearing that some of them might have taken part in the Haitian Revolution. In 1804, Claiborne wrote a letter to then secretary of state James Madison, sharing his concern: "At present I am well assured, there is nothing to fear either from the Mulatto or negro population," he said, beginning by attempting to assuage any immediate fears the president and his cabinet may have had, "but at some *future period*, this quarter of the Union will (I fear) experience *in some degree*, the misfortunes of St. Domingo [Haiti], and *that period* will be hastened, if the people should be indulged by Congress with a continuance of the African-trade." Claiborne said that he would attempt "to prevent the bringing in, of slaves that have been concerned in the insurrection of St. Domingo."

According to historian David Brion Davis, "For nearly seventy years the image of Haiti hung over the South like a black cloud, a point of constant reference by proslavery leaders."

In the 1811 uprising in Louisiana, as the men marched along the bends of the river—drums rumbling, flags held high above their heads—they attacked several plantations with an assortment of knives, machetes, muskets, and other scavenged weapons, killing two white men and destroying property in their wake. The conspirators had laid the groundwork for several months through careful and secretive planning, and using coded language so as not to tip off unsympathetic eavesdroppers. At first, the surprise held. The farther they marched, the more men joined and the more weapons they accrued. Still, not many of the enslaved fighters had guns, and it would take only a small number of armed troops to stop their liberatory march.

Within forty-eight hours, local militia and federal troops suppressed the rebellion. Deslondes briefly escaped the initial wave of slaughter by hiding in the swamp but was quickly captured and executed. His hands were chopped off, the bones in his legs were shattered by bullets, and he was burned over a bale of straw. Many of the rebels were slaughtered on-site, their heads cut off and posted on stakes that lined the levee, a warning to other enslaved people that this was the price to pay for rebellion. Naval officer Samuel Hambleton wrote: "They were brung here for the sake of their Head, which decorate our Levee, all the way up the coast. They look like crows sitting on long poles."

Unlike other rebellions, such as Nat Turner's or John Brown's, the 1811 slave revolt has received little attention in the collective public memory.[*]

---

[*] In November 2019, artist Dread Scott led a reenactment in which hundreds of people, dressed in nineteenth-century garb, retraced the path of the 1811 rebellion, marching twenty-six miles over two days from LaPlace, Louisiana, to New Orleans.

There are no notes of what was said between the co-conspirators, little that gives us insight into what Deslondes may have been thinking. What is undoubtedly true is that each of the people assembled that evening knew the risk of their involvement.

Commodore Shaw captured the planters' sense of fear that pushed them to respond with such violence against those who had participated in the insurrection, and make an example to the larger enslaved population. "Had not the most prompt and energetic measures been thus taken, the whole coast would have exhibited a general sense of devastation; every description of property would have been consumed; and the country laid waste by Rioters." After the slaveholders' worst fears came to fruition, the backlash was brutal. Alarmed enslavers in Louisiana invested resources in training local militias, and slave patrols began surveilling Black people with increasing frequency in addition to limiting their ability to congregate in large groups.

Meanwhile, the federal government committed to defending the institution of slavery by officially granting Louisiana statehood, as a slave state, in 1812. Louisiana remained a state until 1861, when it seceded from the Union. In a speech at the time, Louisiana's commissioner made the state's priorities clear: "Louisiana looks to the formation of a

Southern confederacy to preserve the blessings of African slavery."

My mind wandered back to the exhibit in front of me. I looked at the rest of the bodiless figurines, observing the ridges in their tortured faces and adjusting my feet along the uneven brick beneath me.

These faces exemplify how the Whitney Plantation is unlike almost any other plantation in the country. In a state where plantations remain the sites of formal celebrations and weddings, where tours of former slave estates nostalgically center on the architectural merits of the old homes, where you are still more likely to hear stories of how the owners of the land "treated their slaves well" than you are to hear of the experiences of actual enslaved people, the Whitney stands apart by making the story of the enslaved the core of the experience.

On my way to the Whitney Plantation, the highway was lined with yellow wildflowers that danced from their roots every time a car drove by. Smoke seeped up into the sky from the refineries in the distance. Birds that had flown south from an unpredictable winter rose and fell together, beating their dark wings along the endless sky. The plantation is about an hour southeast of Baton Rouge and two hours southeast of the Louisiana State Penitentiary, the maximum-security prison known as Angola. The radio began crackling, the music becoming more static than melodious, as the land shifted from urban to pastoral—farmland on one side and levees on the other. Lost in the white noise of the radio, I must have been driving twenty miles above the speed limit, distracted by the clouds ahead, which looked like a kaleidoscope of calla lilies. The double yellow line on the single-lane highway swerved back and forth like it was trying to lose someone's trail.

I saw the signage for the plantation and turned onto the gravel road leading to its entrance. I was scheduled to meet John Cummings, the owner of the Whitney from 1999 to 2019, who had invested close to ten million dollars in the plantation.[*]

The land that is now the Whitney Plantation was originally purchased, in 1752, by a German immigrant to Louisiana named Ambroise Heidal (his family would later change their last name to the more French "Haydel"). When Ambroise died, his youngest son, Jean Jacques Haydel, took possession of the land—and, like many southern Louisiana planters in the early nineteenth century,

---

[*] Cummings donated the Whitney in 2019, making it a nonprofit.

entered the sugar trade. In 1820, Jean Jacques extended the property to his sons, Marcellin and Jean Jacques Jr. The brothers then purchased an adjacent plantation, extending their proprietorship farther downriver. Marcellin's widow, Marie Azélie Haydel, ran the plantation after his death and oversaw its most productive years. Under her watch, the plantation was one of the most successful sugarcane enterprises in all of Louisiana, producing over 350,000 pounds of sugar in 1844. By the time of her death, Marie Azélie Haydel was one of the largest slaveholders in the state. Following the end of the Civil War, the plantation came into the possession of Brandish Johnson. He renamed it Whitney, the surname of one of his sons-in-law. When the Civil War ended, many of the people formerly enslaved at the Whitney stayed on and continued to work the land.

Descendants of people enslaved at the Whitney still live in the areas surrounding the former plantation. A few now work at the Whitney—ranging from a director-level position to tour guides to the front desk. But much of the community still suffers from the intergenerational poverty that plagues many formerly enslaved communities more than a century and a half after emancipation. Poverty is common in Wallace, Louisiana, the area encompassing the Whitney, where over 90 percent of the population is Black. Wallace is also one of a series of majority-Black communities lining the Mississippi River from Baton Rouge to New Orleans that—as a result of their proximity to petrochemical plants—form what is known as Cancer Alley. Neighborhoods here have some of the highest cancer risks in the country, and chemical emissions from these plants are linked to cardiovascular, respiratory, and developmental ailments. Civil rights leader Reverend Dr. William J. Barber II put it this way when describing the landscape of factories and refineries along the Mississippi River: "The same land that held people captive through slavery is now holding people captive through this environmental injustice and devastation."

I was early for my meeting with John, so I followed Yvonne Holden, the director of operations for the Whitney Plantation and my impromptu guide for the day, as she led me on a tour of the plantation. Yvonne spoke with eager yet judicious conviction. She shared a profusion of historical facts but was careful to acknowledge when she was unsure of something, reminding me to check other sources to confirm. She was casually dressed, wearing a dark teal blouse, black jeans, and a pair of faded grey, low-cut Converse sneakers, their white laces bouncing lightly as she walked. She had light brown skin and black, curly hair pulled into a tight bun atop her head.

Born and raised in Chicago, Yvonne worked

for years in the city's food and beverage industry, specifically in the world of fine wine. After about ten years, she started to find herself increasingly unsatisfied with the work, a sentiment that was compounded by the incessant racism and sexism she said she experienced in the restaurant industry, making it difficult for her to move up and exhausting for her to navigate. "I [couldn't] be the person in those spaces, not at that time, constantly talking about how I was constantly being put at a disadvantage. Not only because I was a woman but because I was a Black woman, and how those things pretty much created these hurdles that were too high for me to jump over. I could have carved out a career. I still can carve out a career, but I wanted to do something more meaningful and attached to the community."

Sort of on a whim, in her thirties, she moved to New Orleans in 2015 with hopes of transitioning to a new career, in an affordable city that would provide her with the financial and social flexibility to explore interests she might not have otherwise been able to.

I soon learned that her own family history was entangled in the work she does. Her grandmother was born and raised in Mississippi and her grandfather in Arkansas. Her grandfather, who was ninety at the time of our conversation, had been nine years old when, in 1938, he and his sixteen-year-old brother decided to leave the state, hoping to escape the racial terror so many in the South experienced. But by the time they left, white Southerners had already watched the Great Migration pull well over a million Black people from the South, and with them, the cheap labor many white landowners had grown accustomed to. In order to prevent the mass migration from continuing at such a high rate, Yvonne said, they started stopping trains of Black people heading north, forcing the passengers off or forcing the entire train to turn back. The family lore is that the two boys walked all the way from Forrest City, Arkansas, to Chicago, Illinois. "It would make more sense that they hopped a train at least part of the way," Yvonne later told me. "Two young Black men walking the flat state of rural Illinois in the thirties would have definitely attracted the sort of attention that they were trying to escape from."

The fear that Yvonne's family felt—that so many Black folks living in the Jim Crow South experienced—had been somewhat of an abstraction to her until she made the trip to another museum dedicated to documenting the history of racial terror in this country: the National Memorial for Peace and Justice, in Montgomery, Alabama. Operated by the Equal Justice Initiative, a nonprofit organization founded by civil rights attorney Bryan Stevenson, the museum, among other functions, documents the history of lynching throughout the South, naming the people killed in each county across each state. "I found the county where my granddaddy was from and saw the people who were lynched there," she said. This was what Yvonne's grandfather and great-uncle had been running from.

The experience of visiting that museum changed her. Yvonne started to understand "exactly what legacies are. They're not just the things we choose. A lot of them are the things that we don't choose. So that also made me realize exactly how close my family is to this history."

When she learned that the Whitney Plantation was hiring tour guides, she jumped at the opportunity. She began to immerse herself in the historical literature around slavery, spending hours poring over piles of thick texts to better understand what slavery was for herself but also so she could communicate this history effectively.

"Although the individuals enslaved here probably were not my *direct* ancestors...this is an ancestral space. So it is a healing space. Working here became more of a calling than anything else."

Our first stop was a large white church, its flaking facade covered in a thin coat of dirt stained onto the building's exterior. Two Gothic windows with twelve panes each pointed to the roof, where black shingles lay atop one another. The door whistled as it opened, and the cinnamonwood floor moaned under us as we stepped inside and closed the door behind us. This church, built by freedmen, was established after the war and sits off the dirt road. They originally called it the Anti-Yoke Baptist Church, a statement against their former bondage and a homonymic tribute to Antioch, the cradle of Christianity.*

The old church was not originally on this plantation but was donated to the museum by the congregation that has occupied it since the late nineteenth century, a move that not everyone approves of. I had heard sentiments that the church and other exhibits not original to the plantation—like a trio of jail cells that sit at the center of the plantation grounds and were built in Pennsylvania in 1868—undermine the historical integrity of the Whitney. "It's sort of like taking the frame off a Rembrandt, keeping the frame and getting rid of the artwork," explained New Orleans preservation architect Robert Cangelosi Jr. in an interview with the Baton Rouge–based newspaper *The Advocate;* his firm has worked on a number of area plantations. "You must have integrity of site and location. Imagine moving a plantation from a rural setting to downtown New Orleans because

---

* In 1890, the congregation changed "Anti-Yoke" to "Antioch."

the tourism is greater—it's just not appropriate." Others I spoke to, however, feel as if these additions are part of a project that strengthens the Whitney's role as a space of memory beyond the plantation itself. Some see it as akin to an artistic endeavor, meant to use a range of different exhibits, original and not, to communicate the conditions of Black oppression. As historian Jessica Marie Johnson observed about the jail cells after her visit to the Whitney, "To bring a Pennsylvania prison built, more than likely, after emancipation into physical confrontation with slave cabins literally dabbles in blackness as a racialized assemblage and paints it on the landscape." She asks, "Does it matter, then, that the black people imprisoned in the structure may or may not have been slaves? What is freedom in a world of slaves? What is incarceration?"

Inside the church were two rows of wooden pews separated by hexagonal white columns. Scattered throughout the church's interior—standing next to the pews, sitting on the floor, hiding in the corners—were several hand-carved statuettes. There were more than two dozen life-size clay sculptures of small children, each one so alive despite its inanimateness, intricately detailed from the contours of their lips to the bridges of their noses. My heart jumped when I turned the corner and saw them because, just for a moment, I thought they were real children. Their clothing was simple and sparse: the boys were wearing pairs of over-sized overalls, though some were in only shorts, leaving their chests exposed. Some were wearing bucket hats that sat just above their eyes. The girls were wearing simple dresses, some of them with their hair wrapped underneath cloths tied around their heads, and others with small locks falling onto their foreheads. Their eyes were hollow and tender. Rays from the sun shot through the Gothic windows of the church and fell directly onto the figurines, as if they were wearing the sunlight as a shawl.

These statues are *The Children of Whitney*, designed specifically for the plantation by artist Woodrow Nash to add a new layer to the landscape of the plantation. "There's so many misconceptions about slavery," Yvonne said. "People don't really consider the *children* who were brought over, and the children who were born into this system, and the way to get people to let their guard down when they come here is being confronted with the reality of slavery, and the reality of slavery is child enslavement."

Children sustained and embodied the institution of slavery, especially after the formal end of the transatlantic slave trade in 1808. By 1860, there were nearly four million enslaved people, 57 percent of whom were under the age of twenty. In a harrowing description of the conditions some slave children lived in, Francis Fedric, who was born enslaved in Virginia and escaped in his forties, wrote in his autobiography, "Children feed like pigs out of troughs, and being supplied sparingly, invariably fight and quarrel with one another over their meals." Children under ten were 51 percent of total Black deaths in 1850 (compared to 38 percent of white deaths). Put differently, as Mississippi planter M. W. Phillips wrote, "Not one-fourth of the [slave] children born are raised."

"I know me personally"—Yvonne's voice became softer—"when I came in this church for the first time...I burst into tears when I saw these statues." Her eyes moved slowly from one figurine to the next. "Each visitor gets a lanyard with an image of this, and the image is paired with an excerpt from the Federal Writers' Project. A slave narrative."

The Federal Writers' Project plays a significant role at the Whitney, enhancing its ability to center the voices of enslaved people. Created as part of the New Deal's Works Progress Administration, the project included an initiative to document the experience of slavery. In the late 1930s, staff collected more than 2,300 firsthand accounts of formerly enslaved people, including 500 black-and-white photographs. The material was edited into seventeen volumes.

Yvonne considers these stories to be among the

most important documents on record in US history, and she is always struck by how few people seem to be aware of their existence. "There are so many tragedies embedded in this history," she said. "But for me, one of the most profound ones is [that] people couldn't record their own histories. And so these narratives that we have from the 1930s are the only things that we really have to give us insight outside of, of course, Frederick Douglass, Harriet Tubman, Harriet Jacobs, and the like. We do have some narratives of people who were able to escape to freedom and write about their experience while they were still alive, but on the whole . . . we lost that history." While Yvonne is correct that the Federal Writers' Project collection represents one of the most important and extensive sets of narratives of enslaved people this country has, historians note that there are other ways that enslaved people told their stories. For example, the voices of formerly enslaved people can be found through interviews with abolitionists. There were also oral history projects involving formerly enslaved people conducted at historically Black colleges and universities—including Fisk University, Southern University, and what is now called Prairie View A&M University—beginning in 1929.

The voices and stories of enslaved people are the foundation of how visitors experience the Whitney. They are especially important because, apart from a single photo of an enslaved man, there are no images or stories of the many people who once lived on the plantation itself. "Their voices are forever gone and silenced," Yvonne said.

While a life like Frederick Douglass's is remarkable, we must remember that not every person who lived through slavery was like Douglass. Most did not learn to read or write. Most did not engage in hand-to-hand combat with white slave breakers. Most did not live close enough to free states in the North to have any hope of escape. No one, enslaved or otherwise, was like Douglass. There were other brilliant, exceptional people who lived under slavery, and many resisted the institution in innumerable ways, but our country's teachings about slavery, painfully limited, often focus singularly on heroic slave narratives at the expense of the millions of men and women whose stories might be less sensational but are no less worthy of being told.

I thought of my primary and secondary education. I remembered feeling crippling guilt as I silently wondered why every enslaved person couldn't simply escape like Douglass, Tubman, and Jacobs had. I found myself angered by the stories of those who did not escape. Had they not tried hard enough? Didn't they care enough to do something? Did they *choose* to remain enslaved? This, I now realize, is part of the insidiousness of white supremacy; it illuminates the exceptional in order to implicitly blame those who cannot, in the most brutal circumstances, attain superhuman heights. It does this instead of blaming the system, the people who built it, the people who maintained it.

In overly mythologizing our ancestors, we forget an all-too-important reality: the vast majority were ordinary people, which is to say they were people just like everyone else. This ordinariness is only shameful when used to legitimate oppression. This is its own quiet violence.

We stepped out of the church and back beneath the overcast sky. Not far from the church was a long stone-white wall lined with tall black granite slabs.

"So this is the first memorial that we come to," Yvonne explained. "It's the Wall of Honor. This memorial is dedicated to the three hundred fifty-four people that we have records of that were enslaved here on this plantation."

Engraved in white on each of the slabs are dozens of names, with each name accompanied by a date of birth and often a tribal affiliation, which, if present, indicates that the person was brought directly to the New World by the transatlantic slave trade as compared to having been born into slavery in the United States.

"We divided the memorial into two sides. In 1752, when this plantation was founded, it was not a sugar plantation. It was an indigo plantation."

Yvonne explained how in the plantation's earliest days, rice and indigo were the centerpieces of southern Louisiana's plantation economy, and the French ships traveling back and forth between Louisiana and West Africa needed to bring over both types of seeds along with people who would know how to cultivate them once they arrived in North America. Enslaved Africans arrived in Louisiana largely from the Senegambia, with over 60 percent of Louisiana's slave population having come from that region.

Yvonne turned back toward the wall. "So this represents people who were enslaved here during that period of time. It also represents people enslaved here during the transatlantic slave trade." She then pointed her finger toward the other side of the memorial, to what she called the "sugar generation." She looked at the wall, almost as if peering through it. "It represents everybody enslaved here during the US domestic slave trade."

In 1795, there were nearly twenty thousand enslaved people in Louisiana, almost three thousand of whom were on the German Coast. Taking effect in 1808, during Thomas Jefferson's presidency, the United States officially prohibited the transatlantic slave trade. While the transatlantic slave trade did not come to a sudden halt, it became a criminal offense to capture and import Africans to the United States. Some ships, however, continued to smuggle in persons from West Africa and the Caribbean. Half a century later, in 1860, the number of enslaved people in Louisiana had multiplied sixteenfold, with over 331,000 enslaved. Much of the increase was due to the domestic explosion of the enslaved population as a result of the internal slave trade, though some of the increase was because of the continued illegal slave trade.

I turned my head to the wall of granite slabs. Part of one such slab read:

Charles Mandingo Nation Born ca. 1764	Jean Nard Nation Born ca. 1764	Lubin Ado Nation Born ca. 1767
Sara Mandingo Nation Born ca. 1774	François Canga Nation Born ca. 1779	Madou Mandingo Nation Born ca. 1781
Constance Congo Nation Born ca. 1759	Dick Soso (Susu) Nation Born ca. 1758	Yéro Poulard Nation Born ca. 1768
Coacou Mina Nation Born ca. 1768	Samba Poulard Nation Born ca. 1768	Valentin Chamba Nation Born ca. 1778

I ran my fingers over the text and felt my skin dip into the stone, each ravine of letters resurrecting a life I would never know.

In addition to names, several of the granite slabs contained excerpts from stories shared in the Federal Writers' Project. The stories added devastating emotional texture to the sea of solitary names, recounting pain, trauma, exploitation, and sexual violence.

Written on the wall in front of me was a quote from Julia Woodrich, born in 1851 and enslaved in Louisiana: "My ma had fifteen children and none of them had the same pa. Every time she was sold she would get another man. My ma had one boy by her moss that was my missis brother's child. You see every time she was sold she had to take another man. Her had fifteen children after she was sold de last time."

Yvonne stood behind me and gave me time to process what I was reading as my eyes surveyed the harrowing texts over and over again. "I'll show you another narrative," she said after about a minute. "This one, she's talking about her sister, and how the plantation owner would come to the cabin to get her sister at night. So I use these as transitions [on the tour] because, in order to really understand slavery, we have to understand what slavery meant for women."

Woodrich's story continued in another vignette

on a slab to the right. "I 'member how my master used to would come and get my sister, make her take a bath and comb her hair, and take her down in the quarter all night, den have de nerve to come around de next day and ask her how she feel." When women were put on slave ships that crossed the Atlantic, it was common for white sailors to rape them during the journey. Sexual violence was ubiquitous throughout slavery, and it followed enslaved women wherever they went.

The violence enacted on Julia's mother and sister are part of a long history in which Black women were seen as both undesirable and sexually objectified. This is the illogic of white supremacy; it does not need intellectual continuity. The temptation is to say that this illogic "dehumanizes" its subject, though some historians argue that such a characterization is incorrect. Historian Walter Johnson aptly notes that the "language of 'dehumanization' is misleading because slavery depended upon the human capacities of enslaved people. It depended upon their reproduction. It depended upon their labor. And it depended upon their sentience. Enslaved people could be taught: their intelligence made them valuable. They could be manipulated: their desires could make them pliable. They could be terrorized: their fears could make them controllable. And they could be tortured: beaten, starved, raped, humiliated, degraded. It is these last that are conventionally understood to be the most 'inhuman' of slaveholders' actions and those that most 'dehumanized' enslaved people. And yet these actions epitomize the failure of this set of terms to capture what was at stake in slaveholding violence: the extent to which slaveholders depended upon violated slaves to bear witness, to provide satisfaction, to provide a living, human register of slaveholders' power."

Julia Woodrich's words lingered. When that man made Julia's sister lie down in his bed he did not have to believe her to be less than human. He simply had to know that she did not have the power to stop him. To be sure, enslaved women often resisted these advances in ways large and small, but they were up against not only the physical power of the person enacting violence against them but also the power of the state, the power of patriarchy, the power of a society. These acts were not only permissible but legally encouraged. There were laws stating that almost any crime committed by a white person against a Black person was in fact not a crime at all.* The illogic

---

* In the infamous Virginia slave codes, for example, it states: "And if any slave resist his master, or owner, or other person, by his or her order, correcting such slave, and shall happen to be killed in such correction, it shall not be accounted felony." (Louise A. Breen, ed., *Converging Worlds: Communities and Cultures in Colonial*

of it all appears to reveal a simple linear truth that is often lost—oppression is never about humanity or lack thereof. It is, and always has been, about power.

I shared some of these parallels with Yvonne, and she nodded before closing her eyes and taking a deep breath, the sort of breath I have to imagine she has taken many times. She reopened her eyes and said that she thought endlessly about this idea of physical agency being stripped from the enslaved, and how one of the most insidious parts of it all was tied to the fact that this stripping away of agency did not end after they passed away. She started talking to me about the role that enslaved people played in the fields of science and medicine, how an enslaved person's body—dead or alive—was the site of experiments that propelled the entire medical field forward.

"A lot of medical schools, during the history of slavery, largely depended on cadavers of enslaved people. That's who they practiced on...Black women's bodies were used in experiments to advance medicine, like the field of gynecology. We learn about 'from cradle to grave' in history, but what about postmortem? What happened to Black people postmortem? It's like their bodies are

---

America, A Sourcebook [New York: Routledge, 2013], 93.)

constantly being exploited at every age, even in their death."

In her book *The Price for Their Pound of Flesh*, historian Daina Ramey Berry writes about how some of the country's top medical schools—places like Harvard, the Universities of Maryland, Pennsylvania, and Virginia—used the corpses of enslaved people, often purchased on the black market, as tools for their research and medical education. "The body trade was as elaborate as the trans-Atlantic and domestic slave trade that transported Africans to the New World and resold African-Americans on our soil," she wrote in an essay for the *New York Times* based on her research. "But when enslaved people died, some were sold again and trafficked along the same roads and waterways they traveled while alive." Medical schools typically used the corpses of executed criminals or unclaimed bodies from prisons and almshouses, itself an abhorrent practice, but when there were not enough of those needed bodies for their anatomy classes, schools paid people to go to cemeteries and dig up the bodies of the enslaved.

Yvonne continued: "We need to also understand that if any children ever were born, that plantation owner, of course, would have been enslaving his own child, which happened all the time. So a lot of our visitors are completely ignorant of this." According to James Roberts, an enslaved man who fought in the Revolutionary War and was sold in 1783 to a Louisiana plantation several years later, "From fifty to sixty head of women were kept constantly for breeding. No man was allowed to go there, save white men. From twenty to twenty-five children a year were bred on that plantation. As soon as they are ready for market, they are taken away and sold, as mules or other cattle."

I asked Yvonne about the visitors to the Whitney and if they were different from the people who might typically visit a plantation. "Most of our visitors are self-selecting," she said. "We don't get many people who come to our site not knowing where they're coming. Which is to say, no one is coming to the Whitney thinking they're only coming to admire the architecture of the Big House. We get people who consider themselves fairly versed in this history." Then she added a caveat. "But ultimately they come from the same education system we all have."

I wanted to get a sense from Yvonne if the white visitors experienced the space differently from Black visitors. I qualified my question with a recognition that any response would be a generalization that doesn't necessarily reflect the sentiments or experiences of an entire demographic of people, but still, I was curious.

"Number one question [we get from white

visitors]: 'I know slavery was bad...I don't mean it this way, but...were there any good slave owners?'"

Yvonne took another deep breath, the frustration from thinking about the persistence of the question visible in her face—the look of someone professionally committed to patience but personally exhausted by the emotional toll it has taken on her. "I really give a short but nuanced answer to that," she said. "Regardless of how these individuals fed the people that they owned, regardless of how they clothed them, regardless of if they never laid a hand on them, they were still sanctioning the system...You can't say, 'Hey, this person kidnapped your child, but they fed them well. They were a good person.' How absurd does that sound?"

The question, even if the visitors are unaware of it, is tied to decades of mainstream historical thought, in part thanks to the early-twentieth-century historian Ulrich Bonnell Phillips, who propagated the idea that there were in fact many kind slave owners who provided a good life for their enslaved workers. Phillips's assertion was built on the premise that chattel slavery was a largely benevolent system designed to uplift, protect, and civilize an inferior African race. In his 1918 book, *American Negro Slavery,* Phillips wrote, "On the whole the plantations were the best schools yet invented for the mass training of that sort of inert and backward people which the bulk of the American negroes represented." As historian Drew Gilpin Faust has written, it wasn't until the 1956 publication of Kenneth M. Stampp's *The Peculiar Institution: Slavery in the Ante-Bellum South* that this widespread interpretation began to change. Stampp's history, unlike many of his predecessors', was written under the fundamental premise that Black and white people were equal, something earlier white historians did not accept as a given.

Black visitors to the Whitney, on the other hand, bring to the plantation their own set of concerns, questions, and anxieties. At times, Yvonne has found that Black visitors want the Whitney to go further when presenting its history to white visitors and tell an unadulterated story of violence and brutality—to throw away the veil and convey what so few plantations have ever been willing to acknowledge. "If we're not talking enough about the brutality—like, how people were beaten, how awfully they were treated, how young girls were raped, and things like that—sometimes people...will think that we are sanitizing this history, if we do not *only* tell it through the lens of depredation. We got these complaints before, totally fine. It's like, 'You guys didn't say enough about what we went through. You didn't tell people this. You didn't tell people this. You didn't tell people this,' and I get it, I really do. It's like, 'I hear you.'"

Yvonne's voice shifted to a mix of empathy, imbued with a sense of resolution. "First and foremost, we're a ninety-minute tour. There ain't enough time. But also, we can't continue to view enslaved people only through the lens of what happened to them...We have to talk about who they were, we have to talk about their resiliency, we have to talk about their resistance, we have to talk about their strength, their determination, and the fact that they passed down legacies. Maybe they're not physical legacies, but they passed down legacies to generations, and those legacies are living well inside of African Americans today.

"If you can't see them for being people, you can't see me as a person. I want to get you to see them, because I know as a Black woman what my challenges in society have been. It's stemming from this history, so if I can't get you to see them, you can't see the person standing in front of you."

The old slave quarters at the Whitney were built from wooden planks laid on top of and alongside one another, each panel shaved from cypress trees that once ornamented the banks of the river. On the small building's facade, the two-century-old planks had been discolored by time and weather. The boards were a muted green that faded halfway down the wood, like the residue of tears that never reached the bottom of its face. The slave quarters sat on several small brick foundations with three unadorned wooden steps leading up to the porch and two entryways. The room felt fragile, like one wrong step might break a piece of history.

Prior to the Civil War, there were twenty-two slave cabins on the Whitney Plantation. While most of the original cabins have been torn down, two survived, one of which we were standing in. Inside, small beams of light sliced through the holes in the wood boards. Bursts of air hissed through the cracks, licking the skin on my face and crawling under my wool hat. "I'm getting our visitors to understand that we have very specific ideas of what comfort is, what food is—and those things don't apply here," Yvonne said as we stood inside the cabin. "This is not a home. This is a structure to house people. It's small, it's noisy, it's exposed to the elements. Everything outside is inside." The emotional power of the structure makes it the sort of place where, no matter how many people are around, you feel like you are the only person there.

The feeling was notably different from my experience of standing inside the cabin at Monticello. While the cabin at Monticello was a powerful re-creation of an old slave quarters, there was something unique about running my hands over a two-century-old piece of wood and knowing that an enslaved person's fingers had once traced those same cracks. There was something about listening to a creak of the floor and thinking how the board must have groaned under the bodies of the people with no choice but to sleep directly on it. "This is how also we link this history to the present," Yvonne said. "Because this cabin, inhabited by enslaved people, continued to be inhabited by their descendants until the year of 1975."

The slave cabins were surrounded by sugar kettles, a few of them original to the plantation: large metal bowls filled with rainwater that had once been used to boil down juice from the cane. The presence of these bowls prompted the telling of a more holistic story regarding the slave trade.

"[This] gives us an insight into the larger economy of slavery, and the fact that a lot of the sugar [produced] here didn't stay in Louisiana. It was sent up north to granulation facilities," Yvonne said. "That gives us an opportunity to talk about the textile industry and the rise of industrialization. And the North—where were they getting that cotton from? It gives us an opportunity to talk about the larger linked economy of banks, insurance companies, slave traders. All of these things, all these cottage industries that ultimately fed into this larger system of slavery, making it so people, when they come here, are not just focusing on the plantation owners. It was the entire society. And it was entire countries.

"It's so easy for people to just look at these plantation owners and be like, 'This history is awful. *They* were the bad guys.'" Yvonne paused. "They *were* the bad guys, but what are the larger implications of a global society? In England, these factory workers were going to work in the nineteenth century, and all of a sudden molasses comes on the market." There in England, for instance, sugar became cheaper and more accessible—something factory workers could buy, Yvonne pointed out. "Poor people can now afford sweetener, which used to be reserved for the elite." I nodded. "And so these individuals are going to work and now they can start purchasing sweetener for their afternoon tea...and then they start to demand [it]. And that is in direct correlation to the people who are enslaved on these plantations. And so it helps people understand that it's not so cut-and-dry. It's not just like, 'Those overseers were sadistic people. The plantations were morally bankrupt and corrupt.' Yes, they were. But also, in Europe, once the appetite for sugar and chocolate and coffee and cheap textiles and all these things started flooding the market, and people can finally buy into this larger system of capitalism and consumption, who is at the other end of it?"

As Yvonne and I walked toward the Big House, John Cummings, his white hair combed over from left to right under a large-brimmed hat, drove toward us in a golf cart whose motor hummed in the chill air. His presence highlighted a remarkable fact about the Whitney Plantation: almost every tour guide I had seen was a Black woman. I pointed this out to Yvonne, and she smiled, nodding approvingly. "We want this to be an African American–run museum predominantly." She clarified that there were some white tour guides, and "we very much believe that white people should be doing this work too," but they felt strongly that a museum centered on the experiences of Black people should be predominantly staffed by Black people.

While the majority of the staff might be Black, John, who bought the property and developed it into a museum at his own expense, is a white man in his eighties.

I first met John a few months before I visited the Whitney, at his second home, an extensive plot of farmland in Middleburg, Virginia. We sat at the table in his kitchen, which smelled like ginger and green tea, as he rolled up his sleeves and leaned back in his chair, brimming with equal parts confidence and vigor. His thick white beard wrapped around the bottom half of his face. His thin-framed, rectangular glasses sat slightly crooked, sliding slowly down his nose when he became especially animated. His southern Louisiana inflection rose and fell slowly and symphonically, with long pauses situating themselves in the middle of each self-deprecating sentence. He is a multi-millionaire engaged in answering the ongoing question of how to use his wealth, a white person who says he has come to understand, in the last quarter of his life, the totality of the oppression that Black people have experienced.

John grew up in New Orleans and attended Catholic schools from kindergarten through college, graduating from Loyola University New Orleans with a business and law degree. He became a successful lawyer, focusing on large class-action tort cases, opening offices in New Orleans, Philadelphia, and Seattle. While he was building and expanding his law practice, John found causes beyond the court. A self-proclaimed liberal, he worked alongside Black activists to reopen the Audubon Park swimming pool in New Orleans when the city kept it closed to avoid making it an integrated facility.

In addition to being an attorney, John had a successful career in real estate. One day in 1998, he said, a friend gave him a call and told him that the old Whitney Plantation, which at the time was owned by the plastics and petrochemicals corporation Formosa, was for sale. At this point he wasn't thinking of it for the site's historical significance; it was simply another potentially profitable real estate acquisition.

The plantation was in bad shape, but John thought he would clean it up and, similar to what had been done with other plantations throughout the South, turn it into a tourist destination.

That changed when he was given a report commissioned by Formosa. The company had hired independent experts to provide a history of the property in an attempt to mollify environmentalists and other advocacy groups concerned about a seven-hundred-million-dollar, two-thousand-acre chemical plant being built beside the Mississippi River and occupying land with such historical significance. While much of the eight-volume document talked about the architecture and infrastructure on the land, it also outlined the plantation's slave-trading past. "I looked at the inventory, and there were one hundred and one slaves then. There was a name, an age, a column for what they did on the plantation," John said. "A dollar amount for every one of them."

After reading the report, John started seeking out more documents about slavery. It was a different piece of inventory, from another plantation, that ultimately pushed him to make the Whitney into a place willing to reckon with the history he was confronting.

"Not at our plantation, but I saw an inventory where the woman was twenty-nine. I forget her name." He leaned forward and brought his hands together. "I'm going to say it twice. There's a job on the plantation that was 'good breeder.' She was a 'good breeder.' Had nine children in eleven years. 'Good breeder.'" He shook his head. "Very few days start without me thinking about that. And that's when I changed. That's when I realized that I could not have this property and make it a tourist attraction that would glorify a life of people who exploited human beings. Couldn't do it anymore. I couldn't."

He continued: "I was embarrassed. Because here was this big shot from New Orleans—thought I was the smartest guy in the world—and I didn't know *that*. *So,* I thought, *what are you going to do about it, man?* I knew, if I didn't know it, everybody I knew with this color skin didn't know about it." He dragged the back of his fingers down his forearm. "[It] was never in our education."

John began the process of educating himself. "As I got into studying slavery, and I've read probably eleven hundred oral histories, [I thought,] *Sooner or later I'm going to get to the one where the woman was not raped or the man was not almost beaten to death or branded or his finger cut off or his ear cut off for trying to run away.* But I haven't gotten there yet." He added: "You get an eerie feeling 'cause it's their words, more or less. And you feel as though someone is talking to you who never had a voice...and all of a sudden, you feel very strange. It's not a feeling of guilt. It's a feeling of 'discovered ignorance.' I don't know how else to explain it. When you wonder, *How could this have happened and I didn't know about it? How could that happen?*"

John has invested more than ten million dollars of his own money into the museum over the course of a fifteen-year restoration effort.

When word got out that John was building a museum dedicated to slavery on a former plantation, some were skeptical of what he was doing and why he was doing it. During a conversation I had with Leon A. Waters, the local New Orleans historian and activist called John "arrogant" and a "chauvinist" and questioned his motives as well as his approach to the Whitney.

John told me that there are people who have suggested he is attempting to make money by exploiting the history of Black suffering, a claim he fundamentally rebukes. "I don't make any money here," he said. "I spent ten million dollars here. And you can check. Send somebody and audit the books. I don't get paid for anything." The volume of his voice was increasing, his tone shifting. "I was putting up a hundred thousand dollars a month just to get it going."

The first day the Whitney Plantation opened, according to John, only four people showed up and "two of them were lost." He guffawed at the memory. "They were looking for another plantation, but I held them there and they went on the tour." Soon, though, word spread, and by the end of its first year the Whitney had had about 34,000 visitors, a considerable number for a plantation an hour away from New Orleans with no other meaningful tourist draw. Steadily, the numbers continued to rise. In 2017, it had 68,000 visitors. When I talked to him at the end of 2018, he hoped to reach 200,000 annual visitors in the next five years (though these plans were interrupted when COVID-19 swept across the country in 2020).

John believes that it is not enough for people to write about slavery from the towers of academia if so many of those works never reach a wide audience. He thinks the Whitney offers something different, something more dynamic. "I've seen some of the greatest empirical studies, and they sit on library shelves gathering dust. Nobody reads them. We want to go to the masses, man. We want to go to the masses."

Clouds slid across the sky as if some invisible hand was pushing them along as Yvonne and I walked over to the main office building on the plantation. Yvonne said she wanted to introduce me to Dr. Ibrahima Seck, John's partner in building the Whitney from its earliest days. Seck, a Senegalese historian and the Whitney's director of research, splits his time between southern Louisiana and the Senegalese capital city of Dakar. When we met, he had just arrived at the plantation from his home in New Orleans. Beneath Seck's coat he wore a black-and-white plaid oxford shirt, every button on the shirt fastened neatly up to his neck. The shirt was tucked into a pair of faded grey jeans that crinkled at the cuffs. His smooth, dark skin made it difficult to know his age. As he spoke, Seck was judicious with his movements—no lifted hand or stroked chin seemed to be done without purpose. While English is his fourth language, he spoke with eloquent fluency. The final consonants at the ends of his sentences would hum in the air above his lips before dissolving into the next word.

Seck was born and raised in a town in northeast Senegal, and went on to become a high school teacher in Dakar. During his time in the classroom, he told me, he was selected by the United States Information Agency to participate in their International Visitor Program, through which he visited several states as part of a cultural exchange program. "Mississippi was part of the trip," Seck said, the *s*'s in "Mississippi" rolling together like the undercurrent of the river that shares its name. "We visited Oxford, and they brought us to see an old Delta blues singer, James 'Son' Thomas. When he started playing I just melted. I said to myself, 'There's something that needs to be investigated here along this river—along the Mississippi River.'"

Listening to Thomas play, Seck heard and felt a direct connection to his homeland. "The Delta blues is so close to our musical culture in the Sahara of Africa," he said. "When we get closer to the desert, that's where you see many people singing along with the African banjo—very sad songs. So I found many similarities there."

Seck knew he wanted to study how this music had crossed an ocean and made its way to this small city in the American South, and he knew that understanding the history of the transatlantic slave trade—specifically the pathway from modern-day Senegal to the mouth of the Mississippi—was where he needed to start.

"Most African Americans don't know much about Africa and Africans, and most Africans don't know much about African Americans. They may know the music. They may know something related to the culture. They don't really know about the history of slavery in the Western Hemisphere," he said. "So I really felt that there's a necessity for us to better know the diaspora, and I was so glad to be able to work on a topic like this."

Seck felt that Louisiana was the perfect place to study. The Mississippi River, he said, was "the main artery through which African culture was introduced here and became a very important part of the definition of American culture and identity."

Seck started taking English language classes at the American Center Dakar while teaching full-time, in addition to beginning his doctorate at Cheikh Anta Diop University in Dakar. Six years after his initial trip to Mississippi, he applied for and received a Fulbright grant, which took him back to the American South. He spent the next few years traveling back and forth between the US and Senegal, eventually becoming an associate professor at the university while continuing to do his research. In 2000, he was introduced to John Cummings by Gwendolyn Midlo Hall, the historian who had built the Afro-Louisiana History and Genealogy database, and who had become a mentor to Seck after he heard her speak in Senegal years earlier.

"From the very beginning I felt a lot of commitment from him," Seck said of John Cummings. "He is someone who can really listen, and once you convince him that this is the right thing to do, nobody can stop him. So from the very beginning I felt that he's not doing this for money. He's giving something to the community."

I asked Seck if he was ever skeptical of John—a Southern white multimillionaire whose actions rubbed more than a few people the wrong way; a man who asked him to cross an ocean to help build something that was only then a flicker in his imagination.

"No, I was not worried," he said, shaking his head. "Sometimes he may say something that may upset some people, but it is not like the willingness to hurt. It is just a misunderstanding." For Seck, no trepidation he might have felt could outweigh the potential benefits of being part of a project that would help people confront what their education had largely avoided, the yawning gap on slavery that he had observed during his brief time in the US.

"The problem with [this] country—and also all around the world—is...miseducation. The miseducation of the mind and hidden history. I saw so much in the documents—in the archives—dived into the archives for so many years, so many things, that I said, 'People need to know this.' Of course people have [written] about those things before I got involved. But I said to myself, 'Books are really good, but who can read a book? Who can have *access* to books?' This needs to be an open book, up under the sky, that people can come here and see."

When people leave the Whitney, Seck wants them not only to be able to connect the dots between the intergenerational iterations of violence but also to understand that the importation of Africans was responsible for both the economic foundation of this country and its culture. "You see children being abused. Women being abused. People being mutilated, decapitated," he said in reference to enslavement. "But I always tell my visitors that we also need to go beyond all of that. Yes, of course, they did suffer a lot. They built the foundation of the economy of this country. But let's also go beyond all of that and see how they contributed to building the culture that all Americans are enjoying today. And also, outside in the world, the culture is everywhere. And what makes American culture so active abroad, outside, has something to do with the culture that was born here on this plantation."

I walked with Yvonne to an area of the plantation called the Field of Angels, which was built to honor the lives of 2,200 enslaved children who died here in Saint John the Baptist Parish between 1823 and 1863. The plot of land had been made into a small brick courtyard surrounded by black granite plaques that were about waist-high and that listed the children's names.

At the center of the courtyard, on an elevated pillar, was a statue of a woman down on one knee. Her chest was bare and a pair of large wings jutted out from just under the shoulder blades on her back. A heavily creased cloth was draped loosely around her midsection, falling over her legs to the ground near her feet. Her hair was pulled into several thick rows of braids tugged horizontally across each side of her scalp. Her neck was smooth and curved, while her head was bent, eyes cast downward, looking at the limp body of the small child in her hands.

My own son was a few months from turning two at the time, while his baby sister was a couple of weeks from making her way into the world. The artist's rendering of this child, cradled in the angel's hands, evoked from me something I was unprepared for. I felt the blood leave my fingers and arrow toward my heart. I felt the saliva bubble up in the back of my throat, and the space around me became swollen with a grief I could not name. I had to actively push out of my head the image of my own child in those hands. I had to remind myself to breathe because I realized I was not.

"These are their death records, names, dates that they died, how old they were when they died," Yvonne said. "And, if all the information was recorded, you also see the name of their mom. Most of the children here died as toddlers—died very young." She scanned the names on the granite slabs. "Most of them died of malnutrition and disease.

"We do know, through others, that sometimes enslaved women would kill their own children, because they didn't want them to grow up in the system. But we can't officially say that here, because we don't know why these children died. But that is something that we do see in this history: women making this really, really unimaginable decision because they understand, especially if they have young girls, what it would be like for them."

After my visit to the Field of Angels, I walked back toward one of the slave cabins. I stood on the porch, looking out over as much of the plantation as my eyes would allow me to see, tracing the uneven cartography of the vast land. The sky had changed to a soft copper. More people had arrived, and the plantation bustled with activity on an increasingly chilly midafternoon.

To my left was the Big House, framed by a row of oak trees whose branches bent like crooked crescent moons, wind chimes singing in their tangled limbs. The leaves had changed color, folded into themselves, and dressed the dirt on the cobblestone path in a thin blanket of brown foliage. The Big House sat at the end of the road, alluring in its decadence, its white facade with a dozen open doors and windows, wind slapping the shutters back and forth against the panes.

Behind me was a memorial of intersecting white stone partitions, with the names of a hundred thousand people enslaved in Louisiana laid out across each black slab. It was similar to the Wall of Honor I had seen earlier in my visit but far larger, with even more names. The walls of this memorial sat like shadows anchored to the ground, a labyrinth of lost voices etched into dark stone. It was staggering to consider the enormity of the number of people, and to consider what that number meant in the context of my own life. I thought about all of the descendants of these names and the lineage of Black Louisianans who came after them. How the intergenerational progeny of the names on these walls were possibly people I passed on the street, people I had gone to school with, people checking out their food next to me in the same grocery store. Perhaps they were members of my own family. Lineage is a strand of smoke making its way into the sky even though we can't always tell where it's coming from, even though sometimes we can't distinguish the smoke from the sky itself.

In front of me a tour passed by, being led by a Black woman—who, Yvonne had told me, was the descendant of one of the people once enslaved here. The visitors listened to her intently, nodding as she shared with them so much of what Yvonne had shared with me. I pulled a piece of paper from my pocket. "An open book, up under the sky." I had written the phrase in my notebook when it fell from Seck's lips earlier that day in reference to the Whitney. After I had written it down, I had torn the page out of my book and folded it into my pocket. I held the paper, shifting the uneven edges of the ripped sheet between my fingers. The ink was now smudged from my body heat and the friction of rubbing against itself. I looked at the bleeding words.

The Whitney exists as a laboratory for historical ambition, an experiment in rewriting what long ago was rewritten. It is a hammer attempting to unbend four centuries of crooked nails. It is a place asking the question *How do you tell a story that has been told the wrong way for so long?* For some, it is a place that doesn't fully live up to its ambition, a scattered assortment of exhibits that fails to tell a cohesive story. For others, it is a necessary, even if imperfect, corrective against a history that has been misrepresented or ignored for so long, a place that does far more good than harm. From both perspectives, it has served as a catalyst for discussion around how plantations should reveal the truth of slavery in ways that few other places have.

I stepped off the creaking porch of the slave cabin and turned around, looking in the direction of the memorial to the 1811 slave revolt, which sits on the plantation's edge. I thought of how I had grown up in Louisiana and had never been taught that the largest slave rebellion in US history happened just miles from the city that had raised me. I had never been taught that the Louisiana Purchase was a direct result of the Haitian Revolution, the uprising that laid the groundwork for all the slave revolts that followed in its wake.

About fifty yards from the slave cabins was a large bell, its cylinder of cast iron widening at the lip as if trying to get a better look at the earth beneath it, its color dulled by years of exposure to the elements. A coiled rope, its pale brown fibers braided tightly together, was tied to the top of the bell and hung down at its side. Historically, the role of the bell on a plantation served two purposes. It was used to signal when it was time to go out into the fields at the beginning of the day and when it was time to return at the end of it. It was also used to summon enslaved people, often when someone was about to be punished, an audible marker of the terror that enslavers maintained. At the

Whitney, this bell has been repurposed, reclaimed. As visitors move through the different parts of the plantation, they are invited to ring the bell in honor of all the people who lived here and died in the struggle for freedom. I pulled on the rope. The bell's metal tongue swung inside its body, as its chime reverberated like a heavy heart.

"I can't change what happened here"

ANGOLA PRISON

My memories of traveling up I-10 West from New Orleans are recollections of trips to Boy Scout camps, to soccer tournaments, and to visit my family in neighboring states. For others, this particular stretch of highway signals a very different kind of journey, one that brings them to the Louisiana State Penitentiary. I watched the city's high-rises dissolve into long stretches of swamp and marshland, watched that marshland turn into swathes of green pastures, watched those pastures give way to yellow sweet gum trees with leaves colored by the changing season.

On the bus ride to the prison, known by many as Angola, I sat next to Norris Henderson, a man I've known for years because of his political work around voting rights. Norris spent nearly thirty years incarcerated in Angola for a crime he maintains he did not commit. He has a neatly shaved bald head and a thin grey-and-black mustache.

Born in 1953, he reminds me of a favorite child-hood football coach, the way he engages each person with the sort of familiarity common to those who have grown up in places like New Orleans, where being family is contingent not on bloodlines but on ties to a shared community—the same set of traditions, the same culture.

Norris told me he has taken this trip to Angola more than a hundred times since he was released in 2003. "I've been home fifteen years," he said, leaning back in his seat. "I've been in Angola, I would venture to say, once a month, every month since I've been home."

Norris sometimes does these sorts of tours in conjunction with a tour of the Whitney Plantation, two hours southeast of the prison, so that the connection between the two institutions, and their respective histories, can be made clear. "If we want to end mass incarceration, we've got to kind of get the history of where it comes from, and how it still exists, and what that looks like." His voice has the texture of an old blues singer, his accent peppered with a quintessential New Orleans lilt. The way the vowels in words like "point" and "joint" evaporate off the tongue, replaced by a soft *r* that turns his language into jazz. The way words like "corner" walk around the edges of the mouth before slipping off into the wind.

Norris is not an official tour guide of Angola,

but after twenty-seven years imprisoned there, he is intimately familiar with the landscape. Since his release, Norris has been an unceasing advocate of criminal justice reform in Louisiana and across the country. Only a few weeks before our visit Norris had successfully led a coalition of incarcerated people, formerly incarcerated people, and their allies to end Louisiana's practice of nonunanimous jury decisions via a ballot measure that had amended the state constitution. Up until that point, Louisiana was one of only two states in the entire country—Oregon being the other—in which someone could be convicted of a felony without the jury coming to a unanimous decision.

In his book *Jim Crow's Last Stand: Nonunanimous Criminal Jury Verdicts in Louisiana,* historian Thomas Aiello describes how the rationale for such a policy is not simply an innocent difference in respective state constitutions but grounded in a history of racism. The policy, stemming from post-Reconstruction white supremacy, was meant to funnel Black people into the convict leasing system, replacing in part the labor force lost as a result of emancipation. The policy also had the effect of suffocating the political and judicial power of Black people in Louisiana.

When the United States acquired Louisiana as a territory in 1803, it had unanimous juries. But following the Civil War, white Democrats across the South sought to subvert the rights of newly freed slaves by imposing a new system of control: convict leasing. The Thirteenth Amendment barred involuntary servitude, "except as a punishment for crime whereof the party shall have been duly convicted." The convict leasing system allowed Black people to be imprisoned for years under spurious charges and be "rented" to companies. These people and institutions, whose businesses had been built on the labor of enslaved people, experienced a vacuum in the years following abolition. But with convict leasing, imprisoned Black men could now be legally forced to provide that labor for their railroads, their plantations, and their businesses.

Many Southern states passed so-called pig laws—in 1876, for example, the state of Mississippi established the theft of any property worth ten dollars or more and any livestock worth a dollar or more as "grand larceny" and thus subject to a sentence as high as five years. "Southerners constantly manipulated laws to drive convictions," said Aiello. "Pig laws did create more convicts, and those convicts were overwhelmingly Black and overwhelmingly leased."

The conditions under convict leasing were often as gruesome as anything that had existed under slavery. So much so that in 1884 C. Harrison Parker, editor of the New Orleans *Daily Picayune,* wrote of the men sentenced to convict leasing at Angola that it would be "more humane to punish with death all prisoners sentenced to a longer period than six years" since the average prisoner sentenced to convict leasing would not live more than six years anyway. As one man told the National Conference of Charities and Correction in 1883, "Before the war, we owned the negroes. If a man had a good negro, he could afford to take care of him: if he was sick get a doctor. He might even put gold plugs in his teeth. But these convicts: we don't own 'em. One dies, get another."

In Louisiana, in order to ensure there were more convictions, and thus more prisoners available for labor, in 1880 the state legislature shifted the requirement for juries from unanimous to non-unanimous. This way courts could allow a few Black people to serve on the jury—in accordance with their new rights as freed persons—but by requiring only nine of the twelve jurors to convict someone of a crime, they effectively subverted any political power Black people, or those sympathetic to them, might otherwise have had. Those responsible for the change did not equivocate in their rationale. The purpose of the 1898 convention, in which the new law officially became part of the Louisiana constitution, was, as summarized by the chairman of the convention's judiciary committee, "to establish the supremacy of the white race." A non-unanimous jury policy would invariably make it easier to convict people—and these convictions were a key part of Louisiana's convict leasing system. Despite its history, the law was upheld in a 1972 Supreme Court ruling and amended only slightly in 1973 from nine out of twelve jurors being needed to convict to ten out of twelve.

The Advocate, a newspaper in Baton Rouge, found that upon reviewing nearly one thousand felony convictions between the years 2011 and 2016, 40 percent of convictions by twelve-member juries had one or two jurors who did not agree with the verdict. Additionally, they found that in these cases, Black defendants were about 30 percent more likely to be found guilty than their white counterparts. Innocence Project New Orleans, an organization committed to exonerating wrongly convicted people, has found that in the last thirty years split juries played a role in upwards of 45 percent of exoneration cases in Louisiana that were eligible for a non-unanimous verdict.

Norris said he thinks that around 35 percent of the people at Angola were convicted by split juries. He then made a point that I had not considered. Throughout the state, non-unanimous juries had long been used by prosecutors as leverage to extract plea deals from defendants. If a prosecutor could go into a room, he said, and tell someone, "Look, all I need to do is get ten of the twelve people on this jury to flip; I don't even need them all to believe me," it instills fear in the defendant that their odds of being found not guilty in court are incredibly limited. "A lot of guys may have pled guilty [before the trial] to avoid having to be confronted with a ten–two or an eleven–one verdict," Norris explained, making it impossible to know the true scale and costs of this law.[*]

The bus made a slow turn onto Highway 66, the road that serves as the prison's only entry point. The entrance to Angola looked as if it could be a truck stop on the side of the highway. There was a large white triangular overhang with a small booth underneath it, the type you see at toll stops on the interstate. Cars entered and exited on either side. At the center of the overhang was a black sign with bold red letters that read LOUISIANA STATE PENITENTIARY. To the right, before we entered, was the Angola Museum at the Louisiana State Penitentiary, a small white building with a long porch that covered the entire front-facing part of the property—the starting point of our tour. We were given time to walk through the museum on

---

[*] In April 2020, the US Supreme Court ruled that non-unanimous verdicts were unconstitutional for cases involving serious crimes, though the ruling applies only to crimes committed after 2018.

our own before we were scheduled to meet our guide for the day, back outside on the bus.

The cool air tiptoed across my skin. It was November, but there were still gnats buzzing about over the soft, wet earth. I was struck by how desolate the landscape felt. How unalive it looked. The sky was grey and endless with sheets of clouds holding everything above it in place. Behind the clouds, small handfuls of light stretched thinly in every direction, and the breeze trembled above the uncut patches of grass in front of the museum.

The first thing I saw inside the museum was the wall behind the checkout counter. On the wall was a twenty-foot-wide image that kept my feet in place. Below the words LOUISIANA STATE PENITENTIARY was a photograph of two dozen Black men being marched into the fields, each of them carrying a long black hoe. They were wearing an assortment of grey sweatshirts and white T-shirts that rendered their bodies almost indistinguishable. To their far right was a white woman on horseback, her long blond ponytail extending from beneath her black cap and down her back. The sun, full and luminous even in the black-and-white image, hung just above the trees in the distance, suggesting that these men were beginning their day. The procession of black skin carrying black hoes into this field further erased the identities of each man. They existed in this photo not as individual people but as a homogenous, interchangeable mass of bodies.

I turned away and then looked back multiple times to make sure I understood what I was seeing. The photo seemed to have been taken recently; it was not a vestige of the past. It was indeed a white person on horseback, herding a group of what seemed to be exclusively Black men into a field where they were forced to work. The unsettling nature and placement of the image was compounded by the fact that it welcomed its viewers into a gift shop stock-piled with an extensive inventory brandishing the Angola name.

As I walked around the relatively small room, there were various T-shirts touting the Angola Prison Rodeo, a biannual event that takes place every Sunday in October and over the course of one weekend in April. There were caps that read simply ANGOLA STATE PEN. There were ashtrays, built from license plates, stacked on top of one another (Angola is where every license plate in the state of Louisiana is made). I thought about the cruel irony of people so restricted in their own movements creating something that facilitated mobility for so many others. There were shot glasses, sunglasses, and T-shirts with the prison's name emblazoned across their breasts. But what stood out most in the gift shop, sitting on a shelf at the far end of the store, was a white mug with the silhouette of a guard sitting in a watchtower surrounded by fencing. Above the picture it said ANGOLA, and beneath the picture it read A GATED COMMUNITY.

I looked around the gift shop once more and wondered whom it was attempting to serve. Who saw the largest maximum-security prison in the country as some sort of tourist destination?

After I left the gift shop, I found a plaque inside the museum noting that the goal of the Angola Museum was to "establish and preserve Angola's past and to educate all who visit about the role this sprawling prison farm has played in our state's history." But as I walked from room to room of the museum, it became clear that the institution was interested only in preserving a history that created clear, misguided demarcations between "criminals" and those who watch over them.

Then I stepped into a room dedicated to the Angola Prison Rodeo. It was filled with posters and photographs from rodeos of the past. There was even a mannequin dressed in a black cowboy hat and large blue cowboy chaps. The self-proclaimed "Wildest Show in the South" brings tens of thousands of visitors to Angola every year. In his book *Slaves of the State: Black Incarceration from the Chain Gang to the Penitentiary,* scholar Dennis Childs describes the scene of the rodeo:

In the first event, a clown places a card table in the middle of the six-thousand-person rodeo arena, around which four prisoners sit and pretend to play a game of cards. A modest monetary prize is awarded to the man who remains seated the longest as a bull attempts to [gore] all four contestants. For the second event, a large number of stripe-clad men attempt to remove a poker chip tied between the horns of a bull. Prisoners are regularly tossed over twenty feet in the air by the two-thousand-pound animals. They also routinely suffer from broken bones, deep lacerations, and concussions as a result of this spectacle. One prisoner is known to have ultimately died from a heart attack resulting from his participation in one of the events.

On the other side of the wall was a glass case holding photographs and memorabilia from several of the movies that have been filmed at Angola. In another room, a large glass encasement, entitled INMATE WEAPONS, displayed dozens of homemade items like shanks made from plastic toothbrushes, knives made from pieces of a broken typewriter, guns sent and smuggled inside.

In another room I found a wall that included photographs of administrators at Angola dating back to 1916. Looking down from the wall were the faces of fifteen white men.* In another room there was a wall of men who had attempted to escape and been apprehended. And in another room a display case held photographs of guards who had been killed by someone imprisoned at Angola. In each room, I caught the eyes of Samora, another person on the tour, and a musician and composer from Oakland, California, with messy black hair hidden beneath an orange beanie. Each time one of us glanced over, the other would furrow a brow, a silent but clear acknowledgment between us that something wasn't right here.

Our walk through the museum continued. In one room there was a replica of a cell that people could step into. In this context, so close to the gift shop, would the cell, I wondered, be anything more than a photo op for someone with their new Angola sweatshirt, smiling behind the bars? Would they pose, with a coffee mug in one hand and a shot glass in the other? In yet another room, a large ball and chain sat on the ground,

---

* Angola has only once been run by a Black administrator: Larry Smith, who served as an interim warden for a period of less than a year between 1989 and 1990. He is not pictured on the wall.

its rusted links snaking across the floor. It weighed about fifty pounds, according to the placard, and when I tried to pick it up I lost my footing. On the placard, it said this "was commonly used in the early days for problem prisoners." I looked at the words again and whispered the phrase "problem prisoners" to feel the discomfort of the euphemism on my tongue.

It seemed much of the museum, almost relentlessly, depicted images of violence. And yet, paradoxically, its curators also sought to couple this violence with a narrative of progress, as if to show how bad the prison used to be and tout how incredibly safe it was now. The brochure of the museum states, "Once known as the 'bloodiest prison in America,' the Louisiana State Penitentiary at Angola has emerged as one of the most progressive and well managed prisons in the country." The final point on a time line in the museum makes the espoused transformation more intimate: "1995–2016 Burl Cain becomes warden, begins massive expansion of education and moral rehabilitation programming; violence inside the prison is dramatically reduced."

Later I spoke with Samora, hoping that our exchanged glances did indeed reflect a shared sense of horror. "Everything was like, 'What's the most sensational thing we can talk about?'" he said. "Which is kind of ironic given the fact that, really, the most sensational and real thing you can talk about...is actually the fact that it was a *plantation* and all the awful shit that happened there. But that was the one thing that wasn't a part of it, but then they wanted to talk about, like, who was the most notorious outlaw and all the crazy weapons that people were trying to use...So they were clearly trying to be like, these are the things that would attract people, but let's avoid the actual thing that's at the center of all this."

The group left the museum and its accompanying gift shop and got back onto the bus to begin the tour inside the prison grounds. Once everyone was settled, Norris introduced us to our official guide for the day—an assistant warden at the prison I'll call Roger. Roger was a tall white man with a calm, even affect and dark, narrow eyes. He smiled as he looked at all of us on the bus, readjusting his jacket as he waited for conversation to die down so that he could begin.

Roger opened by talking to us about the Indigenous population who first lived on this land centuries ago. It was encouraging to hear him begin by naming the land's history. He explained that the Indigenous Americans assisted French explorers in learning how to navigate the river so as to more effectively travel north. "The Tunica shared with the French explorers that if you were paddling north in your canoe and you went through this bayou, you would save about forty nautical miles on your trip north, which was a huge, big deal," he said. "Those are some of the forgotten facts about the discoveries of the lower reaches of the Mississippi River." He continued: "Then we move into the prison phase in 1869. Samuel James obtained a lease from the State of Louisiana to house its inmates. In 1880, he bought eight thousand acres, which we're currently on." James moved some of the state's prisoners to Angola, but many of them were subcontracted to work on levees and railroads. "And conditions were horrible. About ten percent of those folks did not survive under Samuel James's watch. Samuel James died here in Angola in 1894, one of the wealthiest men in the state based solely on the backs of convict labor. In 1901, the state came in and assumed control of the prison, and we've been run by Louisiana since 1901."

My initial sense of optimism began to fade away as Roger continued. He went on to say that this had been "a horrible prison" but quickly pivoted to discuss the positive things the prison was now doing to make life better for the people held captive there, including providing accredited college courses and degrees from the New Orleans Baptist Theological Seminary. While it was encouraging to hear about the progress the prison had made, the time line Roger provided seemed, at best, abbreviated, if not willfully misleading. Roger moved from discussing the Indigenous communities and French exploration of the seventeenth and early eighteenth centuries straight to post–Civil War America—skipping the period in which Angola existed as a plantation worked by enslaved Black people. He mentioned convict leasing without explaining that it was an explicit tool of economic and racial subjugation, in which men were starved, beaten, and housed in former slave quarters. He failed to mention that the land upon which Angola is built had once been the plantation of Isaac Franklin, a man whose business, Franklin and Armfield, became one of the largest slave-trading firms in the United States. The plantation produced 3,100 bales of cotton a year, a yield higher than most other plantations in the South. He failed to mention that Samuel Lawrence James, who purchased the plantation from Franklin's widow, was a former major in the Confederate Army. James agreed to a twenty-one-year lease with the state to purchase access to all of the state's prisoners as long as he was able to keep all of the profits. James subsequently subcontracted the prisoners to labor camps, where—as Roger had told us—they worked on levees and railroads in horrific conditions. A prisoner under James's lease had a greater chance of dying than an enslaved person did.

Upon approaching the building where executions took place, I felt my chest tighten and my mouth turn sour. Inside, the room adjacent to the execution chamber was unremarkable. At its center were two wooden tables brought together, their clean, polished surfaces reflecting the flickering fluorescent lights. The tables were surrounded by ten armless, black, rolling office chairs set to different heights, some slightly reclined as if someone were sitting in them. Next to the back wall were two tall plants—their leaves bursting a full and healthy green. The walls were beige with white trim, and the floor was a neat aggregation of square linoleum tiles. The soft hum of the air-conditioning vibrated throughout the room. With the exception of the large circular seal of the Louisiana Department of Corrections at the center of each table, it would have been easy to mistake this for any other conference room in any other office building. This was not any other conference room. This was the room where the people sentenced to be killed by the State of Louisiana had their final meals. They ate these meals—perhaps a hamburger and french fries, perhaps steak and mashed potatoes, maybe a basket of boiled crawfish and a bowl of gumbo—before being injected with a cocktail that rendered them unconscious, paralyzed their muscles, discontinued their breathing, and stopped their hearts.

In the vestibule between the conference room and the execution chamber, eight mahogany leather chairs were packed tightly together in two rows, the second row elevated slightly behind the first. On the far wall, there was a sliding wooden door, and on the other side of that sliding door were four more chairs—two in front and two behind—seated next to the window.

The victim's family—if they so choose—sit on one side of the sliding door, while witnesses, often the media, sit on the other side. The family of the person being executed cannot be in the viewing chamber for the execution. In front of these chairs, on both sides, was a large glass panel that looked directly into the execution chamber and directly at the table upon which the person would be killed. As we walked into the room and slowly encircled the table at the center, the group fell silent. Many were unable to stare at it directly.

Silent but for a soft symphony of breaths, we were a congregation of lowered heads and sunken shoulders. The table was long and blue-black, its upholstery covering a thin layer of foam padding. Seven discolored brown and black straps, haunting in their stillness, stretched across the width of the bed, each locked and pulled tight. A small pillow rested at the head of the table where the person is meant to lie, and another set of straps would come down over their shoulders. About a foot below the pillow on either side of the bed were the places where the soon-to-be-executed would lay their arms. On each of these arm-length extensions was a leather strap meant to be tightened near the person's elbow. They were noticeably different from the other straps—a faded blend of grey and brown, taut leather that had cracked with age. The straps, with their procession of small notches, dangled below the table. At the foot of the table were two shackles, their silver metal glimmering under the lights. A hot rush of blood pulsed behind my ears, as I felt the shame of being alive in a room built to kill.

On the bus ride to Angola, Norris had told me a story about how this bed, or the one that came before it, had been made. He said that when the State of Louisiana transitioned from the electric chair to lethal injection in 1991, the prison needed a bed on which to lay the condemned. Meanwhile, in the welding shop of the prison, some of the men were handed a new assignment, though they did not know what for. "One of the guys, one of the clerks, happened to see the whole blueprint laying on the drafting table," Norris said, recounting the event, "and went back out in the shop and said, 'Bruh, y'all know what you're building?' They're like, 'What?' 'You're building the damn deathbed.'"

Instead of purchasing a bed, Norris said, the Department of Corrections found it cheaper to direct the prisoners in the machine and welding shops to build it, with each part of the bed assembled separately. Norris paused, shaking his head at the memory. "One of the guys on the welding crew, his brother was on death row."

Upon realizing what they were building, Norris said, the men refused to continue. And as a result, they were locked inside their cells. "The word spread like wildfire, because it was lunchtime when they was getting locked up, and so when it came time for everybody to go back to work after lunch, everybody was like, 'We're not going back to work.'" The prison, Norris said, was essentially at a standstill for three days.[*]

My mind jolted back to the room where I stood,

---

[*]   The incident was reported by the Associated Press in July 1991 ("Prisoners Strike After Two Refuse to Build Execution Bed," July 24, 1991). A prison official acknowledged to the press that "there were some inmates...who refused their job assignment" but said he had "no comment on what that assignment is." Later, said Norris, the warden at Angola took the unusual step of apologizing to the prisoners for the incident.

between the table and the glass panel, looking at the table and then turning my head to look at the chairs on the other side of the glass. The chairs and glass turned this room into a spectacle of state-sanctioned, taxpayer-funded death. The table was a reminder of how fragile our bodies are, how little is needed to extinguish a life.

Robert Sawyer was the first person put to death by lethal injection in Louisiana, in 1993. Childhood abuse left him brain damaged with severe mental impediments—he was executed despite having an IQ of only 68, below the threshold of what is considered intellectually disabled.

Dobie Gillis Williams—another man who suffered from intellectual disability—was killed on January 8, 1999. For his final meal he ate twelve candy bars and a bowl of ice cream.

Gerald Bordelon—who, during his execution, wore a gold cross that his daughter had given him just hours before—turned to the family of his victim in the moments before he was killed, looking at them through the glass, and said, "I'm sorry. I don't know if that brings any closure or peace. It should have never happened, but it did, and I'm sorry."

Each of these three men was found guilty of taking someone's life, but standing in this room, I couldn't understand how taking their lives in return made things any better.

We filed back onto the bus without saying much of anything. The engine started, and the bus's rubber tires spit out clouds of dust behind them.

Earlier, we had visited the law library and the automotive tech shop, where we met John, a fifty-three-year-old who was in charge of the vocational-training program. More than thirty years into a life sentence, he spoke thoughtfully about how, though it seemed unlikely that he would ever be released, his work made it possible to provide mentorship and life skills to men who would be going back into society. It helped give his life a sense of purpose.

The law library was filled with dozens of book-shelves containing old legal texts and small carrels tucked away between them where books and case work could be stored. Here we listened to three men describe their experiences working in the library. I was not allowed to bring any recording device inside the building itself, but I remember how they spoke of the way the law library helped them reclaim a sense of agency, how learning the law made them feel as if they still had control over something in their lives.

I have spent the past several years teaching in prisons and jails, and the tables spread out across the law library reminded me of so many of the classrooms where I had worked with incarcerated writers. As I listened to the men speak about their experiences, it was impossible not to think of all the stories my own students had shared with me about living inside a cage.

It felt incredibly important to hear directly from people incarcerated in Angola, but having an official employed by the prison present us with seemingly preselected speakers lent the impression that the men were giving us presentations they had given on many other occasions to many other visitors. I imagined there was little chance that these men would say anything unfavorable about the prison in front of a prison representative. Such dissent could lead to retribution; there is a long precedent for that. As such, there will always be a limit to the amount of candor an incarcerated person can provide in such a space.

After listening to the men, we returned to the bus. I sat in the fourth row of seats as the shuttle rattled along a narrow dirt road, gravel cackling underneath us. As the bus rolled on, I thought of how slavery—a history with which Angola is inextricably linked—was only being alluded to in a sort of offhanded way. Roger stood at the front with a microphone in his hand, glancing around to see if anyone had a question as we traveled to our next destination. I cleared my throat.

"I was wondering if you could talk a little bit about the prison's relationship to slavery."

I was nervous to ask the question. And I was ashamed of myself for feeling nervous.

Roger paused, then nodded. "He's asked me to talk a little bit about the prison's relationship to slavery," he said, repeating my question, perhaps to buy time, or so people in the back of the bus could hear.

"I'll tell you this," he began, readjusting the microphone in his hand, "and I told you this when we came in: this was one of the bloodiest prisons in America. It was a horrible prison." His voice was sincere and steady. "On the way out I'm gonna show you the Red Hat cell block," he said, speaking of the prison's infamous maximum-security housing unit that closed in 1972. "And we don't make any bones about it. I can't change what happened here when Samuel James took this prison over. This was a . . . this—" He stumbled over his words as he attempted to finish his thought. "[They] housed slaves on this land, and I can't change that. I think it's an interesting situation that we're in, when you go from that, when you're at that level with some of the worst things that have ever happened on a piece of land in America. This eighteen thousand acres has seen more suffering than any eighteen-thousand-acre piece of property in the world probably—when you look at it, it's horrible. But when you go from that, and you go years and years and years, and you get to where we are today with the redemption and the change—then that's what I like to talk about. Our history is our history, and I can't change that."

Roger went on to share how the prison had sent one of its observation towers to the National Museum of African American History and Culture in Washington, DC. The Red Hat cell block was listed on the National Register of Historic Places—more evidence, according to Roger, that the penitentiary was acknowledging its history.

He paused, looked around the bus, and smiled—"I'll get off my soapbox"—before moving on to talk about the prison's hospice, which we passed on our left. A wave of whispers made its way around the small bus.

Roger's "I can't change that" seemed to provide the pretense of acknowledgment while creating distance from personal culpability. It was reminiscent of a refrain laced throughout our country's conversations about the history of racism. I thought about all of the times, growing up, when I had sat in class and heard a white classmate say, "Well, *my* ancestors didn't own slaves," or heard a political commentator on television say, "Why are we still talking about slavery? People need to get over it." Or a politician say, "We can't wallow in the past. It's time to focus on the future." When I hear these deflections, I think of all the ways this country attempts to smother conversations about how its past has shaped its present. How slavery is made to sound as if it happened in a prehistoric age instead of only a few generations ago.

In his 1935 book, *Black Reconstruction in America,* W. E. B. Du Bois wrote that the story the country tells about its relationship to chattel slavery is willfully distorted. "Our histories tend to discuss American slavery so impartially, that in the end nobody seems to have done wrong and everybody was right. Slavery appears to have been thrust upon unwilling helpless America, while the South was blameless in becoming its center...One is astonished in the study of history at the recurrence of the idea that evil must be forgotten, distorted, skimmed over."

If in Germany today there were a prison built on top of a former concentration camp, and that prison disproportionately incarcerated Jewish people, it would rightly provoke outrage throughout the world. I imagine there would be international summits on closing such an egregious institution. And yet in the United States such collective outrage at this plantation-turned-prison is relatively muted.

It's not that people don't know. Angola prison has been regularly and casually referred to as a plantation by state authorities and media for over a century. When many people say "Angola is a prison built on a former plantation," it is often made as an unsettling observation, not as a moral indictment. Is it because our collective understanding of slavery, and its inherent violence, is so limited? Or is it that violence experienced by Black people is thought less worthy of mourning? White supremacy enacts violence against Black people, but also numbs a whole country—Black and white—to what would in any other context provoke our moral indignation.

I still wasn't satisfied with the answer Roger had provided, so after he responded to a question from someone else in the group by discussing the positive programming the prison was doing, I raised my hand again.

"On that note," I began again, "you're showing us lots of and talking a lot about some of the stuff that you all do really well, which is really wonderful to see. I'm curious about what things you think you all could be doing better."

In hindsight, I should have asked my follow-up question more directly, but in the moment, I was concerned with sounding condescending or disrespectful. I was occupying two identities: as a Black man who grew up in Louisiana, I felt a sense of responsibility to demand more from a place that had enacted so much violence on my community; as a PhD student at an Ivy League school, I didn't want to come across as someone who had dropped in to critique a place I had no personal ties to. I didn't want to dismiss the reforms. It's important that prisons are not dangerous for the people kept in them. It's important that people are prepared for life if they leave and allowed the opportunity to live a meaningful life for however long they are imprisoned. But simply because something has been reformed does not mean it is now acceptable. And even if something is now better, that does not undo its past, nor does it eliminate the necessity of speaking about how that past may have shaped the present.

Roger talked about how the prison had no control over what happened in the state legislature, and that it needed that body to pass certain laws in order for them to help prisoners more effectively. He talked about the extremely low recidivism rate for people convicted of murder, but reminded us that without a change in sentencing laws, Angola could not simply release its prisoners. I was astonished by the lack of institutional contrition, the refusal to admit what was right in front of us. I have no way of knowing Roger's intentions, but it was evident that he had little interest in talking about the role slavery had played in shaping Angola, which in its early days had a "big house" of "the old Southern plantation style" on the grounds, in which the person responsible for all of the people held here—the warden—lived with his family.

Some prison employees and their families are also given free housing on the grounds, and well into the twentieth century guards and other prison employees used the labor of those incarcerated for their own personal use. In a book about Angola published in 1990, Patsy Dreher, whose father was a guard captain at Angola, is quoted looking back nostalgically on her time living on the grounds: "Angola was a pleasant place to live back then. A vegetable cart came by every morning. What you didn't get in pay, you got in benefits. You...could get inmates as cooks, yard boys, house boys; you could have two or three of them if you wanted. We had an old cook named Leon who cried like a baby when he got paroled; he said ours was the only home he had known in a long time."

I brought up my concerns with Norris. He looked at me and said, "Sometimes people wanna let dead dogs lie."

But I didn't want that. I wanted the prison to create a sign at the entrance naming that it had been a plantation. I wanted markers erected in the places where incarcerated people had died, and for the first and the last sentence of every tour to begin with the word "slavery." I wanted Angola, where 71 percent of people are serving life sentences and three-quarters of the population is

Black, to not pretend as if that was a coincidence. What I wanted more than anything was for this prison to not be here, holding these people, on this land, with this history. It all felt so profoundly irredeemable.

While Roger may have been unwilling to provide more than a perfunctory acknowledgment of the prison's relationship to slavery, the relationship is clear to those who have experienced incarceration themselves. Generations of men who have been incarcerated at Angola or elsewhere have been more than willing to name that connection.

Monroe Green, who arrived at Angola in 1957, was explicit: "I saw a big farm. There were a lot of men in the fields. The living conditions were like on those slave ships coming over here, with the quarters filled with slaves."

A poem from Mark King in a 1992 issue of Angola's award-winning prison magazine *The Angolite* draws direct comparisons between the brutality of slavery and the conditions and treatment of the people in Angola.

A century of forced labor, blood and pain.
Lives wasted, buried in the shame.
Slavemasters oversee their daily tasks
Hidden behind century-old sadistic masks.
The world has passed this deathly land by.
The inhabitants still ask why.

Angola Prison

In 1998, Chuck Unger said the people held at Angola have "become modern-day slaves for the state. We work at hard labor for practically nothing and we make people rich."

Incarcerated activist and writer Mumia Abu-Jamal has noted, "If there ever was a question of *the slave parentage of the American prison system,* one glance at the massive penitentiary known as Angola...removes all doubt."

In 2000, Lane Nelson, who wrote in *The Angolite,* observed that "Angola's turbulent history is stitched to the present by threads of oppression" where "people have been held in bondage on this land for more than 200 years." Uninterested in obscuring the past and its relation to the present, Nelson stated unequivocally that Angola "still conjures historical images of Southern slavery."

And in 2018, prisoners refused to work after a confrontation between workers and guards. The organization Decarcerate Louisiana released a set of demands on behalf of striking workers, including a call for a national conversation on how state prison farms had come to hold so many people of African descent against their will. "We are urging that local, state, and federal governments who currently hold hundreds of thousands of African Americans on prison farms across the country be investigated for antebellum criminality, involuntary servitude and slavery."

At another stop, the bus came to a halt in the middle of a dirt road that we could not see the end of, that melted into the fields in the distance. On our left were two conjoined buildings, white with red trim. One had black shingles laid across its slanted roof. The buildings were surrounded by chain-link fencing that had been weathered into penny rust and muted silver, messy tangles of barbed wire sitting on top of them. The grass was a puzzle of brown patches, though green enough to not look wholly forgotten. Clouds continued to coat the sky with a thin membrane of light grey as the sun hummed softly behind them. These were the buildings known collectively as the Red Hat cell block.

The Red Hat cell block was constructed after an attempted escape in 1933. Located in the prison's Camp E, it became Angola's most restrictive and harshest housing facility—a dark scar that rose from the skin of this vast land. Forty cells lined its corridor, each room measuring five by seven feet. The block became known as the Red Hat because when the men went out to work in the fields, they wore straw hats that had been dipped in red paint to make them easily identifiable.

As I stepped inside the cell block, the soft echo of my shoes against the floor bounced off the bars of each cell. The cells had heavy sliding steel doors that locked into place against the concrete walls. The sun crept around the door on the opposite end of the corridor, casting long shadows of our bodies onto the floor. I stepped into the first cell on my right and became acutely aware of my body in the confined space. On my left, a slab of grey concrete rose from the floor, a place for the condemned to lay their head. At the opposite end of the slab, and just a few inches to the right, was a small grey sink, wet and discolored, mold blooming in its crevices. Another foot to the right and low on the wall was a toilet. The paint on the floor, on the walls, and on the toilet was peeling off from the duress of prolonged exposure to the changing seasons.

I stood in the middle of the cell and stretched my arms out; with my left hand I could run my fingers over the cold, uneven concrete, and with my right hand I could nearly reach the steel bars of the cell door. This was not the width of the cell; this was the length. I sat at the edge of the concrete slab, and when I extended my legs I could touch the wall. I lowered my feet again to the ground and let the smallness of the cell wash over me. I looked up at the small square window and the streaks of light scissoring through its four vertical bars. I thought of the people who had lived in these cells, who had slept on these slabs.

In recollections of their time at the Red Hat, the

men who lived there described the cell block as infested with rats and other vermin. Albert Woodfox, who spent forty years in solitary confinement at Angola, recounts, "There was a toilet in the cell but they kept the water turned off, so it didn't work. You had to use a bucket in the corner which could only be emptied when you were let out every few days for a shower. They wanted you to smell the stench of your own body waste while eating."

In his memoir, Billy Wayne Sinclair, who was once on death row at Angola, said that the men held on the Red Hat block were given the leftovers from other prisoners' meals and that those meals were delivered to them in wheelbarrows. Sinclair described the Red Hat during the 1940s and 1950s as "Angola's torture chamber" and outlined a culture of violence and callousness, not from the prisoners but from the guards. "Inmates sent to the Red Hats were brutally beaten by convict guards going in, beaten on a daily basis, and beaten coming out. They were fed bread and water twice a day. Some inmates were broken; others died from abuse and neglect. Some sent to the Red Hats during that era simply disappeared, never to be seen or heard from again."

Adjacent to the cell block, and accessible via a small though haunting antechamber, was a single-room building, empty but for the electric chair near its back wall. The original chair is no longer there. It sits in the museum up the road. But a replica sat in its place.

I looked around; no one else was in the room with me. I walked over to the chair and sat down. My shoes became draped in a tangle of cobwebs at its base. The chair was long, wooden, and perpendicular. I am around six feet tall, and once I was fully seated, my feet dangled a few inches from the ground. I imagined the leather straps that hung from the arms of the chair being tightened around my forearms and my waist. My dangling feet—and my body, tied to the chair—would create a sense of helplessness, leaving me feeling both heavy and weightless. Next to the chair was an entwinement of wires connected to a box that would produce the fatal electric shocks.

Louisiana began using the electric chair in 1941. The original electric chair was known by the men at Angola as "Gruesome Gertie." At first, the chair was not based at a single location but traveled to the parish where the condemned person was imprisoned. In 1957, however, Gruesome Gertie retired from its traveling and found a home on the Red Hat cell block at the Louisiana State Penitentiary.

The chair has the infamous distinction as the site of the country's first-known botched execution by electrocution.

Willie Francis, a seventeen-year-old Black boy

from Saint Martinville, Louisiana, was placed in the electric chair on May 3, 1946. He was charged with murdering a pharmacist named Andrew Thomas in 1944, but in the decades following his death, serious questions were raised about Willie's culpability. Months after Thomas was killed, the Saint Martinville police had failed to apprehend anyone for the murder. Saint Martinville's sheriff called the chief of police in Port Arthur, Texas, and told him to arrest "any man" from Saint Martinville found in Port Arthur, in a last-ditch effort to resolve the case. Willie, visiting one of his sisters in Port Arthur at the time, had been arrested, mistakenly, on a separate drug charge. The charge was dropped, but the police began questioning Willie about Thomas's murder in Saint Martinville instead. Soon police had a signed confession from Willie. The boy had no counsel present. Given his age and the circumstances of his arrest, it is unlikely that such a statement could exist devoid of coercion, threats, or violence from the officers in their interrogation room. Willie pleaded not guilty and was put on trial in front of a jury of twelve white men. Willie's lawyers called no witnesses, refused to make an opening statement, and offered no objections. Two days after the trial began, Willie was convicted of murder. It took the jury fifteen minutes to deliberate. He was sentenced to death.

It is difficult to imagine what a person feels in the moments before they are to be executed. Willie's words provide a small piece of insight into an otherwise unfathomable experience:

Everybody was watching me as I walked out. I looked at the Sheriff and he nodded, so I walked across the room and sat down in the chair. He took the handcuffs off and the men began strapping me into the chair. They put one strap around my leg and around my waist and tied my arms down, too. I knew then how real it was to have to die. I had it in my mind deep. It was so quiet in there everybody was looking at me so funny. It was the realest misery I ever knew, to see them watching me. It seemed like they would come close to my eyes and then move away from me. I wished they had kept still because I was already dizzy. I was cold and my hands were all wet. I couldn't feel my neck and my head but they say I was soaking with perspiration. They kept on fixing the machine and connecting the wires to my head and to my left leg.

But the machine Willie was being connected to had been improperly assembled. The prison guard responsible for its assembly, Captain Ephie Foster, along with a prisoner assisting him, had been drunk while setting it up earlier that day. As a result, the electrocution did not kill Willie, but it did torture him.

> The best way I can describe it is: Whamm! Zst!
>
> It felt like a hundred and a thousand needles and pins were pricking in me all over and my left leg felt like somebody was cutting it with a razor blade. I could feel my arms jumping at my sides and I guess my whole body must have jumped straight out...I thought for a minute I was going to knock the chair over. Then I was all right. I thought I was dead...Then they did it again! The same feeling all over. I heard a voice say, "Give me some more juice down there!" And in a little while somebody yelled, "I'm giving you all I got now!" I think I must have hollered for them to stop. They say I said, "Take it off! Take it off!" I know that was certainly what I wanted them to do—turn it off. I really thought I was dead then.

Willie's father found an attorney to take on his son's case. The lawyer argued that subjecting Willie to *another* attempted execution would amount to cruel and unusual punishment. The case made it all the way to the United States Supreme Court. Ultimately the Court ruled 5 to 4 against Willie.

He was killed, by electric chair, just a little over a year later, on May 9, 1947. Willie recounted the events that led to that moment:

> I know how it felt to have them read a death warrant to me, I know how it feels to sit in a cell waiting for the day they will lead me to the chair again. I sure know how it feels to sit in that chair and have them strap me in and put a mask on my eyes. I know how it feels to have the shock go through me and think I am dead but find out I am not.

I sat in the chair and thought of Willie Francis's reflection, an observation both profound and devastatingly youthful: "Boy, you sure feel funny when you know you're going to die; almost like you know something only God should know."

Only a few minutes after we entered the Red Hat we were told it was time to get back on the bus. I kept sitting in the chair and clutched my hands on its rough wooden edges before lifting myself up and walking toward the haze of the door. As I stepped out of the Red Hat, the air smelled like smoke even though nothing was on fire. Or maybe everything was.

At the time of our visit, the state of Louisiana had sixty-nine people on death row, meaning individuals who have been sentenced to death for crimes they have been convicted of. The average person remains on death row for more than a decade as they appeal their sentence or wait to be executed. Two-thirds of the people on death row in Louisiana are Black; an estimated one out of every twenty-five people who are sentenced to death in the United States is innocent.

"We're the only prison, I'd venture to say, in America that would allow people [to visit] death row. The other states would never do that—they'd freak out with that," Roger said proudly as we pulled up to the building where death row prisoners were housed.

"I'm gonna step up a little bit on this soapbox here and I'm gonna throw it out because no one has asked me," Roger said, though it was unclear what he was alluding to. "So one of the things that you haven't asked me about is solitary confinement. Solitary confinement does not exist in Louisiana. Solitary confinement denotes solid, steel doors devoid of human contact. And I'm gonna prove this to you right now, when we go to death row."

Louisiana had taken steps to make death row a less restrictive experience for the people housed there. Roger implied that the Department of

Corrections had done this of their own moral accord. What Roger did not mention was the history of recent lawsuits that appear to have pushed the state to make substantive changes to the way it treated those on death row.

In 2013, three men on death row sued Angola for "appalling and extreme conditions" caused by extreme heat. Their attorneys asserted that the conditions of the unit violated the cruel and unusual punishment clause of the Eighth Amendment. The lawsuit claimed that during the summer of 2011, the heat index on death row at times reached 195 degrees Fahrenheit. For a staggering eighty-five days between May and August 2012, the heat index rose above 126 degrees. Death row units did not have any air-conditioning systems, only fans. And, according to the lawsuit, "[d]uring the summer, the bars of the cells are hot to the touch and the cinder block walls release additional heat." It also claimed that the people housed on death row often chose to sleep on the concrete floor of their cells "because the floor is slightly cooler than their beds."

After three years, a federal judge ruled that the prison was in violation of the Eighth Amendment once the heat index surpassed 88 degrees, and the judge required remediation measures to address the heat (though the prison was not forced to install air-conditioning units). Later, the US Court of Appeals for the Fifth Circuit overturned the requirement to keep the heat index of the death row unit below the 88-degree maximum the plaintiffs had urged. In 2016, Jimmy LeBlanc, secretary of the state's Department of Public Safety and Corrections, claimed that providing air-conditioning for the people on death row would open a "Pandora's box," potentially forcing the state to provide air-conditioning to many other prisoners.

In 2017, another lawsuit challenged the use of solitary confinement on death row. The suit alleged that forcing people to spend twenty-three hours a day in a windowless cell with little or no interaction with other people caused severe physical and mental harm. Wilbert Rideau, who spent more than a decade in solitary confinement, described the experience:

I spent twelve years in cells that were variations of solitary confinement...I think I have never before or since felt the bone-cold loneliness that I felt on death row, removed from family or anything resembling a friend, and just being there, with no purpose or meaning to my life, cramped in a cage smaller than an American bathroom. The lonesomeness was only increased by the constant cacophony of men in adjacent cells hurling shouted insults, curses, and arguments—not to mention the

occasional urine or feces concoction. Depriva-
tion of both physical exercise and meaningful
social interaction were so severe in the early
days of Louisiana's death row that some men
went mad while others feigned lunacy in
order to get transferred to the hospital for the
criminally insane, where they had freedom of
movement, interaction with others, and an escape from their date with the electric chair.

Less than two months after the lawsuit was filed,
the Louisiana Department of Corrections imple-
mented a series of policies that loosened some
of the death row restrictions. The department
claimed that the lawsuit against the prison was
not at all connected to the changes on death row,
though the timing is difficult to overlook.

Previously, no two people were allowed out of
their cells at the same time. Each person had one
hour a day to walk up and down the tier, take a
shower, or make a phone call. They were allowed
outside three days a week during that single hour,
in separate fenced-off enclosures—areas that the
lawsuit compared to dog cages. When they were
allowed to leave their tier, it was often in shackles,
no matter the distance they were going.

Since May 15, 2017, however, men on death row
have been afforded four hours, together, outside
their cells. They no longer have to wear shackles

every time they leave their tier, they are no longer forced to be in separate outdoor cages when exercising, and on our visit we would see four men playing basketball while two guards stood watch. Roger's bet was that we would think of this arrangement as generous, though for me it could only be understood relative to the reprehensible alternative that had been in place for so long.

I had spent years calling the death penalty inhumane but only began to truly understand how inhumane when I saw the table in Angola upon which it is carried out. I had taught writing and literature in prisons for years but had never seen a place as difficult to write about as the Red Hat cell block.

I was confronted with that feeling when the bus pulled up to death row, which was separate from the execution chamber. The pathway to the front door of death row was polluted by a spiral of barbed wire on either side. Inside was a front desk that looked as if it might be the front desk of any office building during the holidays. Christmas decorations were strewn across the wall in November. To the right was a door that opened into a vestibule, sterile and silent like an abandoned hospital wing. The bottoms of our shoes squeaked against the clean tile floor as we were led down into the antechamber.

This experience, more than any other at Angola,

is the most difficult to clearly recount, as I felt pulled out of my own body in the few short minutes we spent there. The death row unit was set up like a small, single-floor panopticon, the dull colors of the room holding the light hostage. A round control room sat at the center of the unit, with large clear windows that would allow the guards to observe everything that surrounded it. From that room, correctional officers could see into each of the tiers on the unit, sections that extended outward from the center like the legs of a large steel spider. In the reflection of the glass surrounding the control room, I could see a ghostly outline of my body staring back at me.

There were about seventy men total on death row, and each of the tiers held approximately twelve people, each in individual cells. In between the tiers and the control room was a circular path that allowed for constant observation. It took only about a minute to walk around the entire unit. The space was small and compact, and we were a carousel of cautious bodies uncertain of how to move inside it.

We had arrived during the period of time when the men were allowed out of their cells—two hours in the morning and two hours in the afternoon—but had to stay on their tier.

As we walked around the unit, we could see into each tier, and they could see us. Some of the men were doing calisthenics, some were talking to one another and looking out of the windows on the tier, some were on a computer, some were on the phone. As we walked by each of them, they looked in our direction. Some waved. Some smiled. Others didn't. It felt like a profound invasion of privacy to be there, unannounced, walking around in what was essentially their home. And yet I wanted to come across as amicable, to wave back when waved to. The group tacitly settled on nodding to those we passed and keeping our collective silence. The air seemed too fragile for anything else.

We circled the room, walking clockwise, so each time we looked to the right we were followed by the faint reflections of our bodies in the glass panes of the control room. I could not help but feel that something rancid had settled in me, like my presence made me complicit in what was happening here. The incessant, multidimensional surveillance tightened my chest. Before I could fully come to terms with the gravity of where we were, the humanity of who we were seeing, we were quickly ushered out, leaving the men behind.

My eyes narrowed as they adjusted to the light outside.

Right before we got on the bus, a voice emerged from behind us. "Norris, is that you?" Norris turned around, smiled, and then embraced a man dressed in the attire all incarcerated people at Angola wear, and whose name I did not catch.* They laughed and patted each other on the back, and Norris promised they would catch up more during his next visit.

Being with Norris over the course of these hours made it clear how much he meant to the people who remained incarcerated inside Angola. Every person we walked by knew him by name, and he knew theirs, their faces glowing when they saw him. It was evident how much he was a part of the recent history of the institution, and that his work meant so much to so many of the people there. "It's challenging when I leave, because I'm leaving people that I care about," he told me. "It's like some folks are there who I met when I first got there, and they're still there after I'm gone. That's the hardest part about it, seeing people and finding out about other folks who may have passed on."

The average sentence at Angola is eighty-seven years.

"I know I inspire them," he continued. "But at the same time they give me the energy to keep

---

* Some of the incarcerated people in Angola, depending on how long they've been there and on the security level at which they're kept, are able to move with relative freedom inside the prison.

fighting, because I know what I'm fighting for. It's right in front of my face. So that's what keeps me there. It lets me know exactly why I'm in this fight, and why it's so important to stay in this fight."

As we drove toward the exit of the prison, the sun cast a late-autumn shadow of our bus along the fields. From the window, we saw a group of two dozen men in white-and-blue sweatshirts with garden hoes methodically rising in their hands and then falling to the earth. Their bodies were set against a backdrop of trees that had tumbled into autumn, draping them in a volcanic sea of red and orange. It had been one thing to see Black men laboring in the fields of Angola in photographs but it was quite different to see it in person. The parallel with chattel slavery made it feel as if time was bending in on itself. There was no need for metaphor; the land made it literal. I wanted so desperately to ask the bus driver to stop, to be able to get off the bus and go speak with these men. I don't know what I would have said. I wanted voices to add texture to the images these men had become. I wanted them to be more than their bodies. More than flesh and fields and tools and emblems of a history no one here seemed willing to sit with. I did not want to remember them as silence. But as quickly as we saw them, they began to recede. My neck craned and shifted, straining to keep them in my sight for another moment. As we drove off, I watched them fade into the distance, their bodies melting into the grey sky—a throng of tangled silhouettes disappearing into the vast expanse of land.

As we rode along the levee lining the river, the barrier that kept the prison from flooding during heavy storms, I looked out the window one last time and saw miles and miles of land bathed in the purple-orange hue of dusk. The earth resembled a quilt, patches of land crowned in cages and patches of land made of quiet, open fields. A flock of birds, small and black, pushed and pulled against the sky as they moved in unison over the fields. They swerved and dipped and bent their bodies around each slice of wind, flying over the levees and toward the river, as if to look down and wonder, *What is a fence if you can fly right over it?*

I turned and asked Norris, "How much did you get paid when you worked in the field?"

"They give folks an allowance. First six months when I came to prison, you didn't earn anything," he said. "The first six months you're paying off all your clothes that we got to give you while you're here. Now, go figure." Norris chuckled. "Six months going to pay for clothes for a lifetime."

But how much does someone make after the period is finished? I asked.

"Jobs in the field? Seven cents an hour."
I leaned in, thinking I had misheard.
"Seven cents," Norris said again.*

"This place really is just like the plantation was. Just to utilize all the free labor that they can get," Norris continued. "They lost all that free labor to emancipation, and now how are we going to get that free labor back? You got all these folks wandering around with no real skills, don't know what to do, well, we can create laws to put them back in servitude, and that's what they've done. Where do they work? They go right back to working convict leasing, working these same plantations that they were freed from."

---

* According to a representative from the prison, those working in the field make between two and twenty cents an hour. With regard to prison labor, as Whitney Benns has written in *The Atlantic* ("American Slavery, Reinvented," September 21, 2015), Angola is not the exception; it is largely the rule. Incarcerated workers have not reaped the benefits of the labor movement over the course of the past century, in large part because they are not understood to be "employees." As Benns writes, incarcerated workers are not explicitly stripped of employee status in statutes like the Fair Labor Standards Act or the National Labor Relations Act, but on the multiple occasions in which people in prison have sued a department of corrections to receive standard minimum wage for their work, the courts have stated that incarcerated workers are not protected by such laws, as the relationship between said person and said institution is not primarily economic in nature.

I asked Norris what stood out to him in his memories of the field.

"Picking cotton," he responded, without any hesitation. "Man…it's like knowing your history, knowing what our folks went through, and all of a sudden, having one of these cotton sacks in your hand." He cupped his hand and then closed his fingers around the bag we were both imagining in his grasp. His knuckles were dark and cracked, and when he reopened his hand he rubbed the inside of his palm with his thumb.

"I think that's the biggest challenge more than anything else," he continued. "Not the work but just the mindset of being there and knowing you're kind of reliving history, in a sense. I'm going through the very same thing that folks fought and died for, so I wouldn't have to go through it, and here it is all over again."

"I don't know if it's true or not, but I like it"

BLANDFORD CEMETERY

Ken was tall and slender with thin, greying hair, and a pair of glasses atop his forehead, ready at any moment to, with a nod, drop down to his nose. Tours at Blandford Cemetery were scheduled to begin every hour. At 9:55 a.m. I was the only person there. "Looks like it's just you and me," he said, smiling and rolling up his sleeves.

The cemetery was as still as a cloudless sky. The soft din of lawnmowers buzzed in the distance, their vibrating bodies held by Black men steering them in between tombstones draped in Confederate flags. The scent of freshly cut grass—a commingling of green blades and dry earth—swept across the field. The oldest marked grave at Blandford Cemetery dates back to 1702, but what this land is best known for took place more than a century and a half later. Buried here in Petersburg, Virginia, are the bodies of roughly thirty thousand Confederate soldiers, one of the largest mass graves of Confederate servicemen in the South.

I walked through this field and observed the names carved into each ashen tablet. JAMES. WRIGHT. COTMAN. I did not know if they were first names or last names, soldiers who fought in the Civil War or their descendants. It is a cemetery full of bodies that have long watched over this land, and of newly buried bodies just becoming acquainted with the earth.

The entrance to the cemetery was marked by a large stone archway ornamented with the words OUR CONFEDERATE HEROES and two smaller archways on either side of it. Two Confederate flags sat at the bottom of the columns framing the main archway and flapped gently in the wind. The first dragonflies of spring whipped through the light breeze, their translucent wings pulsing against the warm air, their unbridled bodies somersaulting past one another. I watched them dance through the air, land atop a headstone, and pause. I watched their wings twitch once, twice, then take off again, their bodies governed by the wind. I watched and, somewhat mystically, wondered whether these might have been descendants of the dragonflies that flew over this land during the war, more than a century and a half ago. I imagined them zipping past the bullets that turned men into ghosts, their wings warm with beads of blood. I imagined them landing on top of bodies that were strewn on top of bodies, circling the smoke billowing from burning soil.

Ken looked down at his black watch. It was 10 a.m. He led me out of the visitor center and up a set of stone stairs toward the church. The Blandford Church is a russet brick building with a festoon of tombstones in front of it. It was built as an Anglican church, part of the Church of England. But as the city of Petersburg grew, largely because of its proximity to the Appomattox River, which was a central means of trade throughout the region, the congregation decided in 1806 that they wanted to move to a more central location in the city. In order to do so, however, they had to go through a process of deconsecration, in which they formally declared that the building was no longer a church.

"When they do that, doors, floors, pulpit, pews, windows, all come out of this building. It is totally gutted," Ken said. The church, then a brick shell of itself, sat largely abandoned for ninety-five years.

"I want to jump forward," Ken said as a couple who had arrived late hustled up the hill to join us. Ken welcomed them, shared a brief summary of what he had previously said, and began telling the story of how this land was transformed into one of the largest cemeteries in the state.

"A year after the Civil War, there's a young

lady in town named Nora Davidson. She is very much a daughter of the Confederacy," said Ken. Davidson was headmistress at a school for young women, and she took her students to Blandford Cemetery to put flowers and flags on the graves of Confederate soldiers the year after the war. She was part of a group of women who, as Ken put it, were "disappointed because they felt that the Southern soldier had not been treated with the same dignity and honor that the Northern soldiers had. Southern soldiers, often when they fought and died, were buried where they fell. The South didn't have the resources to take you back to Georgia or Maryland or Texas or North Carolina.

"The ladies felt they wanted to do something about this. So they formed something called the Ladies' Memorial Association. Their mission was to...exhume the bodies of the Confederate soldiers they could find, and bring them into this now larger cemetery and rebury them." The Petersburg Ladies' Memorial Association was one of many that organized throughout the South in the aftermath of the Civil War, hiring laborers to find bodies and rebury them in Confederate cemeteries. "Well," Ken said, "it took them fifteen years." He dabbed at a line of sweat on his forehead with the edge of his sleeve. "They found almost thirty thousand sets of Confederate remains."

But, Ken said, there was a problem. Most of the bodies exhumed were not identifiable. New forms of artillery had been introduced during the Civil War that left men's bodies ravaged in a way that had previously been unseen in standard warfare. Sometimes all that was left was a leg or an arm or a head with no body attached. "The trouble with the Civil War soldier was there was no standard identification. No one wore dog tags. No one had ID bands," Ken said. Of the roughly 30,000 soldiers buried at Blandford, only about 2,200 are identified.

After fifteen years of collecting the remains, the women decided they needed a focal point around which to dedicate the cemetery. The city of Petersburg gave them the old church, which had been all but abandoned for almost a century, to refurbish and make into a living memorial to the slain Confederate soldiers. The Ladies' Memorial Association commissioned Tiffany Studios, owned by the world-renowned artist and specialist in stained-glass windows Louis Comfort Tiffany, to lead this project. As Ken continued talking, I briefly swiped open my phone and looked it up: Louis Comfort Tiffany was part of the famous New York Tiffany family, and it was his father who had started the company Tiffany & Co.

The problem for the Ladies' Memorial Association was that the women could not afford to pay a company as renowned as Tiffany's to complete the project. "In 1901, Mr. Tiffany sold a window like that, this size, for seventeen hundred dollars. If you do the math, that is forty-nine thousand dollars in today's equivalent dollars," Ken said. And the Ladies' Memorial Association needed more than a dozen windows. But ultimately Tiffany Studios gave the women a discount: only three hundred fifty dollars per window, a much more manageable price but still prohibitive for the organization.

"So the solution was they would go to the Confederate states and the border states and say, 'If you raise the money, we will put in a window in your honor in this memorial for the Southern soldier.' And that's how all the windows got populated," Ken said, waving his hands as if they held magic wands.

Ken grabbed a pair of keys from his pocket and fidgeted with the door of the church before pushing it open. As we stepped inside the church, a hazy darkness wrapped around my skin. At first, all I could see were the silhouettes of old pews and rings of stained-glass windows traced by sunlight. As my eyes adjusted, the contours of the room became more distinct and the images in the windows sharpened. Each stained-glass window was a mesmerizing display of craftsmanship, a canvas of dazzling blues and greens and violets exploding from each pane. On each window stood a Christian saint surrounded by a burst of colors, the texture of the glass making it seem as if the pious figures were stepping out from the thick panels.

"Three things in the window: seal, figure, and inscription," Ken said, approaching the first window nearest the door, a towering, magnificent piece of glass with Saint Mark holding a scroll and looking into the distance. Each window commemorating a state's soldiers depicts a saint, with a state seal at the top of the window and an inscription at the bottom. Below Saint Mark, written in black in a golden box, was: TO THE GLORY OF GOD AND IN MEMORY OF SOUTH CAROLINA'S SONS WHO DIED FOR THE CONFEDERACY+++HE DOETH ACCORDING TO HIS WILL IN THE ARMY OF HEAVEN AND AMONG THE INHABITANTS OF THE EARTH.

In the other windows were the saints Bartholomew, Paul, John, Peter, James the Less, Philip, Thomas, Matthew, Luke, and Andrew. Beneath each of them was an inscription praising the valor of the Confederate soldiers who fought in the war.[*] My eyes moved back and forth from the images of the saints to the inscriptions under their feet, the dissonance growing with every second.

---

[*] There are fifteen windows in total. Of the thirteen windows dedicated to states, eleven have saints (Maryland's and Arkansas's don't, and are smaller). One window is dedicated to the Ladies' Memorial Association, and the last one depicts a cross, known as the Cross of Jewels.

Ken went on to outline the aesthetic history of each window in the church with meticulous detail, making his way from window to window, reciting his practiced presentation with precision and depth. There was little discussion, however, of anything beyond the windows.

I asked Ken if many of the people who visited these grounds and came on these tours were Confederate sympathizers.

"I think there's a Confederate *empathy*," he said, altering the language slightly. "You're here primarily for the beauty of the windows, but a lot of people don't know about it and a lot of people who do come have Confederate empathy. People will tell you, 'My great-great-grandmother, my great-great-grandfather, are buried out here.' So they've got long Southern roots, which go back into the 1860s and before." He shuffled the keys in his hand, looking for the one that would lock the church door. "But an awful lot of people come from Michigan and Minnesota and Montana because they want to see the beauty of the windows."

I tried to be more direct.

I asked Ken how he personally—and Blandford as an institution—thought about addressing the history and symbolism of Confederate iconography in the church and throughout the cemetery. Was it okay to only talk about the windows and not to say anything about the Confederate cause they were built to honor?

"Very simple," Ken responded. "As they say, 'You're not from around here.' I am not a Southerner."

I didn't quite understand what Ken was saying.

"My father was in the military, so I was raised primarily north of the Mason-Dixon Line. So I don't have the Southern upbringing. I don't have the War of Northern Aggression or the states' rights war," he said, referring to the alternate names the Civil War is sometimes called by those sympathetic to the Confederate cause. "Is it possible that this church in 1735 may have been built probably with slave labor? Absolutely. When the balcony was used up here, and the congregation was small, did slaves stay up there? Perhaps."

Ken said that the lack of discussion around these topics was potentially tied to the demographic makeup of the cemetery's visitors. "Our visitor population is overwhelmingly white, because again, what this is, it's not that a Black population doesn't appreciate the windows, but sometimes in the context of what it represents, they're not as comfortable." He went on: "In most cases we try and fall back on the beauty of the windows, the Tiffany glass kind of thing."

Perhaps it was not simply that Black people did not come to a Confederate cemetery because they didn't want to be in the space; perhaps Black people did not come to these spaces in large part because of how the story of the Confederate cause was told. I was tempted to tell Ken about the Whitney Plantation: how a great many people assume that Black Americans would have no interest in visiting the land upon which their ancestors were enslaved, but my visit to the Whitney had shown me that if a place was willing to tell a different story—a more honest story—it would begin to see a different set of people visiting. For me, coming to a Confederate cemetery and hearing Ken speak about the beauty of a set of windows without exploring what they were meant to memorialize, was not unlike going to a plantation and listening to a talk about the decorative infrastructure of the enslaver's house without mentioning the enslaved hands who built it.

We stepped back into the visitor building, filled by a late-morning light that showered each glass encasement housing pieces of the cemetery's history. Ken pointed to a woman behind the counter. "She's my boss," he said in what felt like an attempt to pass me off to someone else, or at least to share the burden of questions I was throwing his way.

At this point the woman came over and stood just a few feet away from Ken. She smiled and I smiled back.

Martha had a kind face with large tortoiseshell

glasses that sat high on her nose. I asked her if the cemetery was concerned that, by presenting Blandford in such a positive light, they might be distorting its connection to an army and a cause that was violent, racist, and treasonous.

"Absolutely," she said. "And when people ask—I've been here for eighteen years—people often ask what do I personally feel is the true cause. And I say, 'Well, you get five different historians who have written five different books, I'm going to have five different answers.' It's a lot of stuff. But I think from the perspective of *my* ancestors, it was not slavery. My ancestors were not slaveholders. But my great-great-grandfather fought. He had federal troops coming into Norfolk. He said, 'Nuh-uh, I've got to join the army and defend my home state,' and that's what he did. It was not a slavery issue, but that's just for that particular individual. I always try to tell people, it was a lot of things that came together."

She continued: "It was interesting, when I came to work in the church—my whole point is to learn about the interesting early history and talk about what the women did. Again, as a woman I like to talk about women's history and say they've been through a lot, but this is how they helped to get through their grief of perhaps a husband, father, son dying, trying to take care of those remains, because again, the federal government took care of the Union Army. There was nothing done for the Confederates, so it was important to them. And this is what their result was, this beautiful chapel. To think you can walk in there and, as Ken was saying, just enjoy this little Anglican church that is restored to be this beautiful chapel. I think you could take the Civil War aspect totally out of it and enjoy the beauty."

I made a note of Martha's invocation of her lineage as the starting point of our conversation. It did not feel incidental, but central to how she thought about the war and what it represented.

"You were talking about how for a lot of people they can come in here and just see the windows and appreciate the history and décor of the church," I said. "But for me, as someone who is a Black American, someone whose ancestors were enslaved, it is very difficult for me to disentangle any of it. I think there's a profound dissonance, even to *be* here. I've never been to a Confederate cemetery except at this moment." Ken walked back in our direction. "I think I experience it probably in a very different way than a lot of your visitors."

As I said all of this, Martha and Ken nodded. "Unfortunately, we don't often get that," Ken said. "What would you guess, Martha—eighty-five, ninety percent of our visitors are white?" Martha nodded.

If I had to guess, I imagined even that number was understating the percentage of white visitors.

Ken stepped away again, and I continued my conversation with Martha. As we spoke, I looked down on the counter where handouts for a Memorial Day event hosted by the Sons of Confederate Veterans were piled up. My focus trailed off. Martha's words became an indecipherable din as I reached down and grabbed one. Martha's gaze followed the direction of my hand. Her face turned red and she thrust her hand down quickly to flip the paper, covering the rest of the leaflets.

"Don't even look at this. I'm sorry," she said nervously. "I will tell you from a personal standpoint I'm kind of bothered."

I looked at the flyer again, this time focusing on the photograph of the guest speaker for the event: Paul C. Gramling Jr., then the commander in chief of the Sons of Confederate Veterans.

"I don't mind that they come on Memorial Day and put Confederate flags on Confederate graves, that's okay," she said. "But as far as I'm concerned, you don't need a Confederate flag on—" She stumbled over a series of sentences I couldn't follow. Then she collected herself and took a deep breath.

"I hate the fact that people use that as in-your-face kind of stuff," she said. "If you're just talking about history, it's great, but these folks are like,

'The South shall rise again.' It's very bothersome. It's peaceful, but I went to one because I was invited and I wanted to see and I said I will never do it again. These folks can't let things go. I mean, it's not like they want people enslaved again, but they can't get over the fact that history is history."

Martha started talking to me about how *preservation* was different from *celebration*, an idea that made sense to me in the abstract. I asked Martha for her opinion of the Confederate monuments in Richmond that had gotten so much attention since the 2017 white-nationalist rally in Charlottesville.

"I would like to see the monuments staying up, but with context," she said. "Because again, I understand where people are coming from, but if we can't have them where they are, we've got to have them somewhere.

"The thing is, my personal opinion, and I will tell you this, I don't think that Robert E. Lee would have been pleased with all this deitizing. He was a very humble person. I don't think he'd be happy at all with the controversy," she said. "He did what he thought was right. He did do an awful lot. Again, he was in the US Army before he took on the Confederate [States of America], the CSA. But I—just from personally reading things about him, I don't think he'd be happy at all to know [about] all these statues of him everywhere.

I don't think he'd be happy to know that there's a controversy about Monument Avenue, because he was just much more humble than that."

More people were coming into the visitor center, and I didn't want to keep either of them from their work. I thanked Ken and Martha for their time. We shook hands, and I made my way out the door, the wind slapping against the thousands of tombstones around me.

I thought about Martha's admiration for Robert E. Lee and her assertion that he would not have liked the statues that had been raised in his name. Perhaps Martha was right, as Lee's words suggest that he likely would not have advocated for Confederate monuments to be erected. In an August 1869 letter he wrote, "I think it wiser, moreover, not to keep open the sores of war but to follow the examples of those nations who endeavored to obliterate the marks of civil strife, to commit to oblivion the feelings engendered."

Lee's hesitancy to erect memorials after the war, however, should not be considered exculpatory or a reflection of his desire to move toward an egalitarian society in which Black people were equal to their white counterparts. As historian Kevin M. Levin notes, Lee remained outwardly reconciled to defeat, but privately he was troubled about emancipation and the end of slavery.

Robert E. Lee was a slave owner who led an army predicated on maintaining and expanding the institution of slavery. A letter Lee wrote to his wife in 1856 is often used as a means of demonstrating that Lee couldn't have fought for the Confederacy in order to protect slavery because he believed slavery was "a moral & political evil." Devoid of additional context—and an acknowledgment of the fact that Lee owned enslaved people—this assertion might seem to shield Lee from allegations of racism and bigotry. And yet two sentences later:

I think it however a greater evil to the white man than to the black race, & while my feelings are strongly enlisted in behalf of the latter, my sympathies are more strong for the former. The blacks are immeasurably better off here than in Africa, morally, socially & physically. The painful discipline they are undergoing, is necessary for their instruction as a race, & I hope will prepare & lead them to better things. How long their subjugation may be necessary is Known & ordered by a wise & merciful Providence. Their emancipation will sooner result from the mild & melting influence of Christianity, than the storms & tempests of fiery Controversy.

While Lee believed slavery would one day come to an end, he also seemed to believe it was up to God when that happened. It was a view common of those in Lee's world. He, and his fellow enslavers, had no control over it. Everyone, including the enslaved, were simply meant to wait for divine intervention.

As a slave owner, Lee was ruthless in breaking up families. According to historian Elizabeth Brown Pryor, "By 1860 he had broken up every family but one on the estate." When three of Lee's enslaved workers escaped, he had them hunted down and, when they were returned, had them beaten in a spectacle of cruelty. A testimony from one of the people who attempted to escape reads:

[W]e were immediately taken before Gen. Lee, who demanded the reason why we ran away; we frankly told him that we considered ourselves free; he then told us he would teach us a lesson we never would forget; he then ordered us to the barn, where, in his presence, we were tied firmly to posts by a Mr. Gwin, our overseer, who was ordered by Gen. Lee to strip us to the waist and give us fifty lashes each, excepting my sister, who received but twenty; we were accordingly stripped to the skin by the overseer, who, however, had sufficient humanity to decline whipping us; accordingly Dick Williams, a county constable, was called in, who gave us the number of lashes ordered; Gen. Lee, in the meantime, stood by, and frequently enjoined Williams to "lay it on well," an injunction which he did not fail to heed; not satisfied with simply lacerating our naked flesh, Gen. Lee then ordered the overseer to thoroughly wash our backs with brine, which was done.

During the war, Lee was, like his contemporaries, disturbed by the sight of Black soldiers in Union ranks. White soldiers under his command ruthlessly executed Black soldiers who attempted to surrender during the infamous Battle of the Crater—the first time Lee's Army of Northern Virginia had faced large numbers of Black troops. The Battle of the Crater is helpful not only in contextualizing Lee but in contextualizing the cemetery itself.

"You can connect this directly to the Blandford Cemetery," Levin later told me. "The Confederate counterattack that pushed back the Union advance, including an entire division of Black soldiers, began just steps from Blandford. These men were told that Black soldiers were present on the battlefield and it infuriated them. Roughly two hundred Black soldiers were murdered after surrendering either during or after the battle. There are references to the Crater inside the church. In short, the Blandford Church is on the Crater battlefield."

For whites in the Confederate Army, seeing these Black men in Union uniforms represented a profound and infuriating turning point in the war, one that tapped into their worst impulses. The use of Black soldiers was a threat to the entire social order the South had been predicated on. Black soldiers in the Union Army did not simply reflect a new demographic composition of their military opponents; Lee's army saw Black soldiers as participants in a slave revolt, an insurrection of the most nightmarish proportions that was being actively supported by Lincoln and the US government. The Confederate government put in place policies that officially considered Black soldiers slaves participating in an insurrection, and thus subject to re-enslavement or execution. Their white officers, as enablers of the insurrection, could also be executed.

When Lee's men encountered the Black soldiers in battle, they expressed explicit disdain for their Black adversaries. In his book *Remembering the Battle of the Crater*, Levin cites the reflections of a number of Confederate soldiers: "It had the same affect [*sic*] upon our men that a red flag had upon a mad bull," remarked one South Carolina soldier. Another, David Holt of the 16th Mississippi Infantry Regiment, remembered, "They were the first we had seen and the sight of a nigger in a blue uniform and with a gun was more than 'Johnnie

Reb' could stand." (Johnny Reb was a character meant to symbolize a typical Confederate soldier.) Holt said that "[f]ury had taken possession" of him, adding, "I knew that I felt as ugly as they looked." Per Laban Odom of the 48th Georgia, "Our men killed them with the bayonets and the but[t]s of there [*sic*] guns and every other way until they were lying eight or ten deep on top of one enuther [*sic*] and the blood almost s[h]oe [*sic*] quarter deep." Another soldier in the same regiment wrote: "The Bayonet was plunged through their hearts & the muzzle of our guns was put on their temple & their brains blown out others were knocked in the head with butts of our guns. Few would succeed in getting to the rear safe."

Confederate soldiers were no less brutal after Black troops had surrendered. Levin outlines how soldiers described in detail what happened after the fighting ceased. Jerome B. Yates of the 16th Mississippi remembered: "Most of the Negroes were killed after the battle. Some was killed after they were taken to the rear." According to Henry Van Lewvenigh Bird, "The only sounds which now broke the silence was some poor wounded wretch begging for water and quieted by a bayonet thrust which said unmistakably 'Bois ton sang. Tu n'aurais de soif.' [Drink your blood. You will have no more thirst.]" James Verdery called it "a truly *Bloody Sight a perfect Massacre nearly* a Black flag fight."

Levin argues that such violence was meant to convey to Black people still trapped in the claws of enslavement behind Confederate lines that no such insurrection, be it inside or outside the confines of war, would be allowed. The *Richmond Examiner* unambiguously captured the sentiment many Southerners held at that time, asking General Mahone and his men not to relent: "Shut your eyes, General, strengthen your stomach with a little brandy and water, and let the work, which God has entrusted to you and your brave men, go forward to its full completion; that is, until every negro has been slaughtered...butcher every negro that Grant sends against your brave troops, and permit them not to soil their hands with the capture of a single hero."

After the Battle of the Crater, captured Union prisoners—white and Black—were made to march through the streets of Petersburg. Levin argues that the display was meant as a message to civilians that this is what was at stake if the war was lost: race mixing and the end of white supremacy.

In the years following the war, Robert E. Lee did not become open to the creation of a society based on racial equity; he actively opposed it. He argued, for example, that Black people should not have the right to vote. "It is true that the people of the South, together with the people of the North and West, are, for obvious reasons, opposed to any system of laws which will place the political power of the country in the hands of the negro race," he explained in a letter signed by other former Confederate leaders in 1868. "But this opposition springs from no feelings of enmity, but from a deep seated conviction that at present the negroes have neither the intelligence nor other qualifications which are necessary to make them safe depositories of political power."

The contrast between Lee's racist views and his sanitized image was not just realized by people of future generations; it was named and identified—particularly by Black writers and activists—soon after Lee's death. In 1870, upon seeing the blossoming of Lee's deification, Frederick Douglass denounced the "bombastic laudation of the rebel chief" and was disgusted by the fact that he could "scarcely take up a paper...that is not filled with *nauseating* flatteries of the late Robert E. Lee."

It was clear, too, in the early twentieth century, when W. E. B. Du Bois wrote in a 1928 essay:

Each year on the 19th of January, there is renewed effort to canonize Robert E. Lee, the greatest confederate general. His personal comeliness, his aristocratic birth and his military prowess all call for the verdict of greatness and genius. But one thing—one terrible fact—militates against this, and that is the inescapable truth that Robert E. Lee led a bloody war to perpetuate slavery. Copperheads like *The New York Times* may magisterially declare, "Of course, he never fought for slavery." Well, for what did he fight? State rights? Nonsense. The South cared only for State Rights as a weapon to defend slavery...No. People do not go to war for abstract theories of government. They fight for property and privilege, and that was what Virginia fought for in the Civil War. And Lee followed Virginia...Either he knew what slavery meant when he helped maim and murder thousands in its defense, or he did not. If he did not he was a fool. If he did, Robert Lee was a traitor and a rebel—not indeed to his country, but to humanity and humanity's God.

It is not simply that statues of Lee and other Confederates stand as monuments to a traitorous army predicated on maintaining and expanding the institution of slavery; it is also that we, US taxpayers, are paying for their maintenance and preservation. A 2018 report by *Smithsonian* magazine and the Nation Institute's Investigative Fund (now Type Investigations) found that over the previous ten years, US taxpayers had directed at least forty million dollars to Confederate monuments, including statues, homes, museums, and cemeteries, as well as Confederate heritage groups. And in Virginia, the subsidizing of Confederate iconography is a more than century-long project.

In 1902, as Jim Crow continued to expand as a violent and politically repressive force, the state's all-white legislature created an annual allocation of the state's funds for the care of Confederate graves. *Smithsonian*'s investigation found that in total, the state had spent approximately $9 million in today's dollars. Much of that funding goes *directly* to the United Daughters of the Confederacy, which received over $1.6 million in funds for Confederate cemeteries from the State of Virginia between 1996 and 2018.

Cemeteries filled with Black and formerly enslaved people have never received commensurate financial support. The Virginia legislature passed the Historical African American Cemeteries and Graves Act in 2017, to demonstrate its commitment to making amends for this injustice, but at the time of the *Smithsonian* investigation less than a thousand dollars had been used. (Virginia has increased its level of support since then, and established a fund specifically for nineteenth-century African American cemeteries in 2020, a step to make up for over a century's worth of neglect.)

Across the street from Blandford Cemetery, a smaller, more understated burial ground stood.

The People's Memorial Cemetery was purchased by twenty-eight members of Petersburg's free Black community in 1840. Buried on this land are enslaved people, an anti-slavery writer whose burial site is recorded among the National Underground Railroad Network to Freedom sites; Black veterans of the Civil War, World War I, and World War II; as well as hundreds of other Black Petersburg residents.

The contrast between the two was conspicuous in ways not dissimilar to that between the two cemeteries at Monticello. There were far fewer tombstones at the People's Memorial Cemetery than at Blandford, and those there were indiscriminately scattered across the brown grass. There were no flags ornamenting the graves. There were no hourly tours available for people to remember the dead. There was history, but also silence.

In the weeks that followed, I kept revisiting the way Martha had swiftly flipped over the event flyer, the way her face had turned a hot and revealing red, the shame she had expressed at me having seen that this event was being held on the grounds she presided over. If she had not responded this way, I don't know that I would have felt so curious about what she was trying to hide. But at that point I decided to find out what Martha was so ashamed of.

Wary of making a trip to a Sons of Confederate Veterans (SCV) commemoration celebration alone, I drove back down to Petersburg on Memorial Day morning with a friend, William, a white graduate student with blond hair, dimples, and a vivacious spirit. William and I had been good friends since college, and as a former preschool teacher, he is one of my children's favorite playmates. Following the death of his father, William began exploring his own ancestry and coming to terms with the fact that his ancestors included plantation owners and someone who had fought in the Confederate Army. This trip, he said, would be part of his own journey in reckoning with that.

As we turned into the cemetery, lines of cars were parked alongside the road, and people were walking up a hill toward a large gazebo. I was struck by just how casual the event was—what seemed like a couple hundred men and women sitting alongside each other in uneven rows of folding chairs they had brought themselves. Children laughed and played tag around the trunk of a towering tree. From teenagers to the elderly, people came together and hugged, guffawing and slapping one another's backs with an easy, familiar delight. It felt as if I was walking in on someone else's family reunion.

Dixie flags bloomed from the soil like milk-weeds. There were baseball caps emblazoned with the Confederate flag, biker vests ornamented with the seals of each seceding state, and lawn chairs marked with the letters UDC, the abbreviation for the United Daughters of the Confederacy. To my left and my right were more—and more massive—Confederate flags, its rebel insignia billowing in the wind. In front of the gazebo were two flags, one Confederate, one US, standing side by side as if seven hundred thousand people hadn't been killed under the weight of the epic conflagration between them.

Without lawn chairs, we stood in the back of the crowd so as not to block the view of anyone sitting down and also so as not to be conspicuous.

The event began with an honor guard, a dozen men dressed in Confederate regalia marching in front of the crowd, carrying rifles with long bayonets resting on their left shoulders. Their uniforms were the color of smoke; their caps looked as if they had been bathed in ash. Everyone in the crowd stood up from their chairs as they made their way across the face of the gazebo. Some stood at attention and lifted their right hands to their brows in salute; others lifted their phones to take photos of the wistful procession. After the honor guard made their way from one side of the gazebo to the other, they stood at attention as the master of ceremonies asked everyone to remove their hats and recite the US Pledge of Allegiance. This was followed by an acoustic rendition of "The Star-Spangled Banner" with the crowd joining in. Then, seamlessly, the guitarist strummed his guitar once more and the crowd began a spirited rendition of the famous song "Dixie":

Oh, I wish I was in the land of cotton
Old times there are not forgotten
Look away! Look away! Look away! Dixie Land

The song was originally written in the 1850s to be performed as part of a minstrel show in which white actors dressed up in blackface. Over time, it became the de facto Confederate anthem, and the song would play as Confederate soldiers prepared to enter battle. The song became a symbol of "massive resistance"—a movement to prevent school desegregation that grew to encompass resistance to civil rights more broadly—in the mid-twentieth century. The Ole Miss marching band even played it on the football field; they performed while wearing Confederate-inspired uniforms. I looked around as everyone sang in unison, lifting their voices in an almost paradoxically mellifluous tribute to a fallen ancestral home. A home never meant for me.

A variety of other speakers came to the podium

under the gazebo to speak, each of them praising the soldiers buried under our feet and castigating those who might espouse objections to such eulogizing.

"This cemetery," one said, "this is as important as any [other cemetery] in the Confederate States of America. Lest we never forget the trials, the tribulations that they fought, died, and went through, and their families."

"While those who hate seek to remove the memory of these heroes," another said, "these men paid the ultimate price for freedom, and they deserve to be remembered."

As we stood there listening, I pulled out a small journal and began taking notes. I tried to be subtle, but it felt as if my pen was loudly screeching against the page each time it touched the paper. I felt eyes on me, as more than a few people turned around in their seats and looked with puzzlement, and likely suspicion, at the Black man they had never seen before standing in the back of a Sons of Confederate Veterans crowd. A man to my right, not so subtly, took out his phone and began recording me with its camera. People continued to turn their heads. The stares began to crawl over my skin. I slowly closed my notebook and stuck it under my arm, looking up toward the gazebo, doing my best to give off the sense that I was unfazed. Without moving my head, I scanned the crowd again. The man in front of me had a gun in a holster on his waist. Virginia is an open-carry state.

Paul C. Gramling Jr., the commander in chief of the Sons of Confederate Veterans at the time, was the keynote speaker. I recognized him from the flyer Martha had tried to hide from me weeks before. Gramling wore a tan suit with a white oxford shirt and a straw boater tilted down just a touch over his forehead, as if it were meant to spin on its own axis. He had long dark-blond hair that fell down the back of his neck and rested on his shoulders, and a thick goatee that covered his lips. As he stepped to the podium, his face emerged from the shade of the gazebo and was soon bathed in the soft angles of afternoon light.

Gramling began his speech by sharing a story about the origin of Memorial Day. "I've read several people writing about Memorial Day and how it started. I come across one the other day. I don't know if it's true or not, but I like it. And I wanted to share that with you this afternoon."

He read aloud an account of a Memorial Day ceremony that took place on April 25, 1866, in Columbus, Mississippi, when a group of women "decorated the graves of both Union and Confederate soldiers," he said, his voice like an old rocking chair sliding back and forth on its crescent legs. "The [United Daughters of the Confederacy] will forever honor all of our country's heroes with undying devotion and that of our Confederate dead, who have earned their rightful place to be included as American veterans. We should embrace our heritage as Americans, North and South, Black and white, rich and poor. Our American heritage is the one thing we have in common, and it is what defines us."

I was fascinated by the conciliatory equivocation of his tone, and his desire, it seemed, not to push a demarcation between the Confederacy and the United States but to assimilate the memory of the Confederacy more fully into the country's historical consciousness. Confederate soldiers, according to this narrative, were US military veterans just as those who had fought in World War I, World War II, Vietnam, Korea, and Iraq. It did not seem to matter that they had fought *against* the US; he believed they should be remembered as US veterans themselves.

Gramling's speech sounded so much like similar Memorial Day celebrations after the end of Reconstruction, when orators exclaimed that this day should be one of reconciliation, paying tribute to the sacrifices made by both Confederate and Union soldiers without accounting for what the war had actually been fought over. Former Confederate general Roger A. Pryor went so far as to claim that the war was not caused by slavery at all, that—as Lee maintained—slavery would come to an end if

God deemed it so. "[I]mpartial history will record that slavery fell not by any effort of man's will, but by the immediate intervention and act of the Almighty himself; and in the anthem of praise ascending to Heaven for the emancipation of four million human beings, the voice of the Confederate soldier mingles its note of devout gratulation."

"I don't know if it's true or not, but I like it"—that comment, spoken at the start of Gramling's speech, had been strikingly honest and deeply revealing. I was struck by the cavalier framing Gramling used.

The idea for Memorial Day is often attributed not to Columbus, Mississippi, but Columbus, Georgia, which inspired Mississippi's event even though it occurred a day later.* In 1866, the Ladies' Memorial Association in Columbus, Georgia, selected April 26th—the anniversary of Confederate general Joseph E. Johnston's surrender to Union general William T. Sherman—to pay tribute to the Confederate dead. Other states had other dates they used to mark the earliest celebrations of Memorial Day—or "Decoration Day" as it was often called.

---

* The Ladies' Memorial Association in Columbus, Georgia, publicized the event in newspapers, hoping that other places would hold similar celebrations. The newspapers in Columbus, Mississippi, got the date of the proposed event wrong, so they accidentally held it a day too soon.

For example, May 10, the anniversary of Stonewall Jackson's death, and June 3, the birthday of former Confederate president Jefferson Davis.

Many places throughout the South lay claim to being the originators of Memorial Day, including Blandford Cemetery. According to the official website of Petersburg, Virginia, the first Memorial Day was celebrated on the grounds of Blandford in June 1866. The story is at least as much a matter of interpretation as of fact. According to historian David Blight, the first Memorial Day ceremony was actually held in Charleston, South Carolina, in May 1865, before Confederate women honored grave sites in Georgia or Mississippi or Virginia. In the archives of Harvard, Blight found reports from both the *New-York Tribune* and the *Charleston Daily Courier* detailing an event conducted by Black workmen, mostly freed slaves, who buried and commemorated fallen Union soldiers. Confederates had taken control of Charleston's Washington Race Course and Jockey Club and converted it into an outdoor prison, where they kept Union prisoners of war. The conditions of the prison were so terrible that nearly 260 Union soldiers died and were subsequently buried in a mass grave behind the racetrack's grandstand. Blight describes what happened next:

After the Confederate evacuation of Charleston black workmen went to the site, reburied the Union dead properly, and built a high fence around the cemetery. They whitewashed the fence and built an archway over an entrance on which they inscribed the words, "Martyrs of the Race Course."

The symbolic power of this Low Country planter aristocracy's bastion was not lost on the freedpeople, who then, in cooperation with white missionaries and teachers, staged a parade of 10,000 on the track. A *New-York Tribune* correspondent witnessed the event, describing "a procession of friends and mourners as South Carolina and the United States never saw before."

The procession was led by 3,000 black schoolchildren carrying armloads of roses and singing the Union marching song "John Brown's Body." Several hundred black women followed with baskets of flowers, wreaths and crosses. Then came black men marching in cadence, followed by contingents of Union infantrymen. Within the cemetery enclosure a black children's choir sang "We'll Rally Around the Flag," the "Star-Spangled Banner" and spirituals before a series of black ministers read from the Bible.

I wondered if Gramling had ever come across this history, which was largely forgotten in favor of interpretations more aligned with the Lost Cause.

The Lost Cause is a movement that gained traction in the late nineteenth century that attempted to recast the Confederacy as something predicated on family, honor, and heritage rather than what it was, a traitorous effort to extend and expand the bondage of Black people. The movement asserted that the Civil War was not actually about slavery, that the soldiers and generals who fought in the war were honorable men who did so simply for their families and communities, not because of any racist antagonism. The myth of the Lost Cause not only subsumed those sympathetic to the Confederate cause but also laid its claim to broad swathes of the American consciousness. It attempted to rewrite US history.

The first Memorial Day, as Blight describes it, received significant press coverage at the time. But after Reconstruction was defeated, and as white Democrats took control of state politics, the story of the event disappeared from official records and public consciousness.

As he continued his speech, Gramling turned his attention away from history and began describing a talk he had given that addressed the present-day controversy around Confederate monuments standing across the country. "I told them that we have a common enemy today and that common enemy seeks to eradicate this country's moral fabric. I told them that if they were to succeed in eradicating all things Confederate, what comes next?" I was struck by the stillness in his face, how serious his eyes were as they scanned the crowd. "Our enemies know that if they can take us out, the rest of this country is going to be easy for their picking. Now, thirty years we have been dealing with people trying to take away our symbols. When these monuments were erected over one hundred years ago, in our towns, they were erected in these cities and these towns, the whole town was involved in it. I know in Shreveport [Louisiana], where I'm from, we have a monument there, in Caddo Parish Courthouse, and at the dedication of that monument in 1906, there was hundreds of thousands of people there at the dedication."

People in the crowd nodded. My ears prickled with nervous heat.

"But to think about these men that lay here, buried, that look like that up there..." He pointed in the direction of what looked to be a thirty-foot statue of a Confederate soldier to the crowd's right. "If you take a good look at him, that was all there was to it as far as dealing with the elements, [dealing with] the enemy. And to know that we have thirty thousand of these men buried here, known only to God. And then I think about all the monuments across this country that naysayers are decrying, 'Get rid of them. That offends me. I don't like it.'...I refer to them as the American

ISIS." He looked out into the crowd, who murmured affirmation, and his face contorted with delight. "I have even written about this in the *Confederate Veteran,* in my article, because they are nothing better than ISIS in the Middle East. They are trying to destroy history they don't like. And like I said, once they go through the Confederate symbols—US symbols, Christian symbols, will be next."

Each syllable of Gramling's words were cigarette embers being pushed onto my skin. I thought about all of my friends back home in New Orleans who had spent years fighting to have the Confederate monuments removed. So many of them were teachers committed to showing their students that we did not have to accept the status quo as unchangeable. Others were parents attempting to build a better world, a better city, for their kids, one that did not include slave owners lifted up on sixty-foot pedestals. And many were our elders, veterans of the civil rights movement who had taught us so much about what these statues represented and who, decades ago, had laid their bodies on the line fighting against what these statues represented. I knew these people. None of them were terrorists.

Gramling continued, urging all who were present to understand the true meaning of the Confederacy and to "take back the narrative." "We've got to be able to stand up and say, 'We are more than just this.'" He pointed to the Confederate flag to the left of the gazebo. "We are both of these." He extended the index finger of his opposite hand in the direction of the US flag to his right, so that his arms were now outstretched as if he were blessing the flags that flanked him.

As he began to wind down, Gramling proudly noted how he and the Sons of Confederate Veterans sought to advance their cause by repackaging a well-worn rhetorical maxim. He exclaimed, "When I say that we need to make Dixie great again, some of you might have seen this on our website. We have a baseball cap that says 'Make Dixie Great Again.' It's very similar to the other red cap that I've seen coming out of Washington, DC, 'Make America Great Again.' But I'll submit to you that in order to make America great again, we've got to make Dixie great again."

As Gramling stepped away from the podium, the crowd gave him a rousing round of applause. Two men in front of us holding large Confederate flags began to swing them through the air with unsettling fervor. I turned to William. He raised his eyebrows and let out a long, heavy exhale. We both did a quick glancing survey of everything in front of us and behind us, as if we were small animals who felt unfamiliar vibrations in the earth beneath us.

The remainder of the program was filled with another singer and shorter remarks from a man who reasserted many of Gramling's previous points. As the event concluded, different representatives of the United Daughters of the Confederacy and the Sons of Confederate Veterans laid wreaths at the base of the statue of the Confederate soldier. The honor guard then turned toward the large stretch of cemetery, lifted their rifles toward the sky, and fired into the air three times. I felt my knees buckle at the sound of the first shot, and a thrust of adrenaline hurtled through me. The boom of the rifles reverberated throughout my body. I shut my eyes for the second shot, and again for the third. I felt a tightening of muscles inside my mouth, muscles I hadn't known were there.

As of 2019, according to a report from the Southern Poverty Law Center, there were nearly two thousand Confederate monuments, place names, and other symbols that remained in public places across the country.

The creation of these monuments was not a harmless commemoration or merely an attempt to remember fallen Americans. The creation of any monument sends a message, whether intentional or not. I think of the statues around the country of people who presided over Native American genocide or forced resettlement, and how a young Indigenous child might experience that pedestaled figure.

The erection of Confederate monuments in the early twentieth century came at a moment when many Confederate veterans were beginning to die off in large numbers. A new generation of white Southerners who had no memory of the war had come of age, and the United Daughters of the Confederacy had raised enough money to build memorials to these men. The goal, in part, was to teach the younger generations of white Southerners who these men had been and that the cause they had fought for was an honorable one. But there is another reason, not wholly disconnected from the first. These monuments were also built in an effort to reinforce white supremacy at a time when Black communities were being terrorized and Black social and political mobility impeded. In the late nineteenth century, states began implementing Jim Crow laws to cement this country's racial caste system. Social and political backlash to Reconstruction-era attempts to build an integrated society was the backdrop against which the first monuments arose. These monuments served as physical embodiments of the terror campaign directed at Black communities. Another spike in construction of these statues came in the 1950s and 1960s, coinciding, not coincidentally, with the civil rights movement.

The organization at the forefront of funding and building Confederate memorials and monuments, the United Daughters of the Confederacy (UDC), was founded in 1894 as an amalgam of women's groups and associations that had first emerged during the Civil War. The UDC alone is responsible for erecting more than seven hundred memorials and monuments across the country, according to the *Washington Post,* over four hundred of which are on public grounds. And while the vast majority of these monuments are in the former states of the Confederacy, testaments to the Lost Cause can be found all across the country, including, at the time of this writing, in California, Washington State, South Dakota, Delaware, New York, and Massachusetts.

Those who support these monuments contend that to push back against them is to unfairly apply today's moral sensibilities to a bygone era. This assertion, however, ignores the objections of that era's Black writers and activists. Frederick Douglass wrote in 1870 that "[m]onuments to the 'lost cause' will prove monuments of folly, both in the memories of a wicked rebellion, which they must necessarily perpetuate, and in the failure to accomplish the particular purpose had in view by those who build them. It is a needless record of stupidity and wrong."

Douglass remained a fierce critic of the Lost Cause in the immediate aftermath of the war and over the course of the rest of his life. In 1871, he spoke with great fervor about the danger of forgetting why the war was fought:

> We are sometimes asked, in the name of patriotism, to forget the merits of this fearful struggle, and to remember, with equal admiration, those who struck at the nation's life, and those who struck to save it—those who fought for slavery, and those who fought for liberty and justice.
>
> I am no minister of malice. I would not strike the fallen. I would not repel the repentant; but may my right hand forget its cunning and my tongue cleave to the roof of my mouth, if I forget the difference between the parties to that terrible, protracted, and bloody conflict.

In 1931, W. E. B. Du Bois attacked the decision to erect Confederate monuments as ahistorical and irresponsible:

> The most terrible thing about War, I am convinced, is its monuments—the awful things we are compelled to build in order to remember the victims. In the South, particularly, human ingenuity has been put to it to explain on its

war monuments, the Confederacy. Of course, the plain truth of the matter would be an inscription something like this: "Sacred to the memory of those who fought to Perpetuate Human Slavery." But that reads with increasing difficulty as time goes on. It does, however, seem to be overdoing the matter to read on a North Carolina Confederate monument: "Died Fighting for Liberty!"

The myth of the Lost Cause does not begin or end with the Confederate monuments. The myth seeps into many other facets of state-sanctioned life. In eleven states there are a total of twenty-three Confederate holidays and observances. As of 2020, in both Alabama and Mississippi there is Robert E. Lee Day, Confederate Memorial Day, and Jefferson Davis's birthday; in South Carolina there is Confederate Memorial Day; in Texas there is Confederate Heroes Day. In both Alabama and Mississippi, Robert E. Lee's birthday is celebrated on the same day as Martin Luther King Jr. Day.

The myth of the Lost Cause has also been propagated through media, literature, and postwar propaganda. These fictions often have included denying that the war was ever about slavery, or depicting slavery as a benign or even mutually beneficial institution. On February 22,

1896, thirty-five years after Jefferson Davis's inauguration as president of the Confederacy, former Confederate general Bradley T. Johnson explained that slavery was "the apprenticeship by which savage races had been educated and trained into civilization by their superiors."

After the war ended, white Southern writers took the baton from Confederate leaders and continued to paint slavery not as an institution defined by violence and exploitation but as a mutually beneficial arrangement of eager Black enslaved people and kind white enslavers. Thomas Nelson Page, a writer from Virginia who was just twelve years old when the war ended, exemplified this misguided nostalgia in stories that appealed to white Northerners and Southerners alike. Using his conception of nineteenth-century Black dialect, he wrote about enslaved people who longed for the era of slavery to return. In *Marse Chan: A Tale of Old Virginia,* Sam, a formerly enslaved Black person, says:

> "Dem wuz good ole times, marster—de bes' Sam uver see!…Niggers didn' hed nothin' 't *all* to do—jes' hed to 'ten' to de feedin' an' cleanin' de hawses, an' doin' what de marster tell 'em to do; an' when dey wuz sick, dey had things sont 'em out de house, an' de same doctor come to see 'em whar 'ten' to de

white folks when dey wuz po'ly. Dyar warn' no trouble nor nuttin'."

The Lost Cause was not an accident. It was not a mistake that history stumbled into. It was a deliberate, multifaceted, multi-field effort predicated on both misremembering and obfuscating what the Confederacy stood for, and the role that slavery played in shaping this country.

As the event began to disband, I looked around to see if there might be anyone willing to talk with me. William and I split up, to try to generate multiple conversations.

I walked over to a man a few yards away who had been taking pictures of the event with his camera, its black strap resting on the back of his neck. I introduced myself, and he dropped the camera from his eye and turned around. Jeff had a long salt-and-pepper ponytail that fell past his shoulders and down his back. His denim vest, adorned with Confederate badges, hung comfortably over his round frame. His face was damp from the summer's heat, and beads of sweat rolled down his forehead before he swept them from the top of his brow. He told me he was sixty-three years old and had several ancestors who fought for the Confederacy.

The sun hung like an orange orb above us. I wiped my forehead too and asked Jeff what he thought of the event we had just experienced. "Well, I think if anyone never knew the truth, they heard it today," he said, nodding as if to affirm his own words. "They found out that the Confederate soldiers—and we also mention these Union soldiers and other wars that we were involved in, and we try to be fair and honest about it," he said as an aside before resuming, "about exactly what happened and each individual that fought in these battles, under the circumstances, were trying to do it for freedom. Whatever they believed in, we're all trying to do it for freedom. And I know that the Confederate side tries to honor the Union's a lot, even though some people think we despise them, but we don't. We all know that they're respected soldiers and we're trying to continue honoring them, be it through their flag, which is the American flag, and the monuments. We have them here in Petersburg. We have the Union and we have the Confederate monuments. We do have a Monument Avenue also. And they need to be there for generations in the future because they need to know the truth. They can't learn the truth if you do away with history. You'll never learn. And once you do away with that type of thing, you become a slave. And if anybody knows education, if you don't have it, you become a slave to people."

I was startled by his choice of words but could not tell whether or not that language was intentional and meant to be provocative or a matter of rhetorical coincidence.

"I think everybody should learn the truth," Jeff said, licking his teeth and wiping his forehead once more with the back of his hand.

"And so in your mind, what is that truth?" I asked.

"The truth of it is what really happened."

I nodded, waiting to see if he had more to say.

"Well, basically everybody always hears the same things, 'It's all about slavery.' And it wasn't. It was about the fact that each state had the right to govern itself," he said.

He then pointed to a tombstone about twenty yards away.

"So, you know, you look at that Mr. Richard Poplar—where is his grave marker—over there, Black gentleman. He was captured and sent to two prisons up north and he was a Confederate officer and they told him that if he would, a Black gentleman, 'If you would say they forced you to fight for the Confederacy, we will set you free.' He said, 'I will not leave my men.' He said, 'Because I know what happened. You invaded the South.'"

But the Confederate Army forbade free Black people from serving in their army as soldiers, much less as officers. Poplar's story, I would later come to discover, was central to the story people in Petersburg told about the war. His 1886 obituary read:

> When the Sussex Dragoons were formed at the beginning of the war, and when they became Company H, of the Thirteenth Virginia Cavalry, Richard attached himself to the command. The Sussex Dragoons were a wealthy organization, and each member of the company had his own servant along with him. From April 1861, until the retreat from Gettysburg, Richard remained faithfully attached to the regiment.

The commemoration of Poplar seems to have begun in 2003, when the local chapter of the Sons of Confederate Veterans pushed for an annual "Richard Poplar Day." In 2004, the mayor of Petersburg signed a proclamation declaring one, and calling Poplar a "veteran" of the Confederate Army who served in the 13th Virginia Cavalry. A headstone for Poplar was also put in place at Blandford near where his body was believed to be buried, just a few yards from where I stood with Jeff. But as Levin notes, the characterization of Poplar having "attached" himself as a "servant" seems to indicate that he was not enlisted as a soldier. Poplar's 1886 obituary suggests that he was a cook for the soldiers, not someone engaged in combat. This mythmaking is not unique to Poplar. There have been claims that up to one hundred thousand Black soldiers fought for the Confederate Army, that Black men fought under General Robert E. Lee, and that these men valiantly died as part of racially integrated regiments willing to sacrifice their lives to save the South. There is no evidence to support this.

The myth of Black Confederate soldiers emerged in the 1970s, pushed by the Sons of Confederate Veterans. This story was a response to changing public perceptions of the Civil War in the years after the civil rights movement—away from Lost Cause mythology and toward recognition that slavery was central to this conflict. The SCV appears to have thought that if it could appropriate the stories of men like Richard Poplar, it might, despite an avalanche of evidence to the contrary, protect the Confederacy's legacy. A Confederate sympathizer could argue, if the war was fought over slavery, why were Black soldiers fighting for the Confederates? If Black soldiers fought for the Confederates, how could it be considered racist to fly the Dixie flag?

The idea of using enslaved people during the war had been suggested by Confederate general Patrick Cleburne, but the proposal was scoffed at by the majority of Confederate leadership because it undermined the entire basis upon which the war was being fought. Leadership found themselves in a position in which they could choose to perpetuate slavery or give everything they had to win the war and secure independence—a choice many Confederate leaders were unwilling to accept. Robert M. T. Hunter, a senator from Virginia, is reported to have said, "What did we go to war for, if not to protect our property?" Another Confederate leader, General Howell Cobb, was even more explicit: "If slaves will make good soldiers our whole theory of slavery is wrong."

In a last-ditch effort to salvage the war, just weeks before Lee would surrender at Appomattox, the Confederacy did approve legislation that would allow Black people to fight for the Confederacy. But by then it was far too late. The war had effectively already been lost.

As I continued speaking with Jeff, he began talking about how Lincoln's aggression and the imposition of federal rule on the Confederacy escalated tensions and ultimately led to war.

"It's like I said, it's like me going in your house and telling you how to live in it. You have the right to live in your house, your way. As long as there is not a real major threat or nothing. And that's what he tried to do."

I wanted to understand what if any role Jeff thought slavery had played in the war's origin story; I asked him if he thought it was a part of the reason the Civil War began.

"Oh, just a very small part. I mean, we can't deny it wasn't there. We know slave blocks existed. But the fact is, there was a small amount of us, small [amount of] plantations in the South that had them. Now, if you want to go after them, that's one thing, but you're coming after my family too."

The idea that slavery was "just a very small part" of why the Civil War began is not unique to Jeff; it is reflective of decades of Lost Cause propaganda.

While running for the presidency in 1860, Lincoln opposed the expansion of slavery into new territories, but he promised not to interfere with slavery in any of the fifteen states where it already existed. Despite his promise, many Southern leaders perceived Lincoln's election as a direct, abolitionist threat to their enterprise. According to historian Edward Bonekemper, before he was inaugurated, the seven states with the highest numbers of enslaved people per capita, as well as the highest percentage of family slave ownership, seceded from the Union. An additional four would follow.

Confederate declarations of secession and records from secession conventions show that these states were wholly committed to the institution of slavery—a commitment that far surpassed their commitment to the Union. If they had to choose between slavery and unity, these states unequivocally chose the former. The following are excerpts from several declarations of secession, speeches presented at secession conventions, and other documents related to secession (italics are my own):

Mississippi: Our position is *thoroughly identified with the institution of slavery*—the greatest material interest of the world. Its labor supplies the product which constitutes by far the largest and most important portions of the commerce of the earth. These products are peculiar to the climate verging on the tropical regions, and by an imperious law of nature, none but the black race can bear exposure to the tropical sun. These products have become necessities of the world, and a blow at slavery *is* a blow at commerce and civilization... There was no choice left us but submission to the mandates of abolition, or a dissolution of the Union, whose principles had been subverted to work out our ruin.

South Carolina: A geographical line has been drawn across the Union, and all the States north of that line have united in the election of a man to the high office of President of the United States whose opinions and purposes are hostile to slavery. [Lincoln] is to be entrusted with the administration of the Common Government, because he has declared that that "Government cannot endure permanently half slave, half free," *and that the public mind must rest in the belief that slavery is in the course of ultimate extinction.* This sectional combination for the submersion of the Constitution, has been aided in some of the States by elevating to citizenship, persons, who, by the Supreme Law of the land, are incapable of becoming citizens; and their votes have been used to inaugurate a new policy, hostile to the South, and destructive of its beliefs and safety.

Louisiana: The people of the slaveholding States are bound together by the same *necessity and determination to preserve African slavery.*

Texas: We hold, as undeniable truths, that the governments of the various States and of the Confederacy itself, were established exclusively by the white race, for themselves and their posterity; that the *African race had no agency in their establishment; that they were rightfully held and regarded as an inferior and dependant* [*sic*] *race,* and in that condition only could their existence in this country be rendered beneficial or tolerable.

Florida: This party, now soon to take possession of the powers of the Government, is sectional, irresponsible to us, and driven on by an infuriated fanatical madness that defies all opposition, *must inevitably destroy every vestige of right growing out of property in slaves.*

Alabama: [T]he election of Mr. Lincoln is hailed, not simply as a change of Administration, but as the inauguration of new principles, and a new theory of Government, and even *as the downfall of slavery.* Therefore it is that the election of Mr. Lincoln cannot be regarded otherwise than a solemn declaration, on the part of a great majority of the Northern people, of hostility to the South, her property and her institutions—nothing less than an open declaration of war—for the triumph of this new theory of Government destroys the property of the South, lays waste her fields, and inaugurates *all the horrors of a San Domingo servile insurrection,* consigning her citizens to assassinations, and her wives and daughters to pollution and violation, to gratify the lust of half-civilized Africans.

And the drafters of Virginia's ordinance of secession left no doubt as to why they were separating from the Union:

Virginia: The people of Virginia in their ratification of the Constitution of the United States of America adopted by them in Convention on the twenty-fifth day of June in the year of our Lord one thousand, seven hundred and eighty-eight having declared that the powers granted under the said Constitution were derived from the people of the United States, and might be resumed whensoever the same should be perverted to their injury and oppression; and the Federal Government, having perverted said powers, not only to the injury of the people of Virginia, but to *the oppression of the Southern slaveholding States.*

If these primary sources were not enough, we can look to the Constitution of the Confederate States, which avows in Article IV, Section 3:

In all [new] territory the *institution of negro slavery, as it now exists in the Confederate States, shall be recognized and protected* by Congress and by the Territorial government; and the inhabitants of the several Confederate States and Territories shall have the right to take to such Territory any slaves lawfully held by them in any of the States or Territories of the Confederate States.

Indeed, the man who would become president of the Confederacy, Jefferson Davis, in his farewell speech to the US Senate on January 21, 1861, after his home state of Mississippi had declared secession, made clear that any threat to slavery was a threat to the sovereignty of his people:

It has been a conviction of pressing necessity—it has been a belief that we are to be deprived in the Union of the rights which our fathers bequeathed to us—which has brought Mississippi into her present decision. She has heard proclaimed the theory that all men are created free and equal, and this made the basis of an attack upon her social institutions; and the sacred Declaration of Independence has been invoked to maintain the position of the equality of the races... *When our Constitution was formed, [the institution of slavery] was rendered more palpable, for there we find provision made for that very class of persons as property; they were not put upon the footing of equality with white men—not even upon that of paupers and convicts; but, so far as representation was concerned, were discriminated against as a lower caste, only to be represented in the numerical proportion of three fifths.*

The conflict is also evident in the compromises that members of Congress sought in order to prevent secession and war. In December of 1860, as the rumblings of war became increasingly more forceful, Kentucky senator John J. Crittenden introduced what would become known as the Crittenden Compromise, which proposed six constitutional amendments and four congressional resolutions aimed at preventing the South from leaving the Union. Upon introducing the amendments Crittenden said the following: "The questions of an alarming character are those which have grown out of the controversy between the northern and southern sections of our country in relation to the rights of the slaveholding States in the Territories of the United States, and in relation to the rights of the citizens of the latter in their slaves. I have endeavored by these resolutions to meet all these questions and causes of discontent." Each of the six articles and four resolutions were specifically tied to the issue of slavery. Article 2, for example, stated: "Congress shall have no power to abolish slavery in places under its exclusive jurisdiction, and situate within the limits of States that permit the holding of slaves." Article 4 said: "Congress shall have no power to prohibit or hinder the transportation of slaves from one State to another, or to a Territory in which slaves are by law permitted to be held, whether that transportation be by land, navigable rivers, or by the sea." Altogether, the amendments would have guaranteed the permanent existence of slavery in states south of the line demarcated by the 1820 Missouri Compromise. One amendment even attempted to make it impossible for future amendments to overturn the other five. The proposal was supported by the majority of Southern politicians, but Northern Republicans, including Lincoln, refused to accept it.

One of the most egregious features of the Lost Cause is the dramatic about-face that occurred after the war. When the war ended, the leaders of the Confederacy attempted to walk back or completely deny the centrality of slavery to the formation of the Confederacy. In 1881, two decades after his farewell speech to Congress, Jefferson Davis published a history of the Confederacy claiming that slavery had nothing to do with the Civil War and that there would have been a civil war even if no American ever owned a slave. Alexander Stephens, vice president of the Confederacy, maintained that the explicit rhetoric in his infamous 1861 Cornerstone Speech, in which he stated that slavery was "the immediate cause of the late rupture and present revolution" and the

Confederacy was founded on "the great truth that the negro is not equal to the white man," had in part been newspapers misquoting him. The reporters' notes of the event, taken contemporaneously and published widely, he said, "were very imperfect."

There is no shortage of documentation demonstrating that the Southern states seceded and began sowing the seeds of war in order to defend slavery. To look at primary source documents and convince yourself that the central cause of the war was anything other than slavery requires a remarkable contortion of history.

Two children ran behind me chasing a ball that had begun rolling down the hill. Jeff smiled as he watched them and dabbed his brow with a cloth before placing it back in his pocket. He told me that he does not call the country's deadliest war the "Civil War" because it distorts the truth. "We call it the 'War Between the States' or 'of Northern Aggression, against us,'" he said. "Because what they call the Civil War is not really the Civil War. Southern people don't call it the Civil War because they know it was an invasion . . . If you stayed up North ain't nothing would've happened."

When Jeff said "nothing would've happened," I wondered if he had forgotten the lives of millions of Black people who would have remained enslaved. For these people, the status quo that Jeff seemed beholden to would have meant remaining in bondage. Or did he remember but not care?

A mosquito buzzed in Jeff's ear and he swatted it away with his hand. As he spoke, it became clear that his connection to this land was not rooted in mere historical intrigue but that it was a part of his lineage. "I've been coming here ever since I was four years old," he said.

He told me he had seventy-eight family members buried in the cemetery dating back to 1802. He frequently comes to visit the tombstones of his family members.

"Some nights I just sit there and just watch the deer come out," he said, pointing over to the gazebo, his voice becoming soft. "I sit here all the time and I just enjoy the feeling. I reminisce. I know there's some Revolutionary War guys here and veterans from other wars. To me, it's like I want to preserve history, and save what I can for my granddaughters and other people." He looked again at the gazebo, his eyes scanning its white frame bathed in the shadows of the trees around it.

"This is a place of peace. The dead don't bother me. It's the living that bother me."

It was clear that the Confederacy, and the flag flown in its honor, meant something very specific to Jeff. But for myself, and so many people I love, it meant something different, something far more sinister and violent. Jeff was quick to assert that he believed the symbolism of the flag had become distorted by "other groups" who stole it and have used it as a symbol of hate, which according to Jeff it was never intended to be.

Though he didn't say it explicitly, it sounded like Jeff was talking about the Ku Klux Klan. I asked him directly what he thought about people likening an organization like the Sons of Confederate Veterans to the KKK.

"No, they're not the Klan," he said, speaking with renewed conviction, his jaw stiffening. "No, that's what I was just saying. Even the Klan will admit that that flag does not mean that at all. It means something else to them. They just like the flag. They took our flag and used it. They use a Christian flag too and all that. But the thing you've got to remember, like I said, here in this area, the Sons of Confederates are representing their ancestors."

Founded in 1896 in Richmond—the former capital of the Confederacy—the Sons of Confederate Veterans describes itself as an organization of around thirty thousand members that aims to preserve "the history and legacy of these heroes, so future generations can understand the motives that animated the Southern Cause." It is also the oldest hereditary organization for men who are descendants of those who fought for the Confederate Army; membership "is open to all male descendants of any veteran who served honorably in the Confederate armed forces."

While the organization publicly denounces any association with hate groups or racist ideology, according to the Southern Poverty Law Center, the Sons of Confederate Veterans has been suffused with internal discord between those interested primarily in the preservation of history and those who want to use the group as a mechanism to propagate hate. Hate and extremism are not absent from the history of the SCV; in fact, they are central to it.

There are members like Kirk Lyons, co-founder and chief trial counsel for the Southern Legal Resource Center, a group that has served as a de facto legal arm of the neo-Confederate movement, largely taking cases involving the Confederate flag. Lyons defended white supremacists, including a former Klan leader, and anti-Semitic activists in court during the 1980s and 1990s. In a speech from 2000, Lyons outlined his vision for the society he hoped the Sons of Confederate Veterans would build: "The civil rights movement I am trying to form seeks a revolution...We seek nothing more than a return to a godly, stable, tradition-based society with no 'Northernisms' attached, a hierarchical society, a majority European–derived country." And there are members like Ron G. Wilson, who during his two years as the SCV's commander in chief, from 2002 to 2004, suspended approximately three hundred members of the group who spoke out against racism, according to a Southern Poverty Law Center report.

Even beyond the infighting, the foundational project of the Sons of Confederate Veterans cannot be disentangled from white supremacy. As the Southern Poverty Law Center and a group of New Orleans lawyers put it in a recent amicus brief: "Although the Sons of Confederate Veterans has disavowed racism in its official pronouncements in recent years, the group is still deeply invested in elevating and legitimizing its version of the Confederacy's 'history' and 'traditions,' which implicate an inherently racist, white supremacist vision of society."

The organizational lineage the Sons of Confederate Veterans enjoys can be traced directly to the Ku Klux Klan; the Klan was founded by former Confederates as a secret society before it became a terrorist group, and the early Klan was filled with Confederate veterans. Before the Sons of Confederate Veterans came into existence, its predecessor was an organization called the United Confederate Veterans (UCV). For a time, they existed as separate groups. At the seventeenth annual reunion of the UCV in 1907, the commander of the

SCV gave an address praising Nathan Bedford Forrest, the first grand wizard of the KKK and a former Confederate general:

Great and trying times always produce great leaders, and one was at hand—Nathan Bedford Forrest. His plan, the only course left open. The organization of a secret government. A terrible government; a government that would govern in spite of black majorities and Federal bayonets. This secret government was organized in every community in the South, and this government is known in history as the Klu Klux Clan [sic]...

Here in all ages to come the Southern romancer and poet can find the inspiration for fiction and song. No nobler or grander spirits ever assembled on this earth than gathered in these clans. No human hearts were ever moved with nobler impulses or higher aims and purposes...Order was restored, property safe; because the negro feared the Klu Klux Clan more than he feared the devil. Even the Federal bayonets could not give him confidence in the black government which had been established for him, and the negro voluntarily surrendered to the Klu Klux Clan, and the very moment he did, the "Invisible Army" vanished in a night. Its purpose had been fulfilled.

Bedford Forrest should always be held in reverence by every son and daughter of the South as long as memory holds dear the noble deeds and service of men for the good of others on this earth. What mind is base enough to think of what might have happened but for Bedford Forrest and his "Invisible" but victorious army.

The United Daughters of the Confederacy, too, has publicly distanced itself from hate groups, especially following the August 2017 attack in Charlottesville. A statement on their website says, "Our members are the ones who have spent 126 years honoring [Confederate soldiers'] memory by various activities in the fields of education, history and charity, promoting patriotism and good citizenship. Our members are the ones who, like our statues, have stayed quietly in the background, never engaging in public controversy" and that the organization "totally denounces any individual or group that promotes racial divisiveness or white supremacy. And we call on these people to cease using Confederate symbols for their abhorrent and reprehensible purposes."

However, they too have a more complicated history. As historian Karen L. Cox remarks in her book *Dixie's Daughters,* "UDC members aspired to transform military defeat into a political and cultural victory, where states' rights and white supremacy remained intact."

Heidi Christensen, former president of the Seattle, Washington, chapter of the UDC, before leaving the organization in 2012, said, "In their earliest days, the United Daughters of the Confederacy definitely did some good work on behalf of veterans and in their communities. But it's also true that since the UDC was founded in 1894, it has maintained a covert connection with the Ku Klux Klan. In fact, in many ways, the group was the de facto women's auxiliary of the KKK at the turn of the century. It's a connection the group downplays now, but evidence of it is easily discoverable—you don't even have to look very hard to find it."

In 1914, Laura Martin Rose, who served as the historian and president of the UDC's Mississippi chapter, published *The Ku Klux Klan; or, Invisible Empire,* which effusively praised the Klan and engaged in the worst of racist tropes. "The negro considered freedom synonymous with equality, and his greatest ambition was to marry a white wife," she wrote. "Under such conditions there was only one recourse left, to organize a powerful Secret Order to accomplish what could not be done in the open. So the Confederate soldiers, as members of the Ku Klux Klan, and fully equal to any emergency, came again to the rescue, and delivered the South from a bondage worse than death."

In the opening pages of the book, Rose leaves no ambiguity about the relationship her organization has to the book she has written, stating that the book "was unanimously endorsed by the United Daughters of the Confederacy" and that "co-operation pledged to endeavor to secure its adoption as a Supplementary Reader in the schools and to place it in the Libraries of our Land."

The latter point, regarding schools and libraries, was key to understanding the UDC's collective founding project. Members did not simply want to erect monuments for the fallen; they wanted to rewrite the public narrative. As Cox notes, they saw children as "living monuments" who would go on to defend the principles of states' rights and white supremacy in ways that no inanimate monument could. The organization developed and distributed lesson plans for teachers, and placed pro-Confederate books in schools and libraries across the South. They told the children that slavery was an institution that benefited both Blacks and whites alike, and that it was rare for there to be a cruel enslaver. They held essay contests in which students would regurgitate these falsities.

Their work proved successful. Many of the children inundated with these messages spread by the UDC during the early twentieth century would grow up to become the segregationists of the civil rights era, and the legacy of the UDC's teachings has contributed to the country's collective ahistoricism and has helped shape the ongoing landscape of white supremacy today.

During our conversation Jeff had shared with me what Blandford Cemetery meant to him and why it was so important to his sense of self. So, in turn, I wanted to share with him what it felt like for me to be here. I told him that because my ancestors were enslaved, and because the Confederacy had fought a war to preserve slavery, it was difficult for me to have much empathy for the Confederates and places like Blandford, which paid tribute to the cause they fought for.

"Well, if you ever read the letters," Jeff said. "It was actually written, you can find them if you look, read the letters of Lincoln himself. What he said about slavery. He did not want Blacks to hold office. And as far as he's concerned, he kept them where they belonged or [sent] them overseas."

Lincoln did have a complicated history with slavery and his stance on emancipation. As historian Eric Foner notes, while Lincoln said he had "always hated slavery" and called the institution a "monstrous injustice," his commitment to ending slavery was not necessarily matched by a commitment to Black equality. While some abolitionists saw the desire to end slavery and build a racially egalitarian society as inextricably linked, Lincoln thought of them as distinct. In a September 18,

1858, speech as part of his fourth senatorial debate with Stephen A. Douglas, Lincoln claimed:

> I will say...that I am not, nor ever have been, in favor of bringing about in any way the social and political equality of the black and white races—that I am not nor ever have been in favor of making voters or jurors of negroes, nor of qualifying them to hold office, nor to intermarry with white people; and I will say in addition to this that there is a physical difference between the white and black races which I believe will forever forbid the two races living together on terms of social and political equality. And inasmuch as they cannot so live, while they do remain together there must be the position of superior and inferior, and I as much as any other man am in favor of having the superior position assigned to the white race.

In fact, for much of his political career Lincoln was a public advocate of "colonization," a plan he pushed for throughout the first half of the Civil War. The idea behind colonization—sometimes called expatriation, the same plan that Jefferson advocated—was that it would be better for both white and Black people if the latter emigrated and resettled in another country, either in Central America, the Caribbean, or Africa. Lincoln thought that abolition paired with colonization was the best path forward, as it ostensibly gave Black people freedom and removed the concern that many Americans had about having to live alongside their Black counterparts. On August 14, 1862, Lincoln brought a group of free Black leaders to the White House in an attempt to convince them to lead a resettlement plan in present-day Panama. The proposal was not met with enthusiasm by the visitors and was roundly rejected by other Black leaders, who saw themselves as every bit as American as Lincoln, when accounts were published in the press. Frederick Douglass scathed Lincoln, saying, "The President of the United States seems to possess an ever increasing passion for making himself appear silly and ridiculous, if nothing worse."

While some supporters of colonization suggested that millions of free Black people posed a threat to the social order, Lincoln claimed that his support was rooted in a fear of white racism. According to Lincoln, white racism was so deeply entrenched that Black people would never have the chance to be equal members of society. Lincoln's position was similar to that of many throughout the North, those who believed slavery should be abolished but who did not want to share a society with or live alongside free Black Americans. As Foner notes, "For many white Americans, including Lincoln, colonization represented a middle ground between the radicalism of the abolitionists and the prospect of the United States existing permanently half-slave and half-free."

It should be noted that Lincoln's position began to change after he signed the Emancipation Proclamation and after he saw two hundred thousand Black soldiers fight on behalf of the Union. A few days before his assassination he endorsed the prospect of limited suffrage for certain groups of Black people, albeit those he deemed "very intelligent" and "who serve our cause as soldiers." There is evidence that Lincoln's position was continuing to evolve on the issue, but because of his untimely assassination after the end of the Civil War, we will never know for sure where he might have ended up.[*]

---

[*]   It is also important to note that Lincoln, and many other figures beyond the Confederacy whom our nation holds in collective reverence and esteem, advanced policies that were destructive to Native American communities. These policies included the Homestead Act and the Pacific Railway Act of 1862, which led to an enormous loss of Native land and resources. Lincoln's administration also presided over the removal of the Navajo and the Mescalero Apache from the New Mexico Territory, forcing most of them to march to a reservation roughly four hundred miles away. More than two thousand of them died on the journey or on the reservation, over a period of a few years. (Sherry Salway Black, "Lincoln: No Hero to Native Americans," *Washington Monthly*, January/February 2013.)

Is Jeff wrong that Lincoln advocated Black inferiority and colonization during a significant portion of his political career? No. The issue, however, is not necessarily the veracity of his comments but the attempt to use Lincoln's record to obscure the fact that, as the war evolved, Lincoln was in charge of an army that was fighting to free four million Black people, while the other side fought to keep them enslaved.

Over the course of my conversation with Jeff, the shade of the gazebo had moved and exposed our faces to the hot sun. I could feel the pearls of sweat emerge on my temple and slide down my cheek before getting lost in the forest of my beard. A pair of children were running up and down the hill, resisting their mother's calls for them to move toward their car. The wreaths that had been placed at the foot of the towering Confederate statue leaned against the grey stone, the tails of the ribbons tied around them rising and falling with the breeze.

Jeff stepped away, and a few minutes later I began speaking with a woman and her son, a thin twenty-year-old with glasses and patches of black beard dotting his jawline. I had noticed the young man as one of the people dressed in Confederate regalia as part of the honor guard. "I was actually a last-minute recruit," he said, introducing himself as Nicholas, his voice quick and nasally. "I didn't even have my gun loaded."

"The last time I dressed up as a Confederate was six years ago and that was at Pamplin Park when I was fourteen years old and having fun," he said.

I asked Nicholas what it felt like to dress up in Confederate regalia, wondering if it reflected his allegiance to any particular side or narrative.

"I guess what it is—even though I'm more sympathetic to the Union side than the Confederate side—at the end of the day I still think that both sides were brave men who deserve to be remembered. So that's what I was doing here."

As I was speaking with Nicholas and his mother, another man dressed in Confederate garb, though much older than Nicholas, approached us and stood a few feet away. I watched him from the corner of my eye, but he was not hiding the fact that he was listening in. It was unclear if he was trying to intimidate me or if he was genuinely trying to join in on the conversation.

"How about yourself?" I said, turning to him, preferring to address him directly rather than have him ominously hovering behind us. "Have you been participating in these sorts of things for a while?"

"Since I was nineteen."

"And how old are you now?" Nicholas's mother asked from behind me.

"Forty-eight," he said.

I turned more fully toward him, introducing my-self and getting his name: Jason. I asked him what this event, and what dressing up as a Confederate soldier, meant to him.

"This time period. This '61 to '65. This is my focus. If you look at my library, it's almost exclu-sively Civil War, other than children's books for my kids. This time period, it just gripped me."

He continued: "[I] took a class on Civil War his-tory and from that someone had mentioned to me, 'You know, what I'd like to have for a job is one of those Civil War reenactors. That would be a cool job, right?' I didn't realize it's all volunteer." He laughed, Nicholas and his mother joining in.

"Are you similar to Nicholas in the sense that you are interested and kind of sympathetic to both sides?" I asked.

"I understand both sides. I understand their way of thinking. Both sides. I *will* be honest: I am more sympathetic towards the Southern cause. And there's so much more to it than what is taught in schools today."

I asked him what he was taught in relation to what he believed the more holistic truth was.

"It is the—how do I put this gently—people are not as educated as they should be. People are growing up being taught 'Civil War is all about slavery,' okay? Then they grow up and they teach [younger people], and then they grow up. And if that's all that you hear every single day, you know, and someone comes up to me and I say, 'Well, that's not exactly true. Let's talk about this'...And they just think I'm crazy. No way. That's like me saying," and he pointed his finger at my chest, "'This is not really a shirt.'"

"So were you taught that slavery, growing up, was the central cause of the Civil War?" I asked.

"That's what the textbooks say," he said.

I asked Jason what he believed the actual cause was.

"Now see, that's a whole conversation," he said. "It's so hard to just put that in a little five-second blurb."

"It's complicated," said Nicholas's mother, a departing word before she and Nicholas excused themselves.

"I will tell you this. I've done a lot of research because I'm interested," Jason said. "They've been taught all their life that Confederates are racist, that this was a war over slavery, these men were fighting to keep slavery legal, and if that's what you grow up believing, you're looking at people like me wearing this uniform, 'Oh, he's a racist.' We used to be able to stand on the monuments on Monument Avenue, those Lee and Jackson monuments. We can't do it anymore. 'Cause it ain't safe. Someone's gonna drive by and shoot me. You know, that's what I'm afraid of. I'm not standing out there for a racist reason."

I thought it was unlikely that someone would shoot Jason for standing in front of a Confederate monument; in fact, groups and individuals that are far more extreme than the Sons of Confederate Veterans—white nationalists, neo-Nazis, and others with obviously hateful views—have received an astonishing amount of protection over the past several years from police officers preserving their right to free speech, even when it costs a city millions of dollars to do so. But there was also an irony in Jason's admission of fear. These monuments had been erected decades ago with the intention of rewriting history and instilling fear in Black communities, and now it was Jason who felt scared to stand in front of the same monuments.

He then pointed to a man down the hill to our right. "See this large man standing right over here," he said. "He was the captain of my reenacting group. He recruited me into this hobby. He's in a international"—he paused—"*interracial* is the word I'm looking for, marriage." He looked at the man. "Anybody who doesn't know him is gonna say he's racist, but then when you see his wife, you may have a different perception. You know what I'm saying?"

While it certainly is not true that being in an interracial relationship means that someone can't be racist, it didn't feel like an issue worth pushing back on for the time being, because I wanted to continue to hear what Jason thought about the war.

I asked Jason whether, through the process of his research, he had found anything that suggested the reason the Southern states seceded was tied to slavery.

"No," he said. "I will say there were politicians who will have very racist quotes and you can look it up. There were probably large landowners who felt threatened by this talk. *What? They wanna get rid of slavery? Well, I can't do this job without the slavery.* So I'm not saying that it didn't exist, that's the narrative, but as far as going to war and putting them through the absolute hell that these men went through, why would they do that? The average age was seventeen to twenty-two for a Civil War soldier. Many of them had never even seen a Black man. The rich were the ones who had slaves. They didn't have to fight. They were draft exempt. So these men are going to be out here and they're going to be laying down their lives and fighting and going through the hell of camp life, the lice, the rats, and everything else just so this rich dude in Richmond, Virginia, or Atlanta, Georgia, or Memphis, Tennessee, can have some slaves. That doesn't make sense. To me it's common sense. No man would do that."

The historian Joseph T. Glatthaar has challenged the argument that Confederate soldiers couldn't have fought because of slavery since very few were slave owners. He analyzed the makeup of the soldiers in the unit that would become Lee's Army of Northern Virginia and pointed out that "the vast majority of the volunteers of 1861 had a direct connection to slavery." In 1861, almost half of those Confederate soldiers either owned enslaved people or lived with a head of household who did, and many more worked for slaveholders, rented land from them, and had business relationships with them.

There also is ample evidence that white Southerners who did not own enslaved people were often still deeply committed to preserving the institution. Historian James Oliver Horton writes about how the press inundated white Southerners with messages about why fighting to prevent the abolition of slavery was essential to preventing enslaved and formerly enslaved people from, in the words of the *Louisville Daily Courier*, rising "to the level of the white race." Without slavery, these papers argued, there would be no difference between poor whites and free Blacks. The *Louisville Daily Courier* warned non-slaveholding white Southerners about the slippery slope of abolition and the dangers of racial equality: "Do they wish to send their children to schools in which the negro children of the vicinity are taught? Do they wish to give the negro the right to appear in the witness box to testify against them?" The paper did not stop there, and went right to the issue it knew animated the most fervor and fear among white Southern men: would non-slaveholding white men accept a society in which they "AMALGAMATE TO-GETHER THE TWO RACES IN VIOLATION OF GOD'S WILL"? Propaganda like this helped to convince non-slaveholding whites that abolition was an existential threat to Southern society. Without slavery, they were told, they would be forced to live, work, and inevitably procreate with their free Black neighbors. This was a proposition that millions of Southern whites were unwilling to accept.

Horton finds plenty of examples of Confederate soldiers saying this for themselves. As he notes, one Southern prisoner of war told the Union soldier standing watch, "[Y]ou Yanks want us to marry our daughters to niggers." An indigent white farmer from North Carolina said that he could not and would not stop fighting, because Lincoln's government was "trying to force us to live as the colored race." A Confederate artilleryman from Louisiana said that his army had to fight even against difficult odds because he would "never want to see the day when a negro is put on an equality with a white person."

Blandford Cemetery

In his book *The Peculiar Institution: Slavery in the Ante-Bellum South,* historian Kenneth M. Stampp contends that white Southerners who did not own slaves still actively supported the institution as "a means of controlling the social and economic competition of Negroes, concrete evidence of membership in a superior caste, a chance perhaps to rise into the planter class." Or as historian Charles Dew said, "If you are white in the antebellum South, there is a floor below which you cannot go. You have a whole population of four million people whom you consider, and your society considers, inferior to you. You don't have to be actively involved in the system to derive at least the psychological benefits of the system."

White Southerners' commitment to the Confederate cause was not predicated on whether or not they owned slaves. The commitment was based on a desire to maintain a society in which Black people remained at the bottom of the social hierarchy.

A man I had seen in my periphery, speaking with my friend William, walked up to Jason and me. We shook hands as he and Jason greeted each other with warm familiarity.

"He's a treasure trove of information too," Jason said, pointing to the man.

I mentioned that I had seen him talking to my friend on the other side of the gazebo.

"I been in his ear good and I gave [William] my telephone number if you need anything else," he said.

I thanked him and told him that was very generous.

He looked at me, his eyes searching my face. His face shifted. "I told him, if you write about my ancestors"—the air was now trembling between us; he leaned in closer—"I want it to be correct. I'm concerned about the truth, not mythology."

A few weeks earlier, after my first visit to Blandford, I had driven thirty minutes north to Richmond. When I arrived at Monument Avenue, I double-parked my car across the street, put my blinkers on, and walked toward the statue of Robert E. Lee a few hundred feet away. I craned my neck to see Lee's statue awash in sunlight, its bronze hue glimmering in the rays of late afternoon. The sculpture was enormous, a twenty-one-foot-tall statue thrust into the sky by a forty-foot white stone base. Lee sat in a magisterial position atop his horse, his general's uniform fastened tightly around his torso, the bottom of the jacket draped across his upper legs. I stood there, looking up at the statue long enough to feel its shadow move like a sundial around me, scanning its frame from the bottom of the pedestal to the top of Lee's head. This statue of Lee was not so different from the one I had grown up around.

I was born and raised in a city filled with statues of Confederate soldiers. White men on pedestals and Black children playing beneath them—where Black people played trumpets and trombones to drown out the Dixie song that still whistled in the wind. In my hometown of New Orleans there are at least a hundred streets, statues, parks, and schools named after Confederate figures, slave owners, and defenders of slavery. For decades Black children have walked into buildings named after people who thought of them as property. My own middle school, Lusher, is named after Robert Mills Lusher, a Confederate and former Louisiana superintendent of education who fought against desegregation and who believed in "the supremacy of the Caucasian race." Every time I returned home I would drive on streets named for those who thought of me as chattel.

"Go straight for two miles on Robert E. Lee."
"Take a left on Jefferson Davis."
"Make the first right on Claiborne."
Translation:
"Go straight for two miles on the general whose troops slaughtered hundreds of Black soldiers who were trying to surrender."
"Take a left on the president of the Confederacy, who

understood the torture of Black bodies as the cornerstone of their new nation."

"Make the first right on the man who allowed the heads of rebelling slaves to be mounted on stakes in order to prevent other slaves from getting any ideas."

So much of the story we tell about history is really the story that we tell about ourselves, about our mothers and our fathers and their mothers and their fathers, as far back as our lineages will take us. Throughout our lives we are told certain stories and they are stories that we choose to believe—stories that become embedded in our identities in ways we are not always fully cognizant of.

For many of the people I met at Blandford, the story of the Confederacy is the story of their home, of their family—and the story of their family is the story of them. So when they are asked to reckon with the fact that their ancestors fought a war to keep my ancestors enslaved, there is resistance to facts that have been documented by primary sources and contemporaneous evidence. They are forced to confront the lies they have upheld. They are forced to confront the flaws of their ancestors. As Greg Stewart, a member of the Sons of Confederate Veterans, told the *New York Times* in the aftermath of the 2015 Charleston massacre, "You're asking me to agree that my great-grandparents and great-great-grandparents were monsters." Accepting such a reality would, for them, mean the deterioration of a narrative that has long been a part of their lineage, and the disintegration of so much of who they believed themselves to be in the world.

But as I think of Blandford, I'm left wondering if we are all just patchworks of the stories we've been told. What would it take—what does it take—for you to confront a false history even if it means shattering the stories you have been told throughout your life? Even if it means having to fundamentally reexamine who you are and who your family has been? Just because something is difficult to accept doesn't mean you should refuse to accept it. Just because someone tells you a story doesn't make that story true.

GALVESTON ISLAND

THE LONG-HELD MYTH GOES that on June 19, 1865, Union general Gordon Granger stood on the balcony of Ashton Villa in Galveston, Texas, and read the order that announced the end of slavery. Though no contemporaneous evidence exists to specifically support the claim, the story of General Granger reading from the balcony embedded itself into local folklore. On this day each year, as part of Galveston's Juneteenth program, a reenactor from the Sons of Union Veterans reads the proclamation at Ashton Villa while an audience looks on. It is an annual moment that has taken a myth and turned it into tradition.

Galveston is a small island that sits off the coast of Southeast Texas, and in years past this event has taken place outside. But given the summer heat, the island's humidity, and the average age of the attendees, the organizers moved the event inside. A man named Stephen Duncan, dressed as

General Granger, stood at the base of the stairwell, with other men dressed as Union soldiers on
either side of him. Stephen looked down at the
parchment, appraising the words as if he had never
seen them before. He looked back down at the
crowd, which was looking up at him. He cleared
his throat, approached the microphone, and lifted
the yellowed parchment to eye level.

"The people of Texas are informed that, in accordance with a proclamation from the Executive
of the United States, all slaves are free. This in-
volves an absolute equality of personal rights and
rights of property between former masters and
slaves, and the connection heretofore existing between them becomes that between employer and
hired labor. The freedmen are advised to remain
quietly at their present homes and work for wages.
They are informed that they will not be allowed to
collect at military posts and that they will not be
supported in idleness either there or elsewhere."

All slaves are free. The four words circled the room
like birds that had been separated from their flock.
I watched people's faces as Stephen said these
words. Some closed their eyes. Some were physically shaking. Some clasped hands with the person
next to them. Some simply smiled, soaking in the
words that their ancestors may have heard more
than a century and a half ago.

Being in this place, standing on the same small

island where the freedom of a quarter million people was proclaimed, I felt the history pulse through my body.

General Granger and his forces arrived in Galveston more than two years after Lincoln signed the Emancipation Proclamation and more than two months after Robert E. Lee's famous surrender. A document that is widely misunderstood, Lincoln's proclamation was a military strategy with multiple aims. It prevented European countries from supporting the Confederacy by framing the war in moral terms and making it explicitly about slavery, something Lincoln had previously backed away from. As a result, France and Britain, which had contemplated supporting the Confederacy, ultimately refused to do so because of both countries' anti-slavery positions. The proclamation allowed the Union Army to recruit Black soldiers (nearly two hundred thousand would fight for the Union Army by the war's end), and it also threatened to disrupt the South's social order, which depended on the work and caste position of enslaved people.

The Emancipation Proclamation was not the sweeping, all-encompassing document that it is often remembered as. It applied only to the eleven Confederate states and did not include the border states that had remained loyal to the US, where it was still legal to own enslaved people. Despite the order of the proclamation, Texas was one of the Confederate states that ignored what it demanded. And even though many enslaved people escaped behind Union lines and enlisted in the Federal Army themselves, enslavers throughout the Confederacy continued to hold Black people in bondage throughout the rest of the war. General Lee surrendered on April 9, 1865, in Appomattox County, Virginia, effectively signaling that the Confederacy had lost the war, but many enslavers in Texas did not share this news with their human property. It was on June 19, 1865, soon after arriving in Galveston, that Granger issued the announcement, known as General Order Number 3, that all slaves were free and word began to spread throughout Texas, from plantation to plantation, farmstead to farmstead, person to person.

A ninety-two-year-old formerly enslaved man named Felix Haywood recalled with nostalgic jubilation what that day meant to him and so many others: "The end of the war, it come jus' like that—like you snap your fingers...Hallelujah broke out...Soldiers, all of a sudden, was everywhere—comin' in bunches, crossin' and walkin' and ridin'. Everyone was a-singin'. We was all walkin' on golden clouds...We was free. Just like that we was free."

The air at Ashton Villa smelled of salt and heat. The street hummed with light traffic. The residence's coral-red brick facade shimmered under the summer sun. Each of the three stories of the Victorian-style house held tall white-trimmed windows with forest-green shutters that opened on either side. A cast-iron veranda extended its shadow over the walkway leading to the front door. Completed in 1859, the villa had served as regional headquarters for both the Union and the Confederate armies during the Civil War, moving back and forth between each of them while the battles that would determine the future of Texas, and of the country, were won and lost. The home was built, in large part, by the labor of enslaved people.

I walked inside and was grateful for the cool air. In the back of the old residence was a large, bright room. I walked in and sat down at one of the two dozen round tables laid out across the long rectangular space, each blanketed by a large white cloth with its trim overhanging the edges. The ceiling was so high it looked like it was running from the people below. A large chandelier was suspended in the middle of the room, its glass ornamentation hanging from curved silver arms, each translucent crystal glimmering under the canopy of light. A man at the front of the room was playing the piano, his fingers gliding along the keys in a series of chords, a preview of each song he planned to share during the event.

The room began to fill with a slow trickle, followed by a gush, of limbs and smiles as the start of the program drew near. As friends, family, and neighbors saw each other, they moved enthusiastically toward the tables, hugging, shaking hands, and squealing with delight at each small reunion. Some wore Juneteenth T-shirts with Pan-African colors embedded in the designs; some were dressed in dashikis and colorful beads. Many looked as if they were on their way to a picnic. The vast majority of the people in the room were Black, though a range of races and complexions were scattered throughout.

The scene was similar to the beginnings of the Black church services I knew as a child. It was a scene of fellowship, a sanctuary less reliant on the building it sits in than on the community it has built. Ashton Villa was brewing with the anticipation of revival.

This was the fortieth anniversary of Al Edwards Sr.'s Juneteenth prayer breakfast. The event has been held annually since Texas House Bill 1016 passed in 1979, a piece of legislation championed by state legislator Al Edwards Sr. that made Juneteenth an official state holiday.

"I'm Major General Granger, commanding general of the District of Texas. This morning we would like to present to you some of the history of those enslaved in the United States until this day, when they were set free. We're glad for you to be here with us. This is a very, very important day in the history of Galveston, the history of Texas, and the history of the United States. On this day the promise of freedom became reality."

A student, a young woman who looked to be about sixteen, walked up to the microphone holding a white placard that read "1492." Everyone in the audience adjusted their chairs and turned their heads to get a better look. She placed the placard over the microphone, her arms extending outward so everyone in the crowd could read what it said on the front, while she read from the other side.

"In 1492, Europeans arrived at the Americas searching for the three *g*'s: gold, glory, and God. Long before enslaved Africans arrived, the Spanish enslaved some of the Native populations against the wishes of Queen Isabella and King Ferdinand."

As she pulled the placard down and walked away from the microphone and toward the wall, the man impersonating Union general Granger spoke again, setting the stage for the next young person to come up. "In 1528," he said, "the first non-Native enslaved person arrived in Galveston."

Another young woman walked to the microphone and did the same as the young woman before her. "The first non-Native slave in Texas was Estevanico, a Moor from North Africa. Estevanico was captured and enslaved by the Spanish when he was a child; he accompanied his master, Captain Andrés Dorantes de Carranza, on the Narváez expedition, which landed at present-day Tampa. In November of 1528, their barges went aground off the coast of Texas. Estevanico, Dorantes, and Alonso del Castillo Maldonado, the only survivors, spent several months living on a barrier island, now believed to be Galveston Island, before making their way in April of 1529 to the mainland."

The man in the Union Army uniform spoke again. "In 1619, the first enslaved Africans arrived." It continued on like this for several minutes, student after student coming up to the microphone, providing a parade of facts in chronological order, leading the listener up to June 19, 1865—Juneteenth.

The students, who ranged from elementary-age children to teenagers, had come from the Nia Cultural Center's Freedom School. The program, part of an initiative run by the Children's Defense Fund, offers six weeks of summer-enrichment programming for young people, with a specific focus on helping them understand their relationship to history.

I watched these young people read to the audience parts of history that placed our country in context. I felt, in that moment, envious of them. Had I known when I was younger what some of these students were sharing, I felt as if I would have been liberated from a social and emotional paralysis that for so long I could not name—a paralysis that had arisen from never knowing enough of my own history to effectively identify the lies I was being told by others: lies about what slavery was and what it did to people; lies about what came after our supposed emancipation; lies about why our country looks the way it does today. I had grown up in a world that never tired of telling me and other Black children like me all of the things that were wrong with us, all of the things we needed to do better. But not enough people spoke about the *reason* so many Black children grow up in communities saturated with poverty and violence. Not enough people spoke about how these realities were the result of decisions made by people in power and had existed for generations before us.

After college, when I was doing more reading on my own, I began to understand all that has happened to our communities, to our people, over generations—it was liberating. I had language to name what I felt but had never known how to say. People sometimes believe that if they talk to Black youth about the historical legacy of slavery—and the intergenerational iterations of systemic racism that followed—young people will feel overwhelmed and shut down. But there is enormous value in providing young people with the language, the history, and the framework to identify why their society looks the way it does. Understanding that all of this was done not by accident but by design. That did not strip me of agency, it gave agency back to me. I watched these young people share this history, and I dreamed of what it might mean if we could extend these lessons to every child. How different might our country look if all of us fully understood what has happened here?

As a group of younger children was preparing to sing, I continued to watch from my end of the room. A small white woman helped to gather the children and put them in their correct positions, moving with a mix of purpose and freneticism, and then looking on with unfettered pride as they sang to the packed room.

Kathy Tiernan had a puff of greying brown hair and wore a large pair of frameless glasses. Her eyes tilted down at their edges, giving them an air of empathy and warmth. She wore a long colorful necklace of beads that hung over a faded Juneteenth T-shirt from a previous year's celebration. Alongside a man named Doug Matthews, she has helped organize the program for a decade now and has seen it evolve from a smattering of disparate, competing events to a more cohesive community celebration. Kathy has been central to ensuring that the next generation of Galvestonians understand the importance of Juneteenth.

"I'm going to tell you that about four years ago, as I looked around the crowd for this Juneteenth breakfast, I saw a lot of older people were not returning," she told me later. "And just like our churches, people were dying off, and their three or four friends who brought them weren't coming back, and I thought, *We need to get kids involved.* And that's when I invited Sue Johnson, who is the director of Freedom School and the head of the Nia Cultural Center, to get her college interns involved in telling more about this day in history."

What Kathy loves most is this project of community education. Older kids teaching younger kids. Kids teaching adults, and vice versa. Learning models that break down and break out of our traditional conceptions of what education should look like.

"For me to see this room filled with people, to watch their faces when the kids are singing, to see them nod when they hear about a piece of history that they maybe hadn't thought about for a while, or are hearing really for the first time—that's a real thrill to me. And when people, more people whose story it is, get involved in their own story, things change. Things change for the better all the time.

"Not with a group of just Blacks doing this—that doesn't work. It's got to be the community involved in this, because that's what made the change. It didn't happen isolated. It happened when Blacks worked together and whites worked together and Hispanics worked together. That's when things work, when we all understand, participate, and care about each other's story. And that's what brings me joy."

Once the children finished singing, Reverend Lewis Simpson Jr., pastor of Saint John Missionary Baptist Church, came up to the podium and led the group in prayer. Leaning on his cane, nodding his head as if it were being lifted and released by an invisible string above him, he outlined the parallels between God's freeing of the Israelites and the freedom achieved by enslaved Black people in America, a parallel that has long been made by Black ministers both during and after slavery.

"You led us out of captivity, and for that, Father, all of us"—he lifted his head—"just say thank you."

I looked around to see every person's head bowed in prayer, as devotional ad-libs cascaded across the room.

After Reverend Simpson stepped down, the

pianist, who had been playing lightly in the background of the prayer, seamlessly transitioned into the beginning of the melody for "Lift Every Voice and Sing," also known as the Black National Anthem.

Originally written as a poem by James Weldon Johnson to celebrate the birthday of the late president Abraham Lincoln, the poem evolved into a song, and the song evolved into something much larger than a tribute to any singular figure. Scholar Imani Perry, in her book about the origins of the song, *May We Forever Stand,* writes that it "was a lament and encomium to the story and struggle of black people" that ultimately became "a definitive part of ritual practices in schools and churches and civic gatherings."

Without anyone having to ask, everyone in the room stood up. Some held pieces of paper with the song's lyrics, but the majority stood simply with their eyes shut and their hands clasped. They did not need to read the words. Their bodies swayed and their lips moved to a hymn that had long been imprinted in their memories.

I half sang and half looked around the room, observing the way people's mouths moved over the words, how the vowels at the center of each lyric stretched out and hung like the laundry on a warm day. Around me was a tapestry of sunlight and song, pain and catharsis, moving through the air.

As I listened to people sing, I imagined the words floating above us, my eyes tracing the curve of each invisible piece of language, while the chords from the piano echoed throughout the room. I felt almost as if I should reach up and grab the words and place them in my pocket, in an effort to carry this moment with me once it came to an end.

When we reached the second verse, I felt something different come over the crowd, and felt something different come over me:

> We have come over a way that with tears has
>   been watered,
> We have come, treading our path through the
>   blood of the slaughtered,
> Out from the gloomy past,
> Till now we stand at last
> Where the white gleam of our bright star is cast.

The crowd had turned into a congregation. My own lips, after an initial wariness, curled around each slice of song and found a home there. I had sung the Black National Anthem countless times—in churches, in schools, at my own dinner table—but hearing the harmony of those words reverberate around me in this place, on this day, moved me in a way I had not experienced before.

When the crowd sang *We have come over a way that with tears has been watered, / We have come, treading our path through the blood of the slaughtered,* I thought of how 154 years ago such a lyric would not have been an abstraction, the blood would not have been metaphoric. I felt as if there was something that had been clenched inside me since Blandford that I was now able to release. I exhaled, able to breathe in a new way.

Over the course of the rest of the program a procession of community leaders, local politicians, and event organizers came up to the podium at the front of the room to speak about why Juneteenth is important and what it means to them.

One of the speeches that stood out was given by Grant Mitchell, a tall middle-aged white man whose family has sponsored the program for several years.

"Today is a day for jubilation," Grant said, leaning on the podium. "We celebrate this day as the day word reached Galveston and then spread throughout the region and into other Southern states that freedom had come to millions and a great injustice had been undone. We celebrate the day we got word our great nation, torn apart, but once again united, had taken one bold and decisive step toward fulfilling a promise at the core of its creed, that all people are created equal. But this is not just a celebration. The path toward justice is long and uncertain. It sometimes moves forward and sometimes winds its way back. So today is also a day of reflection. It is a day to look around and ask ourselves, 'Where are we on that path?'"

It is not enough to study history. It is not enough to celebrate singular moments of our past or to lift up the legacy of victories that have been won without understanding the effects of those victories—and those losses—on the world around us today. The state of Texas currently has a larger Black population than any other state in the country—about 3.5 million Black people call the state home—but as is the case across the country, the Black community experiences profound disparities across income, wealth, education, and criminal justice.[*] Galveston, and the state of Texas as a whole, extols its history as the origin point of our greatest celebration of emancipation. It is, however, worth interrogating the past century and a half to understand what led to such wide racial chasms in a state that prides itself on its history of freedom.

---

[*] Per the 2010 census, Black Texans represented 12 percent of the state's population and 32 percent of the prison and jail population, whereas white Texans made up 45 percent of the state's population and 33 percent of the prison and jail population. Of Black Texans, more than 20 percent live in poverty, compared to 15 percent of white Texans. The infant mortality rate of Black women in Texas is more than twice that of white women. The high school graduation rate is 87 percent for Black Texans and 94 percent for white Texans. The list goes on like this across almost every metric.

As the program came to an end, I walked from my table across the room to where the Union reenactment soldiers were sitting. I introduced myself to Stephen Duncan and pulled up a chair next to him. Stephen had a round white face with a pair of thin, circular glasses that sat high on his nose. His goatee was a mixture of dark grey and white, and when he took off his Union Army cap, he revealed a thinning hairline that extended to the back of his head. Stephen, along with the other four reenactors, was dressed in dark blue Union Army regalia ornamented with gold trimmings. A parade of buttons lined the front of their uniforms and glimmered under the light from the chandelier above. When he spoke, the timbre of his voice was soft and peppered with levity, his intonation that of a neighbor who is always eager to chat. He was an educator in the community as well as an ordained priest.

Stephen told me he joined the Sons of Union Veterans organization after developing an interest in the Civil War and in more deeply exploring his lineage. When he signed up to start doing reenactment work, he said, "suddenly everybody who was looking for a Union person would give me a call, which has happened a lot because most of the people in Texas want to be a Confederate reenactor."

With the program now over, chatter emanated all around us as people formed lines to get the free breakfast being served. Over the din of post-program conversation, I asked him which of his family members had fought in the war.

"I have three [great-great-]grandfathers who fought in the armies of the North. Had one who was a cavalry private and two who were infantry." He fiddled with the golden button at the bottom of his jacket.

"It's such a divisive, horrible time in our history. I mean, we saw the country at its absolute worst. We saw people who thought that it was just fine to hold other people in bondage," he said. "And seeing that we struggled through that and made it through to the other side seemed really important to me."

Talking to Stephen in his Union Army regalia, I was reminded of how the story our country tells about the Civil War often flattens some of its otherwise complex realities. Texas, for example, was a Confederate state, but its citizens were not a monolith. Many Texans were Union sympathizers and did not support the Confederate cause. (The same can be said for many Confederate sympathizers in some states loyal to the Union.) Sam Houston, for example, who served as the first president of the Republic of Texas, in addition to serving as both a senator and a governor of the state, opposed secession and unsuccessfully attempted to keep Texas from joining the Confederacy. He was the only governor in the states that would make up the Confederacy to oppose secession in the lead-up to the Civil War.

During an 1861 Texas political convention in which the state formally decided to secede from the Union, Houston refused to swear an oath to the Confederacy, writing, "In the name of my own conscience and manhood...I refuse to take this oath."

State officials removed Houston from his position as governor, and though Abraham Lincoln reportedly offered him military assistance to prevent Texas from joining the Confederacy, Houston opposed the idea of using force to stay in power.

Though he had been considering it long before, Stephen began participating in reenactments around 2012 at the anniversary of the Battle of Bull Run.

"It's not a cheap hobby," he said, laughing and noting that his full uniform cost about a thousand dollars.

There were limited occasions for him to use his uniform, but in 2015 he was asked by Kathy Tiernan if he would be open to reenacting the role of General Gordon Granger and if he would read General Order Number 3. Stephen jumped at the opportunity.

"It's an incredibly cool thing to be able to do," he said, his voice brimming with delight. "I mean, to stand on the steps and say 'All slaves are free' has got to be the most powerful four words in history."

I asked him what it was like to stand up there and say those words.

"The first time was absolutely overwhelming. We were outside and I was up on the balcony and it felt like a thousand degrees. And I said, 'All slaves are free, let me say it again, all slaves are free.' And they started to chant, '*Freedom, freedom, freedom, freedom.*' Congresswoman Sheila Jackson Lee was here, and she was leading the chant. And I'm just…literally overwhelmed by the power of that."

I asked Stephen why he thought more white people didn't participate in Juneteenth events.

"They think it's just a Black thing," he said. "And my argument is it's not 'a Black thing,' it's an American thing. This is the final bit of freedom for us all. And that's just so important."

During our conversation, people came up to Stephen and the other Sons of Union Veterans and thanked them. A number of people asked the uniformed men if they would pose for photos alongside them, which they did enthusiastically. This was something I had not anticipated.

"I get people who come up to me a lot," Stephen

said. "I'm pretty well known in the community." He took a drink of water. "People will come up and thank me for doing this. And I've been known to wear the blue hat in public. I've got two. I've got my chaplain's hat and my general's hat. And I think every African American who sees the blue hat knows exactly what that means. I get a lot of thank-yous, a lot of smiles."

But not everyone has expressed gratitude to Stephen for what he does here. "I'll get snide remarks from time to time from some of the Confederate folks. 'Oh, isn't that the wrong color?' they'd say."

I told Stephen about my visit, just a few weeks prior, to Blandford Cemetery, and what it was like seeing and speaking with his organizational counterparts, the Sons of Confederate Veterans.

"We know them well," he said, nodding his head and briefly tucking his lips inside his mouth. "Some of them are absolutely delightful human beings." He paused. "And some of them don't think the war ended."

In many ways, the public spectacle of Juneteenth came to serve as an open rebuke to the emerging Lost Cause narrative of the late 1800s. How could anyone suggest the war was not about slavery when Black people across the state and across the country were providing annual public reminders of the war's inextricable link to emancipation? As the Lost Cause mythology continued into the early twentieth century, Juneteenth was not only a celebration but also a seizing of public memory. As historian Elizabeth Hayes Turner notes, "Memories represent power to people who are oppressed, for while they cannot control much of what occurs in their lives, they can own their own memories."

The earliest iterations of Juneteenth in Texas, which began following the end of the Civil War, ranged from ceremonial readings of the Emancipation Proclamation to Black newspapers printing images of Abraham Lincoln in their pages, testaments to a man who had already begun to take on a legendary and even mythical status among many in the Black community. Other celebrations included church services in which preachers had the congregation give thanks for their freedom while encouraging them to be relentless in the ongoing struggle for racial equity. Often there were parades, large displays of song and celebration that shook the streets. And in the afternoons there were massive feasts, the sort of spreads people looked forward to all year: spareribs, fried chicken, black-eyed peas. The smell of collard greens crawled out from between the cracked windows of homes and teased everyone passing by. Recipes for special pastries were exchanged between neighbors and transformed ovens into incubators of sugary, breaded delight. Children dashed back and forth between one another's houses, hoping to get an early taste from a generous neighbor of the feast that was to come. There were picnics, beauty pageants, baseball games, and an endless stream of songs that emanated throughout the streets.

Unfortunately, the public celebrations became less visible. As Republicans abandoned the Black community, Reconstruction was dismantled. Black American second-class citizenship was recodified through Jim Crow laws and enforced through the omnipresent threat of violence, and Juneteenth celebrations were not only unwelcome but often dangerous. With the threat of lynching always there for Black Southerners, some celebrations across the country disappeared from public view and into private homes and Black churches. And as the decades went by and Black Americans still had nothing close to full equality, to some, Juneteenth seemed like an unfulfilled promise. In 1941, the *Houston Informer,* a Black newspaper, wrote, "Negroes are not sure whether to be gay on 'Juneteenth' or to observe the day with sadness. They do not know whether they are actually free here."

By the early 1970s, Juneteenth celebrations slowly

began to reemerge as local cultural organizations throughout Texas, and throughout the country, began to lift up the holiday as a way to celebrate Black culture and Black history. In 1979, newly elected Texas state legislator Al Edwards Sr. introduced House Bill 1016, which would make June 19th a state holiday. Over the course of four months Edwards built a diverse coalition of support across the state legislature. As one Juneteenth celebrant put it, "Even if the American people in the United States didn't really set that day aside for us, I believe they owe it to us anyway... they ought to give the colored man a day for his freedom. It should be a red spot on the calendar and really took aside for." Edwards's campaign proved successful, and in 1979, Texas became the first state to create a holiday in honor of Black emancipation.

In Ashton Villa back at the Juneteenth breakfast, Al Edwards Sr. made his way to his seat, his gait frail and unsteady as he hunched over a walker to keep him upright. His movements were labored, his steps precarious, as his son and grandchildren helped him to his seat.

Born in Houston in 1937, Edwards was the sixth of sixteen children. He graduated from Texas Southern University in 1966 and went on to participate in the civil rights movement alongside Dr. Martin Luther King Jr. and Jesse Jackson. Edwards is often referred to as the father of Juneteenth because of his advocacy for the holiday.

When I sat down to speak with him, his voice was so low and so fragile that I could not understand anything he said. I tried to adjust myself to get as close as possible while still respecting his space, but no adjustment proved helpful. Even though I couldn't hear him, seeing Edwards in person was an important reminder that the stakes of this holiday had once been even greater than they are today. At eighty-two years old, Edwards had lived in a world where thousands of people who had been born into slavery were still alive.

In the Federal Writers' Project database, whose interviews of formerly enslaved people took place between 1936 and 1938, I searched for formerly enslaved people interviewed in and around Galveston whose years on this earth crossed paths with Edwards's.

Mintie Maria Miller, who was born in Tuscaloosa, Alabama, in 1852, before moving to Texas, outlined with devastating detail what it was like to stand on the auction block:

They stands me up on a block of wood and a man bid me in. I felt mad. You see I was young then, too young to know better. I don't know what they sold me for, but the man what bought me made me open my mouth while he looks at my teeth. They done all us that-a-way, sells us like you sell a hoss.

Josephine Ryles was born in Galveston and lived there all her life. She couldn't remember her birthday:

Plenty times de niggers run 'way, 'cause dey have to work awful hard and de sun awful hot. Dey hides in de woods and Mr. Snow keep nigger dogs to hunt 'em with. Dem dogs have big ears and dey so bad I never fools 'round dem. Mr. Snow take [off] dere chains to git de scent of de nigger and dey kep' on till dey finds him, and sometimes dey hurt him, I knows dey tore de meat off one dem field hands.

And William Mathews, who, at eighty-nine during the time of his interview, was able to remember with vivid precision the daily life of someone enslaved:

De slaves git out in de fields 'fore sun-up and work till black dark. Den dey come home and have to feel dere way in de house, with no light. My mammy and daddy field hands. My grandma was cook, and have to git in de cook

pot 'bout four o'clock to git breakfas' by day-
light. Dey et by candles or pine torches. One
de black boys stand behin' 'em and hold it
while dey et...De quarters is back of de big
house and didn't have no floors. Dey sot plumb
on de ground and build like a hawg pen...We
went right on workin' after freedom. Old Buck
Adams wouldn't let us go. It was way after
freedom dat de freedom man come and read
de paper, and tell us not to work no more 'less
us git pay for it.

I had known that Juneteenth was predicated
on the fact that some enslaved people, both in
Texas and elsewhere, had gone on working without knowing they were free. Still, it was something
different to understand how their enslavers purposefully continued to keep them in bondage. In
Jasper, Texas, a woman named Tempie Cummins
described what happened to her and her mother:

Mother was workin' in the house, and she
cooked too. She say she used to hide in the
chimney corner and listen to what the white
folks say. When freedom was 'clared, marster
wouldn' tell 'em, but mother she hear him
tellin' mistus that the slaves was free but they
didn' know it and he's not gwineter tell 'em till
he makes another crop or two.

Cummins said she and her mother escaped soon after. She remembered their master getting his gun and shooting at her mother as they fled.

What Cummins would make clear is that the jubilation of June 19, 1865, was for many short-lived. General Granger's proclamation did not bring about the immediate liberation of enslaved people in Galveston, or in Texas. As historian W. Caleb McDaniel has said about the days, weeks, and years following Juneteenth, "Slavery did not end cleanly or on a single day. It ended through a violent, uneven process."

As word spread about the general order, and formerly enslaved people attempted to step into freedom, there were many whites who began pulling them right back. The former Confederate mayor of Galveston even rounded up Black "runaways" in order to return them to their owners, despite the labels "owner" and "runaway" having no legal merit. One couldn't be a runaway if they were, under the law, free. Many Southerners felt differently. To further complicate the matter, the Union Army officials did not consistently enforce the rights of formerly enslaved people.

Beyond Galveston, formerly enslaved people in Texas did not immediately learn of their emancipation. The geography of the state, and the fact that so many were held in remote areas, meant that plenty of them simply did not hear about the proclamation for weeks or months or in some cases years. As Turner writes, even those who did hear about it had little opportunity to take advantage of it if their enslavers were noncompliant. Rural and remote locations made it difficult to seek refuge behind Union Army lines. Those who did try to leave, like Tempie Cummins and her mother, were often unsuccessful. White vigilantes often rounded up and punished formerly enslaved people who sought to escape. Making matters even more difficult was the fact that Texas was the last state to receive assistance from the Freedmen's Bureau—set up to provide aid to formerly enslaved Black people and impoverished white people throughout the South after the Civil War—with officers from the bureau arriving more than two months after General Granger issued his general order in Galveston. Further, freedpeople were barred from assembling in groups until members of the Freedmen's Bureau arrived.

Former Confederates across the South were unwilling to allow formerly enslaved Black folks to transition smoothly and safely to freedom. They often turned to violence, believing they should have been, at the very least, compensated for their loss of property. A woman named Susan Merritt of Rusk County, Texas, reported that "lots of Negroes were killed after freedom...bushwhacked, shot down while they were trying to get away. You could see lots of Negroes hanging from trees in Sabine bottom right after freedom. They would catch them swimming across Sabine River and shoot them."

Merritt also described how one day a man representing the government showed up and told all of the Black workers that they were free. Still, after the "man read the paper telling us we were free…massa made us work several months after that. He said we got 20 acres land and a mule, but we didn't get it."

When freedom did eventually come, it often still felt out of reach. There was little financial support for the formerly enslaved, and they were given few resources with which to build economic and social mobility. As Felix Haywood said, "We knowed freedom was on us, but we didn't know what was to come with it. We thought we was goin' to get rich like the white folks. We thought we was goin' to be richer than the white folks, 'cause we was stronger and knowed how to work, and the whites didn't and they didn't have us to work for them anymore. But it didn't turn out that way. We soon found out that freedom could make folks proud but it didn't make 'em rich."

In 1863, when the Emancipation Proclamation was signed, Black Americans owned about 0.5 percent of the total wealth in the United States. Today, despite being 13 percent of the population,

Black people own less than 4 percent of the nation's wealth. Despite the role Black Americans played in generating this country's wealth, they don't have access to the vast majority of it.

At the Juneteenth event, I watched Al Edwards II speak gently to his father and greet each person who approached his dad with a soft, though warm, enthusiasm. Al II's voice was low and raspy, like the thin layer of sand that cakes the sidewalk near a beach. He lives in New Orleans with his family but would regularly make trips to Houston to spend time with his aging father.

Even before he attempted to turn the holiday into a statewide celebration in 1979, Al Edwards Sr. had embarked on a campaign to get people to understand the day's significance. He attended churches, did radio spots, and visited community organizations and schools to spread the gospel of Juneteenth. He wanted to take the holiday away from the relatively small house gatherings and secluded celebrations that had marked the previous decades. He wanted to get enough people out in the streets so that, as his son put it, "the city and state could see that a significant amount of our people found it important enough to be recognized and celebrated."

I imagined a young Al Edwards Sr., making his way into the state capitol building, the hot Texas sun beating down on him as beads of sweat slid from his face and onto the collar of his three-piece suit. The passage of the Juneteenth bill was far from certain. "It was a ninety-nine-to-one chance," his son told me. It would take passionate hand-wringing and savvy back-room deals. "He only needed fifty percent plus one," Al said, which meant he needed significant Republican support. These were people who had built careers on political ideas that were harmful to Black people. But Edwards Sr. knew that politics, particularly politics in Texas, could never be built on purity. It demanded you not let old grudges or personal distaste stand in the way. In exchange for their support, Edwards Sr. promised Republican law-makers he would be on their side when they needed him. He was staking his legislative career on the Juneteenth bill's success. "It takes that sometimes," his son said. "It's not enough to be right all the time, it's not enough to be right *some-times*. Sometimes you also have to be a benefit to those who you need a benefit from."

For Edwards Sr., any compromises or sacrifices he made were worth it. He had marched with Dr. King, and making Juneteenth a state holiday was an extension of the work put into motion by the civil rights movement. The holiday would not be established by its official recognition—the Edwards family had always celebrated the holiday—but the legislation provided institutional legitimacy to a community that had been denied it for so long. Edwards Sr. kept pushing, kept hand-wringing, kept arm-twisting, kept sacrificing, and it paid off. He got the votes he needed.

Only seven years old when Juneteenth officially became a Texas state holiday in 1980, Al II did not fully understand the significance of everything that was transpiring with the legislation, but he knew that something significant had just happened. "Of course back then those details didn't land any-where with a seven-year-old," said Al. But when Martin Luther King Jr. Day was declared a federal holiday a few years later, "we sort of realized the significance of that first African American state holiday being passed as a part of *national* history, not just for the state alone. How it was the precur-sor for entertaining the entire push for a national holiday around African American recognition."

"So you think your father's Juneteenth bill was something that propelled the Martin Luther King Jr. Day bill?" I asked him, unfamiliar with the relationship between the two.

"Absolutely," he said. "It made it more palatable and more defensible to have a national holiday named for an African American of Martin Luther King's significance . . . but it was sort of the natural progression. But it took that first thrust for it to get that first thing across the finish line."

I was curious as to whether or not his father, following passage of the bill, had had a sense of how significant the law would go on to be and how important it was in the larger context of the fight to have this country recognize what Black people have had to overcome.

"I think for lawmakers in that period of time—between Jim Crow and the turn of the century—there was so much transition. So he may have spent less time thinking about what the long term or big picture was and more time just in the fight itself. So I don't think he spent a lot of time reflecting on it because at every turn someone was trying to beat it back," he said, his voice becoming firm. "I think he spent more time in the work of it than he spent sort of admiring it. He knew that it needed to be visible and it needed to be stoked and kept alive and it needed to be illuminated in the minds of our people especially, because if it was left untended it was definitely going to be [driven] back. He always had that concern."

Reflecting on what celebrations after the first official Juneteenth were like, he said, "It was a totally different thing. We had fireworks! It was a big deal because Dad was giving it the relevance and significance that US Independence Day has. Because it was essentially our Independence Day, and he wanted to make sure that people understood that we do view this that way. Just as the rest of the nation views the Fourth of July."

Al's comment made me think of Frederick Douglass's famous Fourth of July speech in 1852, in which he stated:

> Your high independence only reveals the immeasurable distance between us. The blessings in which you, this day, rejoice, are not enjoyed in common.—The rich inheritance of justice, liberty, prosperity and independence, bequeathed by your fathers, is shared by you, not by me. The sunlight that brought life and healing to you, has brought stripes and death to me. This Fourth July is *yours*, not *mine*.

I left Ashton Villa and began my trek to Galveston's Old Central Cultural Center, about a half mile away from Ashton Villa. The building was formerly part of Central High School, which was established in 1885 as the first high school for Black people in the state of Texas.

Inside, I met Sue Johnson, who sat across from me in a large red Juneteenth T-shirt as the sound of djembe drums pulsed through the wall behind us. Johnson had a short haircut, a black-and-grey

Afro just a few inches high. Born and raised in Galveston, she said she'd been organizing the Juneteenth event for about thirty years. I asked her how the Black community in Galveston felt forty years ago after the measure passed. Excited? Emotional? Grateful?

"It was more like 'It's about time.' But because we have celebrated Juneteenth in Galveston since 1865, we're just in the mode of celebration of the holiday anyway," she said with a mix of pride and defiance, leaning forward over the table. Even though she believed the State of Texas should recognize the holiday, whether or not the holiday would be celebrated by Black Galvestonians was not predicated on its passage in the legislative body. "The fact that it became a [state] holiday was icing on the cake," she said.

For Sue, Juneteenth is personal, not just because she is a daughter of Galveston but because she has spent her life as a student of this history. She has a profound understanding of the horrors Black people were freed from on the famous June day in 1865.

"I grew up reading a lot of slave narratives and stories about when we were enslaved," she said, massaging her hands as she spoke. "It always touched me. A lot of people don't want to look at that at all, and I must. I feel like I must because if you don't remember where you've been, you can't be sure where you're going. Or you don't have direction or lessons from the past. It's important to me to celebrate the holiday to help especially young people reflect on what was, so that they understand where they are today and where they still must go."

The room we sat in, an old school gym, was large and hot. Three flies buzzed above the table, each of them pirouetting around the others in a symphony of irritation. I asked Sue if she thought young people throughout Galveston, beyond the ones she worked with at the Nia Cultural Center, were aware of what this holiday meant. She took a deep breath, furrowed her brow, and tilted her head from side to side as if weighing the right answer.

"The community, in my opinion, needs to do more to educate rather than just celebrate," she said. "Which is one of the reasons we're doing the event today." She pointed to the walls behind us, still thumping with the sound of the drums on the other side. "The International Day of Drumming and Healing [exists] because it gives us an opportunity to look at the institution of slavery and what it meant not only to be enslaved but to be free."

In my experience—as both educator and student, as researcher and writer—there was little mainstream discussion of who Black people were before they reached the coasts of the New World, beyond the balls and chains. This was something I had heard when I lived in Senegal, a decade prior, that we Black Americans were taught so little of our traditions, our cultures, our voices before we were taken and forced onto ships that carried us across the Atlantic. As Sue pointed out, the risk is that Black Americans understand our history as beginning in bondage rather than in the freedom of Africa that preceded it.

Sue contended that these conversations rarely happen in our own community largely because there is a fear of whom it might offend. Specifically, in the states of the former Confederacy. "In the South, I think there's a hesitance to talk about it openly because nobody wants to offend white people," she said. Sue believed there was an unwillingness "to look at the ugliness of slavery and discuss it, because you talk about what whites did to us, and there's a hesitance to talk about that. They don't want to hear it, so we don't want to say it. You know what I mean?" Her voice grew lower. "Or because it conjures up so much pain, people don't want to talk about it."

In an effort to address what she felt was a lack of history-based education taking place in her community, Sue founded the Nia Cultural Center in the building we were sitting in. Living in Galveston, she found there was an enormous preservation effort taking place, but she was concerned that the city seemed interested only in preserving white history. "There was a lot of preservation of *their* history, but ours was being torn down," she said. Her commitment to restoring the awareness and the iconography of her community was solidified.

"I knew that we needed to tell our story, so I started doing events that promote our history, and not just during Black History Month," she said. "[We attended] living history museums, teaching the kids about local historical figures and events."

And as committed as Sue was to teaching young people in Galveston about the history of slavery and its aftermath, she wanted to go even further back than that. She wanted them to understand that their ancestry, their history, did not begin with the Middle Passage. It did not begin with chains.

"I didn't want them to think, *Oh, we popped up and we became enslaved.* No, we were thriving communities and nations and did amazing things before we were ever found by the white man," she said with an unfettered insistence. "We did so many things that it didn't mean that we came here dumb and we had to learn somebody else's way to become truly educated and actualized. I wanted them to see what they brought to the table, and to try to maintain and preserve who they are, and not think that in order to be successful, I have to let go of my cultural stuff and adopt somebody else's."

Sue said that society doesn't give young people enough credit, and doesn't engage them with the seriousness they deserve. She believes, and she said she has proven in her work, that if you give young people the tools to make sense of their history, you are giving them the tools to make sense of themselves, thus fundamentally changing how they navigate the world. "People don't want to be bothered with young kids, but when you tell them their story, when you introduce them to little-known facts about who they are and their heritage, they light up."

People in Galveston repeatedly asked me if I had been to "the park." If I wanted to understand what Juneteenth meant in Texas, they said, I had to go there. So on a warm September day in Houston, as summer was collecting its things and autumn was peeking around the corner, I went to Emancipation Park, an historic landmark in the city's Third Ward.

In 1872, this piece of land was purchased by a group of formerly enslaved people in the hopes of providing Houston's Black community with a place to celebrate Juneteenth. Today it is the site of one of the oldest annual Juneteenth celebrations in the country. The leader of that original group of formerly enslaved people was a man named Jack Yates, a minister and community leader who was central to the social and political landscape of Black Houston life in the late nineteenth century. I went to Emancipation Park to meet his great-granddaughter, Jackie Bostic, who lived just a few minutes away from the park and who has worked diligently to keep her great-grandfather's legacy alive.

I met Mrs. Bostic in a conference room of the building that was once the park's gym. She moved with a dexterity that belied her eight decades, her curly white hair coiled around her head and her eyes as calm as dusk. Her memories were lucid, and her voice was slow and smooth. Her eyes crinkled at the edges as she spoke.

Bostic grew up in Houston and remembered clearly the days when segregation animated every part of Black people's lives. Her activist sensibilities had been apparent since she was young. "You know, I always challenged what I thought was not right or unfair," she said. "And I couldn't understand how, in many places in the South—in Texas, in Louisiana, in Mississippi, and others—the population, in some areas, was totally Black, but yet you were being forced to abide by rules that were made by somebody else. And that you could not believe that you could overcome that, that you could change that situation. And I could understand the fear, because during the time there were many people being lynched...But there was just always something in me that knew *No, I don't have to live like this, and I'm not going to.*"

Bostic never met her great-grandfather Jack Yates, but it was as if the contours of his being had been concretized in her memory. Yates was born in Virginia and married a woman named Harriet Willis, with whom he had eleven children. His wife and children, however, lived on a different plantation. After the Emancipation Proclamation, Willis's owner moved his operations to Texas so that he could continue to enslave his workers. According to Bostic, when her great-grandfather, who had been freed by his own former enslaver, learned of this, he convinced his wife's owner to allow him to purchase his way *back* into slavery so that he could be with his family.

I wasn't sure if I had heard that right, so I asked her to repeat it. Bostic nodded sympathetically, no doubt familiar with how startling the story of a free Black man paying to be re-enslaved must sound to those first hearing it. It was a devastating truth that revealed the lengths enslaved people would go to in order to prevent their families from being separated. The love he had for his family outweighed every other consideration.

The Yates family moved to Matagorda County, Texas, about ninety miles down the coast from

Galveston. They were there when General Gordon Granger read the proclamation letting enslaved Texans know they were free. It didn't take long for word to reach the plantation, and when it did, Bostic said the slave owner told them that it was up to them. They could stay or they could leave. If they left, he said, he couldn't stop them. But if they stayed, they would have to continue working for nothing. Jack Yates and his family left.

The family moved to Houston, which was then still a new city—less than thirty years old—and they began to lay down roots in what would become the Fourth Ward, forming what was known, appropriately, as Freedmen's Town. On the relative outskirts of the city, more Black families came and settled in a place where they could buy land, and live among a community of freed Black people in the joy and uncertainty of post-emancipation Texas. Yates would come to play a significant role in the community. On his plantation in Virginia he had learned to read and write from the slave owner's son, who was his playmate as a child. More educated than the vast majority of other Black people in Freedmen's Town, he became a minister, constructed a church, set up schooling, and made it so the newly freed people in his community had the civic bedrock upon which to build the rest of their lives.

After several years, Yates turned his attention to finding a place for the community to commemorate what had made all of this possible. Working together with other community members, they collected eight hundred dollars to purchase the land—the first public park in the city of Houston and in the state of Texas. Bostic looked back fondly on her childhood Juneteenth celebrations at the park. "A day of fun, fellowship, good food, playing in the park."

Emancipation Park served as a centerpiece of Houston's Black community for decades moving into the twentieth century. But by the 1970s, the park had become a dilapidated, fractured shadow of its former self, and ceased hosting Juneteenth celebrations altogether in 2007. The cessation served as a wake-up call to community members, and a group called Friends of Emancipation Park dedicated itself to restoring the space. That same year the Houston City Council designated the park a historic landmark, which paved the way for its revitalization. Over the next decade, the park underwent a thirty-four-million-dollar renovation, which included building a gym and recreation center, a new pool, and an outdoor theater. To complement the renovation, the city council also voted in 2017 to rename Dowling Street—which ran adjacent to the park and was named after Confederate commander Richard W. Dowling—Emancipation Avenue.

I asked Bostic what she thought her great-grandfather would think, of both the renovations and the Juneteenth celebrations being held at the park today, 147 years after the founding of the park.

"Well, it's just wonderful to see that people are still, in 2019, able to come to a park that was started by people who had just come out of slavery and had no idea that it would be the park, today, that it was then." Bostic looked around the room and, briefly, out of the window. "You know, it's changed in many ways, but it's still a place for people to come enjoy their families and have good fellowship, and enjoy freedom."

She paused. "It's all about freedom. How important freedom is to them."

One thing that Bostic is especially committed to is ensuring that while Emancipation Park provides a place for people to celebrate Juneteenth, these celebrations don't come at the expense of people understanding what the history of Juneteenth actually is. She, like Sue Johnson, has realized that the work of preserving history must be taken on proactively, that history must be cultivated and nurtured, or else we risk losing it.

"I think my generation," she said, "many getting killed, and beaten, and spit on, and dogs, and hoses, did not understand that you have to keep telling the story in order for people to understand. Each generation has to know the story of how we got where we are today, because if you don't understand, then you are in the position to go back to it.

Her voice began shaking. "I watched so much turned around, that people I know fought for…And I'm watching here, in real time, watching other people not turn it around, because we're not understanding what's happening.

"They may discuss in the school system that you were a slave, but they're not going to talk about what happened after slavery." Her face sank. "How you were emancipated, how others came and took your land…if you got anything at all—how you weren't given anything."

She continued: "They're not going to tell you the real story of how you went and you fought in every war that this country has ever fought, including the Civil War, where the most people have died in this country than in every war we've fought in. They're not going to tell you those things. They're not going to put that in the history books, because they want to glamorize the Confederacy."

The responsibility of passing on this history falls to both the community and the schools. Texas, the home of one in ten public school students in the country, has experienced a number of high-profile embarrassments with regard to how schools in the state have taught Black history, particularly slavery. In 2015, the State Board of Education and publisher McGraw-Hill Education came under fire for providing students with a textbook that described how the transatlantic slave trade brought "millions of workers from Africa to the southern United States to work on agricultural plantations." It seemed to many to be a deliberate obfuscation of the fact that Africans were forcibly and violently stripped from their homelands, not people who were just "workers" who simply agreed to come help cultivate North American land. In April 2018, eighth graders at Great Hearts Monte Vista North charter school in San Antonio were asked to complete a worksheet titled "The Life of Slaves: A Balanced View," which had two columns in which the students were meant to write the "positive" elements of slavery in one and the "negative" elements in the other. A textbook that had been used at the school included a description of how slavery included "kind and generous owners" and enslaved people who "may not have even been terribly unhappy." The Texas State Board of Education has since revised the standards so that, across the state, slavery is understood to have played a "central role" in causing the Civil War.

"It's a subject that nobody wants to touch, because nobody wants to really talk about it," Bostic said. She leaned toward me, and her eyes locked on mine. "But it's what is going to continue to tear our country apart, until we're willing to understand it happened. It really happened."

In Galveston, I walked back to Ashton Villa and felt the heat wash over me. The island's air, still thick and heavy, settled across my skin. I stood on the walkway in front of the house with my back to the street as cars thrummed behind me, waiting at a stoplight. I looked up at the balcony again, squinting and cupping a hand across my forehead to shield my eyes from the light. I marveled at the tight coils of iron glazed by the glint of midday sun and each section's undeviating symmetry. Thin columns of metal rose from the balcony's platform and blossomed like chrysanthemums, a throng of floral spirals and corkscrews that held up the roof above it. A band of sparrows flew overhead and landed atop the roof. Sirens of an unseen ambulance sang in the distance. I grabbed a bottle of water from my backpack, and the condensation dripped over my fingertips. I took a gulp and let the cool drink slide down my throat.

I let my imagination lean into the myth, into the possibility of this origin story being true. I pictured General Granger standing on that veranda, encircled by his commanders, their bayonets pointed toward the sky. I imagined how small the general order he read from might have looked from here—a small scrap of paper that broke the chains of 250,000 enslaved people in Texas—a piece of parchment that could make the earth beneath them quake. I thought about what it might be like to be surrounded by a throng of people as they first learned of their freedom. I imagined my body surrounded by the ghosts of other bodies, these shadows of a singular history whose feet were still firmly planted on the ground. I felt their presence in a way that startled me, almost as if I could feel their skin jostling against my own. All of us looking up at the veranda in anticipation of the news.

I narrowed my eyes and traced the contours of Ashton Villa's facade so I would be able to recall it without a photograph. So I could whisper its name and summon its image whenever I needed to be reminded of freedom.

To my right, about fifty yards away, was a statue of Al Edwards Sr. forty years younger, in his three-piece suit, standing upright and smiling as he lifted HB 1016 into the air with his right hand. The sun, now behind the statue, created a bronze eclipse—a golden hue humming around the figure's sharp edges. This was how Edwards, who passed away about a year after my visit to Galveston, would be remembered: not as the aging man I had spoken to but as a paragon of persistence. The man who officially brought Juneteenth to Texas—and to the country.

As I looked at Edwards's statue and then back at Ashton Villa, I thought about how Juneteenth is a holiday that inspires so much celebration, born from circumstances imbued with so much tragedy. Enslavers in Texas, and across the South, attempted to keep Black people in bondage for months, and theoretically years, after their freedom had been granted. Juneteenth, then, is both a day to solemnly remember what this country has done to Black Americans and a day to celebrate all that Black Americans have overcome. It is a reminder that each day this country must consciously make a decision to move toward freedom for all of its citizens, and that this is something that must be done proactively; it will not happen on its own. The project of freedom, Juneteenth reminds us, is precarious, and we should regularly remind ourselves how many people who came before us never got to experience it, and how many people there are still waiting.

"We were the good guys, right?"

NEW YORK CITY

As WE DESCENDED FROM New York City's Penn Station through Manhattan, the 1 train barreled down the tracks, the doors opening at each stop as passengers buried themselves in their phones, in their books, and in the shoulders of people they love. As we made our way through Manhattan, the train, once full, became incrementally emptier. When we reached the South Ferry stop, the half dozen people left on the train got up from their seats as the conductor announced that this was the last stop. There was no farther south to go without barreling into the river. The wind from the Hudson River wrapped itself around me as I climbed the stairs to exit the subway. I flung my hoodie over my head and buried my hands in my jacket pockets. From the station, I walked the couple of blocks to New York's branch of the National Museum of the American Indian, where a walking tour on slavery and the

Underground Railroad in New York City was set to begin.

A group of about a dozen people had gathered around a woman standing at the top of the building's front stairs with a sign indicating she was the leader of the walking tour. The assembly of people was more diverse than any other I had encountered. When the guide asked us to share where we were from, a cascade of accents swept across the group. There were people from Germany, South Korea, Brazil, Australia, England, Canada, Long Island, and Brooklyn.

Our guide, Damaras Obi, was dressed in an all-black ensemble of leather boots, pants, and jacket with a grey backpack fastened tightly over her shoulders. Her shoulder-length hair was composed of tight black curls, with a faint trace of red highlights dressing their corkscrew tips. Deliberate but inviting, her sense of humor would interweave itself into her monologues outlining some of our nation's darkest moments.

"You can call me D," she told us, adjusting her microphone and smiling at the group. Damaras began by telling us that she was raised in New York City, the daughter of a Nigerian father and a Dominican mother. Her background is relevant, she said, because "I use myself as an example on this tour.

"You guys are going to be receiving a very big

chunk of history today. This is not Black history. This is not New York City or American history. This is world history"—she paused briefly—"that has been completely whitewashed and wiped out of our education systems globally, because history is no longer taught. Or when it's taught, it's taught incorrectly. A lot of the information you hear today is going to make you feel very, very uncomfortable. That's okay." She smiled. "That's what learning and development is as a human being, being uncomfortable. Some of the information may challenge your educational background, as well as your personal beliefs. That's all right as well.

"I'd like to start out by stating that the Underground Railroad was neither underground nor was it a railroad." She looked around. "I see some of you smiling. You would be very surprised at how often I have to make that statement. So today's tour will not be taking place underground in a subway or in a cave."

Damaras continued and explained that at the beginning of the Civil War in the United States in 1861, slavery had existed for well over two hundred years and was a multibillion-dollar industry. Summarizing the work of historian David Blight, she explained how slavery was central to the US economy: by 1860 the nearly four million enslaved people were by far the country's most valuable economic asset; valued at approximately $3.5 billion, they were worth more than all of the country's manufacturing and railroads combined.

Damaras described how slavery has existed throughout history, across the world. People would regularly be enslaved because they were prisoners of war or because they owed some sort of debt. Sometimes, she explained, enslavement would endure only for a specific period of time, and even if you were enslaved for your entire life, your children would not necessarily be enslaved after you.

Slavery in the United States was different. "This New World enslavement," Damaras said, "this chattel slavery, was based off of a racial caste system, a racial hierarchy, and it was wrapped around the European ideology that there was something inherently subhuman or inhuman with the genetic makeup of the African, so the only thing that made you eligible for this lifelong sentence was pigmentation, or the color of your skin.

"Race is a by-product of racism. In fact, race doesn't exist." Damaras said this in the way a person might say water is wet. "Some of you look surprised." She adjusted her feet and straightened her back. "It's a social construct. There has never been any scientific or genetic evidence to back up the concept of race. Despite it being false, it has woven its way into the fabric of all of our societies."

Echoing the work of Barbara Fields and Karen

Fields, whose book *Racecraft* outlines that race and racism are separate, distinct social entities, Damaras made clear that people often believe racism came after the creation of race, when it was in fact the other way around. The authors argue, "*Racism* is first and foremost a social practice, which means that it is an action and a rationale for action, or both at once. *Racism* always takes for granted the objective reality of *race*...so it is important to register their distinctness. The shorthand transforms *racism*, something an aggressor *does*, into *race*, something the target *is*, in a sleight of hand that is easy to miss." A statement like "Black Southerners were segregated because of their skin color," they say, is something students might find in textbooks and never blink an eye at. As Barbara Fields and Karen Fields explain in their book, that passive construction makes it seem as if segregation were completely natural, which absolves the enforcers of segregation—both systemic and interpersonal—from any sort of culpability.

The land we were standing on was the oldest part of New York City, originally founded by the Dutch as New Amsterdam in 1624. When the Dutch arrived, they were met by the Lenape Native Americans, an Algonquian-speaking people who had lived on the land since 10,000 BC. Originally, it is said, their interactions were friendly, but their relations deteriorated as tensions over land increased. Two years later, the Dutch West India Company "purchased" the island of Manhattan from the Lenape for a price of sixty guilders' worth of goods, equivalent today to about a thousand dollars. Damaras held up a copy of the earliest known reference to the purchase, a letter from 1626 reporting the news to the Dutch government. The original contract did not survive, but it may have meant something quite different to the Lenape than it did to the Dutch. "You see, this idea or this concept of owning land or resources—that was a European concept. Owning land to the Native Americans was like owning water or the moon or the stars, and in fact, there wasn't a word for [land] ownership in their Algonquian language."

The first enslaved people to arrive in New York were eleven African men brought to the shores of New Amsterdam in 1626. They were tasked with clearing the land, building homes and roads, and generally helping to lay the infrastructural groundwork of the early Dutch settlement. It's likely that some of the wood they cut from trees in lower Manhattan was used to build ships that eventually carried captured Africans.

According to records from the Dutch West India Company, two years later the company brought over three enslaved African women "for the comfort of the company's Negro men."

"They are forcibly brought here to the New

World, and these men come here bearing names like Peter Portuguese and Anthony Congo. Obviously the Africans don't have names like Anthony and Peter. The very first thing you want to do to an enslaved person is you want to strip them of their identity, and how do you do that? You take away their [given] African names and you replace them with new European names." The captured Africans' last names often indicated where they were stolen from or reflected a connection to the person who took them from their birthplace—this, Damaras said, helped the enslavers keep track of their cargo.

These enslaved people helped build the foundation for much of the land we stood on that day, including Wall Street, just a few blocks away. "Does anybody know why Wall Street is called Wall Street?" Damaras asked. "There was a wall." She laughed, as did we. "My questions will never get more difficult than that, I promise." She showed us a picture featuring a rendering of what that wall had looked like, turning her body in a semicircle to ensure that everyone could see it.

"People say this: 'The wall was built by the Dutch for protection against the Natives.' The Natives had a nasty habit of attacking this wall." Damaras's voice was imbued with mockery. Then she became serious. She pointed out the history of violence against Native Americans by the Dutch and the fact that they were essentially foreign invaders bent on taking Native American land. "So did the Dutch need protection from the Natives or did the Natives need protection from the Dutch?"

While a common narrative is that the wall was meant to defend the Dutch against Native Americans, it was originally built primarily to defend against the British. The Dutch, however, did scramble to defend themselves against Native American attacks, after Dutch forces massacred over a hundred Lenape men, women, and children in 1643, under the orders of Governor Willem Kieft. A twentieth-century account of the story describes the retaliatory attacks as the reason for an early version of the wall that ran along what would be Wall Street:

The red people from Manhattan Island crossed to the mainland, where a treaty was made with the Dutch, and the place was therefore called the Pipe of Peace, in their language, Hoboken. But soon after that, the Dutch governor, Kieft, sent his men out there one night and massacred the entire population. Few of them escaped, but they spread the story of what had been done, and this did much to antagonize all the remaining tribes against all the white settlers. Shortly after, Nieuw Amsterdam erected a double palisade for defense against its now enraged red neighbors, and this remained for some time the northern limit of the Dutch city. The space between the former walls is now called Wall Street, and its spirit is still that of a bulwark against the people.

The wall was reinforced and expanded about a decade later, when Peter Stuyvesant, director general of the colony—after whom one of New York's top high schools is named—ordered enslaved workers to construct a barricade using logs "twelve feet long, eighteen inches in circumference, sharpened at the upper end" across the island of Manhattan.

I watched as the Financial District churned and hummed all around us. Sound emanated from every direction: the staccato of jackhammers cracking blocks of concrete in their search for softer earth; cranes stretching their steel joints to lift rubble from one corner of the street to another; ambulances mazing their way through cars and crosswalks, their red flares howling a loud and urgent incantation. This was a significant contrast to the quiet, insulated mountains that encircled Monticello, or the soft rustling of long grass that surrounded the Whitney, or the haunting silence of Angola.

The group descended the stairs, and when we reached the bottom, Damaras turned her back to the National Museum of the American Indian and ushered us in front of her so that we could see the building's edifice as she spoke.

Located in the Alexander Hamilton US Custom House built in 1907, the museum spans three city blocks with traffic churning on either side of it. Sweeping across the sandy-hued facade of the seven-story structure are a dozen cylindrical columns, each with the head of Mercury, the Roman god of commerce, resting at its peak. The columns frame the windows that reflect slices of the skyscraper sitting across from them. On either side of the steps and sitting at the far corners of the building are four intricate marble sculptures of human figures, each in a different position atop its stone pedestal. Designed by sculptor Daniel Chester French, the four statues are meant to represent the regions of Africa, Europe, America, and Asia. French was also the sculptor of the Lincoln Memorial in Washington, DC.

"Notice how Africa is the only one of these four statues depicted sleeping on her throne. That is because, throughout history, Africa has been known as the Sleeping Continent. She's also the only one of the four statues sculpted lying in a half-naked state. It was playing into the archetype of the African being savage and barbaric in nature. All four of these statues are seated on some kind of throne. Africa's throne is sculpted from a boulder from the inland of the continent. At this time in history, the Africans were not considered human enough to warrant a royal symbol."

In February 1915, French wrote: "It is usual to depict the negro with a snub nose and exaggerated fullness of lips, in fact the lowest type of negro that exists. As a matter of fact there is a type of negro which probably represents some section of Africa in which the nose is aquiline and the whole cast of features handsome and dignified according to our Caucasian ideas. I do not at all mean that this type has not the fullness of form by which the African is distinguished, but that by the laws of composition the face is developed in a natural sequence that stands for beauty according to our European art standards."

Damaras directed our attention to the next statue, depicting Europe. She continued: "Notice the difference between both of the statues. In contrast, Europe sits high and mighty on her throne. She's clothed majestically in robes, and her left fist is on a pile of books, and it's on the globe, symbolic of Europe's past conquest. She's going to be the [continent] to lead us into the future with all of her wisdom and her knowledge."

Damaras paused briefly, then moved to the third figure, depicting America. "Notice how America is the only one of the statues sculpted in action. From the torch of Liberty in her hand, America

the Brave will lead us into a new age of enlightenment." Damaras drew our attention to the object
underneath America's right foot: the head of
Quetzalcoatl, the Mesoamerican serpent god.

Then she gestured to a statue of a Native American man crouched behind America. "That is the
point of the architecture. He is hidden behind her,
as it's symbolic of the Native Americans being
a relic of the past. America is facing forward,
towards our future."

The numbers vary widely, but historian Donald
L. Fixico estimates that there were anywhere from
a few million to 15 million Indigenous Americans
living in North America upon Columbus's arrival
in 1492. By the late nineteenth century, the population had dropped to approximately 250,000.

Damaras finished by telling us how the allegori-
cal sculpture of Asia was made to look as if it were
built on top of a bed of skulls, with a man, woman,
and small child kneeling and groveling at her side
to represent, as Chester wrote, "the hordes of
India, and the hopelessness of the life of so many
of the inhabitants."

This was not the first time I had walked by the
National Museum of the American Indian. How
many times had I walked past these statues without ever considering anything other than their
elegance? I certainly had never considered how
the priorities of genocide, colonization, slavery,

and exploitation had been literally carved into these stones and proudly displayed.

During parts of the seventeenth and eighteenth centuries there were more enslaved Black people in New York City than in any other urban area across North America. Enslaved workers made up more than a quarter of the city's labor force. As the city grew, so did the number of enslaved people. As the American Revolution began, about a sixth of New York's population was of African descent, and almost all of them were enslaved.

In the early days of the Dutch settlement, write historians Ira Berlin and Leslie M. Harris in their anthology *Slavery in New York*, the norms governing slavery were different than they were in later iterations of the institution. There was a racial hierarchy in place, but how people moved within this hierarchy varied. For example, many enslaved people were paid for their work. And some enslaved people who were not compensated for their labor petitioned the Dutch West India Company for what they deemed their monetary due. Some Black people were freed by Dutch authorities and given land between New Amsterdam, in the southernmost part of Manhattan, and the rest of the island. This land, however, was not given out of benevolence but to create a buffer zone between the white settlers and the Native Americans who lived farther north, as tensions between the two were on the rise. As a result, by the middle of the seventeenth century, free Black people made up a third of New Amsterdam's total Black population. Many of these free Black people participated in the social life of the Dutch settlement; they married in Dutch churches, they engaged with the Dutch judicial system, and some took on Dutch names. This did not mean that free Black people were equal members of society—they were not, and were constantly reminded of that. Even "freedom" for Black people came with a conspicuous asterisk—it did not necessarily extend to their children. As Berlin and Harris wrote, "While some blacks gained their freedom, that freedom had been granted to assure the safety of a society committed to African slavery."

In 1664, the British ousted the Dutch and took over the colony—no more of the "half freedom" for enslaved people, as historians have called it, that had existed under Dutch rule. Men and women were largely separated, as women stayed in the city to care for the homes and children of their enslavers, while men were increasingly used as agricultural laborers outside the city. Enslaved people had a difficult time finding partners, and fewer enslaved people were having families of their own. The British in New York became increasingly dependent on the transatlantic slave trade to find new workers, importing an average of 150 enslaved people each year from Africa and the West Indies. According to historian David Brion Davis, around 40 percent of households in British Manhattan owned enslaved people.

But the mortality rate of Black people in New York skyrocketed, as enslaved people were made to work harder than ever before and as an increasing number of Africans with little defense against new diseases were brought to the New World. Even before they arrived on the shores of New York, the death toll was staggering. According to historian Jill Lepore, for every one hundred people taken from Africa, only about sixty-four would survive the trip from the region's interior to the coast. Of those sixty-four, around forty-eight would survive the weeks-long journey across the Atlantic. Of those forty-eight who stepped off the ship in New York Harbor, only twenty-eight to thirty would survive the first three to four years in the colony. Berlin and Harris referred to New York at this time as "a death factory for black people."

The enslaved population pushed back—some subtly, by purposefully slowing the pace at which they worked or pretending to be ill, some conspicuously. The largest rebellion came in April 1712, when between twenty-five and fifty enslaved people rose up and killed nine white people and wounded six more. More than seventy Black people were arrested, forty-three brought to trial, and twenty-three executed—some hanged and others burned at the stake. Following the rebellion, the laws governing enslaved life became even more severe—restricting their movement, preventing them from owning property, and requiring slave owners to pay exorbitant fees if they wanted to free the enslaved people they owned.

The rebellion of 1712 may not have been the only slave uprising in the history of New York. In 1741, after a series of fires erupted across New York, a grand jury concluded that Black arsonists had set them as part of a conspiracy to overthrow chattel slavery. More than one hundred people were arrested. Seventy were sold to work in the Caribbean. Seventeen were hanged. Thirteen were burned at the stake. Lepore describes the response as worse than the violence and hysteria of the Salem witch trials. "Over one hundred and fifty accused witches were arrested in Salem, compared to nearly two hundred conspirators named in New York. But in Salem, only nineteen people were executed (four more died in jail), and, contrary to popular opinion, none were burned at the stake."

Scholars still debate whether the fires in 1741 were part of an organized uprising by enslaved people or if there was another explanation. Regardless, from that point on, the mythology surrounding them significantly altered the trajectory of slavery in the colony. Prior to 1741, almost three-quarters of the enslaved workers in New York had come from the Caribbean. After the alleged plot, New York slave owners acquired the majority of their workers directly from Africa. This way, they thought, enslaved people would have a harder time communicating with one another. And therefore would be less likely to plan a mass rebellion.

Slavery continued to grow in New York as more enslaved people were imported. On the eve of the American Revolution, New York had the highest proportion of enslaved Black people to Europeans of any northern settlement, with approximately three thousand enslaved people in the city and twenty thousand more within fifty miles of Manhattan. On a visit to the colony one traveler complained, "It rather hurts a European eye to see so many negro slaves upon the streets."

Damaras waved us forward and we moved as a group from the museum through the streets of the financial district. She carried a small red flag above her head so we could keep track of her as we pushed through the throngs of people. We walked past bars and delis, rounding street corners that pulsed with thousands of footsteps. As we turned onto Pearl Street, we arrived at a block of bricks that jutted up from the sidewalk, with a golden railing encircling a well that was covered in glass. I looked over the rails and into this hole in the ground and saw deteriorating bricks covered in algae, small plants reaching from one side of the cistern to the other.

The well dated back to the eighteenth century and had been the central water source for inhabitants who lived nearby. The first and final thing an enslaved person did every day was get water from the well for their households, and it was here that they were able to spend time together.

"You are allowed to look that person in the eyes," Damaras said. "You are allowed to say 'Good morning.' The enslaved people who came to this well," she continued, "were able to reclaim their humanity for just twenty minutes out of their day." While I knew what Damaras meant, and understood her remark as being a sort of shorthand for saying that this well was a place where enslaved people were not subject to the same levels of intense surveillance and violence they were in other contexts, I thought again about the formulation of enslaved people's "humanity" and how it is not contingent on certain moments or actions but is central to the very project of the institution. They were human at the well, and they were human away from it.

Leaving the well, we walked northeast on Pearl Street, making our way along the sidewalk in the opposite direction of traffic. The smell of melted cheese and baked bread spilled from a small pizza joint on our left, a half dozen pigeons flocking outside its doors and pecking intermittently at the remnants of uneaten crust left on the ground. Joggers slalomed through us on the narrow sidewalk. Dive bars had cracked their windows to provide customers with a bit of reprieve from the heat of bodies and breath. The chatter of a new weekend fell into the street, the volume ebbing and flowing as people came and went. The Queen Elizabeth II Garden, a small triangular park with smoky-grey stone benches, provided a small burst of flora in an otherwise commercial section of the city.

Damaras stopped at the corner of Water and Wall Streets, just in front of a small plaque. Its text was too small to decipher from afar. She told us to take our time, take a look, and after we were done to meet her on the corner a few yards away. I let a few people go before me. When the others had finished, I stepped up to the green marker and its white text. It read:

On Wall Street, between Pearl and Water Streets, a market that auctioned enslaved people of African ancestry was established by a Common Council law on November 30, 1711. This slave market was in use until 1762. Slave owners wanting to hire out enslaved workers, which included people of Native American ancestry, as day laborers also had to do so at that location. In 1726 the structure was re-named the Meal Market because corn, grain and meal—crucial ingredients to the Colonial diet—were also exclusively traded there.

Slavery was introduced to Manhattan in 1626. By the mid-18th century approximately one in five people living in New York City was enslaved and almost half of Manhattan house-holds included at least one slave. Although New York State abolished slavery in 1827, complete abolition came only in 1841 when the State of New York abolished the right of non-residents to have slaves in the state for up to nine months. However, the use of slave labor elsewhere for the production of raw materials such as sugar and cotton was essential to the economy of New York both before and after the Civil War. Slaves also cleared forest land for the construction of Broadway and were among the workers that built the wall that Wall Street is named for and helped build the first Trinity Church. Within months of the market's construction, New York's first slave uprising occurred a few blocks away on Maiden Lane, led by enslaved people from the Coromantee and Pawpaw peoples of Ghana.

Next to the text was a drawing of the slave market in the early 1700s. Ships were in the foreground, their sails still in the windless rendering of the day. Buildings fanned out into the distance, with what looked like the steeple of a church jutting into the air, the centerpiece of an otherwise shallow skyline. About a dozen people were on the shore, and at its center sat a small pavilion where—looking closely—it appeared as if someone was standing over an enslaved person on his knees.

The marker was conceived by Chris Cobb, an artist and writer who began researching the site in 2011 during the Occupy Wall Street movement. Cobb spent years looking for documentation to prove what many had known. Cobb found a 1716 map by William Burgis in the New York Public Library on which the slave market was depicted; he found what he was looking for. "It was an amazing moment," Cobb said in a 2015 interview. "There it was. The invisible suddenly became visible again. So I photographed it and in Photoshop removed the ship that obstructed the market. That clear view of the market, unobstructed, is what is on the marker."

I did a slow 360-degree turn to get a sense of

the setting. About a block in front of me to my right was a Citibank, its trademark red arc sitting over white letters on a sky-blue background.* To my direct right, Bank of America, its red neon banner gleaming behind its windows. Struck by the presence of these banks and their proximity to the former slave market, I could not help but think of slavery's relationship to some of the country's largest banking institutions.

Two of Bank of America's predecessors, Southern Bank of Saint Louis and Boatmen's Savings Institution, listed enslaved people as potential collateral for a debt in 1863. Citibank also had ties to chattel slavery.

Moses Taylor, a nineteenth-century banker who was the director of the City Bank of New York, Citibank's predecessor, managed the capital coming from Southern sugar plantations and was intimately involved in illegally trafficking enslaved people into Cuba.

The country's largest bank, JPMorgan Chase, was the most deeply entwined in the slave trade. A 2005 statement from the company read as follows: "JPMorgan Chase completed extensive research examining our company's history for any links to

---

* Citibank moved out of the 690-office building in December 2019, though the sign remained when I was there in January 2020.

slavery...we are reporting that this research found that between 1831 and 1865 two of our predecessor banks—Citizens Bank and Canal Bank in Louisiana—accepted approximately 13,000 enslaved individuals as collateral on loans and took ownership of approximately 1,250 of them when the plantation owners defaulted on the loans."

By the early nineteenth century, the New York financial industry became even more deeply entrenched in chattel slavery. Money from New York bankers went on to finance every facet of the slave trade: New York businessmen built the ships, shipped the cotton, and produced the clothes that enslaved people wore. The financial capital in the North allowed slavery in the South to flourish. As the cotton trade expanded, New York City became the central port for shipments of raw cotton moving between the American South and Europe. By 1822, more than half of the goods shipped out of New York's harbor were produced in Southern states. Cotton alone was responsible for more than 40 percent of the city's exported goods.

Once we all made our way back to the group, Damaras explained, "One of the biggest lies we are still telling in this country—and I know because I'm trying to combat it—[is that] during the Civil War we were the good guys, right? New York City was good. Everybody else in the South, they were bad."

She went on: "Here's a small recap. This is what happens. We divide ourselves up into two sections: Southern—Confederate or slaveholding states; Northern—Union or free states. What are we fighting over?" She pauses and scans our faces. "Currency—what our currency was going to be moving forward. The United States of America's economy was founded on the currency of selling human livestock. So we're fighting a war over slavery.' When we teach this story to our children, adults, and people outside this country, we lie and we say that New York...we were never a slave state, we were a free state." Damaras took a deep breath and shook her head. "Guys, what were you just standing in front of?" She pointed to the marker behind us, her voice rising an octave. "Where we're standing"—she pointed emphatically to the ground beneath her—"this is the second largest slave market in the United States of America. The second largest, the first being in Charleston..." Her voice dissolved into the cacophony of the city.

Damaras adjusted her microphone and waited for an ambulance to pass. "Eventually slavery would become so intertwined with our economy that Fernando Wood—he was the mayor of this city during the Civil War," she clarified, "he would say, 'Listen...we should secede from the Union,'" she said, paraphrasing what Wood indeed proposed in 1861 in an effort to protect the city's profitable, cotton-trading relationship with the Confederacy.

Damaras took seriously what it meant for people to understand the relationship between slavery's history and the legacy of racism interwoven in present-day policing, housing, and job discrimination. She did not mince her words, and told the group that Black people in the United States "are second-class citizens."

One person, an older white woman who was on the tour with two friends, took issue with Damaras's characterization. The woman, who said she was eighty years old, told Damaras that she didn't see New York City as prejudiced and that she believed people lived together in peace here.

Damaras nodded her head politely, her eyebrows furrowed, but not in anger. "What I will say…" she began. "Consider the perspective that you don't have the same life experience because you are from a certain class and because you have a certain skin color." The woman, her lips pursed in displeasure, interrupted and said that she came from a working-class background and bootstrapped her way up, implying that other people simply needed to do the same. Damaras listened and nodded along as the woman spoke. Forthright and unapologetic, Damaras spoke with a generosity of spirit, making it possible to ask questions or make comments that might otherwise not have been said. Once the woman finished, Damaras responded, "Yes, well, you're not the same race as many other people in New York, and people's lived experiences may be different from yours. Your perspective might be valid in your social circle; in other social circles it may not be. That's all."

We walked just three blocks down Wall Street and arrived at the New York Stock Exchange, where Damaras described the work of abolitionists like the Tappan brothers, Arthur and Lewis, whose offices were right here on Wall Street. The brothers made their sizable fortunes from their silk business, and they used these fortunes to support New York's abolitionists. Their efforts drew the spite of pro-slavery Americans in both the North and the South. In 1834, for example, a mob ransacked Lewis Tappan's home and burned his belongings in the street.

Damaras told us that New York abolitionists, wary of being found out, would communicate in code. "Hey, good morning. How you doing? Listen, at three p.m. I have a package coming for you down from the Southern line. Make sure to avoid blackbirds. They're going to be out around noon," Damaras said, imitating the kind of coded conversations that might have taken place between abolitionists across the city. According to Berlin, in his book *The*

Long Emancipation: The Demise of Slavery in the United States, slave catchers and kidnappers, indeed known as "blackbirders," congregated in Northern cities, taking part in what became an increasingly lucrative endeavor. New York City, per one abolitionist, became a "slaveholders' hunting ground."

Damaras pointed to one of the buildings behind us and explained that before it was a bank for J. P. Morgan it was the site of an oyster house owned by a free Black man named Thomas Downing. Downing was raised on the Eastern Shore of Virginia, after his enslaved parents were freed. After spending his childhood raking oysters, he moved to Philadelphia, where he spent several years working at an oyster bar. Upon moving to New York, Downing started his own restaurant, aptly named Thomas Downing's Oyster House, which was frequented by wealthy white bankers and merchants in the city. While his oyster business thrived, Downing used his restaurant to provide cover for his other work. "While he's upstairs dining and schmoozing," Damaras said, "underneath his feet, his son George is hiding people in their cupboards."

Despite New York having fully and formally abolished slavery in 1827,[*] slave catchers still roamed

---

[*] In 1799, the state began to institute "gradual emancipation." An Act for the Gradual Abolition of Slavery, 1799, stipulated that a child born to an enslaved woman would be freed but not

the streets looking for fugitive slaves—and even free Black people—to capture and bring back to the South. Slave catchers made little distinction between Black people born free and those who had run away. Parents worried desperately about their children, and for good reason. In the 1830s, a seven-year-old Black boy was "dragged from school on suspicion of being a runaway."

In the nineteenth century, Black people lived in fear that at any moment a slave catcher could snatch them or their children up, regardless of status or social position. In the twenty-first century, Black people live in fear that at any moment police will throw them against a wall, or worse, regardless of whether there is any pretense of suspicion other than the color of their skin.

Downing's story is important because the folklore around the Underground Railroad often overstates the roles of benevolent white people while undervaluing, if not completely erasing, the Black people who were involved. Blacks, both free and enslaved, were central to the abolition movement. New York–based newspapers like *The Colored American*, *Freedom's Journal*, *The Ram's Horn*,

---

until they reached their twenties—twenty-eight for men and twenty-five for women. This way slaveholders were still able to take advantage of a person's most productive years of work under the pretense of "indentured servitude."

and *The Rights of All* lifted up the voices of Black abolitionists and their allies. People like James W. C. Pennington, David Ruggles, Henry Highland Garnet, and Thomas Downing put their lives at risk every time they spoke out against slavery or harbored a fugitive. Black-run organizations, like the New York Committee of Vigilance, came together to protect runaways and Black New Yorkers from the omnipresent threat of slave catchers. As historian Manisha Sinha writes, "New York's black abolitionists kept alive the antislavery impulse even as it atrophied among white Americans."

I remember being taught as a child—sometimes implicitly though often explicitly—that abolitionists were people who wanted to both end slavery *and* extend equal rights to the formerly enslaved. As I grew older, I learned that the story is not so cleanly demarcated. There were certainly those, like the Tappan brothers, who believed in both ending slavery and supporting Black rights, but for many, the goals of antislavery and antiracism did not go hand in hand. The American Colonization Society (ACS), for example, wanted to physically remove Black people and send them to Africa. In its 1823 annual meeting, the ACS calculated that if they removed thirty thousand Black people from the country every year, the United States could completely eradicate its African American population. In 1829, the New York arm of the

ACS concluded that removing Black people from the United States was an effective way to purge the country of a "degraded population."

Others wanted to end the institution of slavery and were open to having Black people stay, contingent on maintaining the racial caste system. At the New York State Constitutional Convention of 1821, Republican delegate Peter Livingston proclaimed to other delegates, "[I]f they are dangerous to your political institutions, put not a weapon in their hands to destroy you." What Livingston meant was that Black New Yorkers could enjoy freedom from slavery, but not the right to vote. The convention would extend the franchise to all white men, while Black men were required to own two hundred fifty dollars in property, a standard the delegates knew few Black men would be able to meet. The laws put in place after this convention shaped the lives of Black New Yorkers for decades. As historian Patrick Rael writes, "Law did not merely reflect popular attitudes, it also reinforced them, lending a new explanatory power to race. It was becoming unnecessary to argue why black people were inferior; blackness itself was becoming sufficient cause for assuming inferiority."

Black abolitionists spoke out against both slavery in the South and the virulent racism that existed in their own ranks. They understood that a successful abolition movement could not simply be antislavery but had to also be founded on principles of antiracism.

The walk from the Stock Exchange to the African Burial Ground—the next stop on our tour—was about fifteen blocks, a straight shot up Broadway. During the walk I struck up a conversation with Pierre, a young man in his early twenties visiting from Hamburg, Germany. Pierre was tall and lanky with blond hair; he had a thick accent and a soft voice. We spoke about our favorite soccer players from the Bundesliga, the German professional league. He lamented that his hometown team could never seem to break into the top tier, specifically past the perennial powerhouse Bayern Munich. I asked him if they had learned about American slavery back in Germany. "Small parts in school," he said. "Normally we see it just in movies, like *12 Years a Slave*."

But you never really address it in depth? I asked.

"We have one year in school that's history of America," he said, "but it's not quite the same as..." Pierre nodded his head toward Damaras to indicate, it seemed, that he was comparing his school education to what he was learning on the tour.

Pierre's English was more than proficient but not

yet fully fluent, and he said that he was learning a lot of new information on the tour, even when he couldn't understand the details of all that was said. It was his first time in the United States, and he was surprised to learn that even today in the US not everyone was equal. He said that he had had a conversation with a Black American who told him that racism was still a big problem. "I was a little bit shocked," he said, "because normally when I hear from America a lot of people say, 'No, it's fine here.'"

Pierre continued: "Before, I have this [in] mind and hear a lot of times the words 'Everyone can do here, the American Dream,'" he said. "It's not a problem where did you come from." He searched for the right word. "It's a land where you can imagine your dreams, make your dreams." More traffic blared around us, ambulance and police and fire sirens coming from what felt like every direction.

"You want to get a job, the white people get it, you don't. Always you have to question 'Is it because of my skin tone?' ... " His voice trailed off. "I can't imagine."

Pierre turned to me. "What do you think—what is for real the problem? Why it doesn't change?"

I thought for a second and responded, "I think part of it is because there's an unwillingness to acknowledge that there's a problem."

"Unwilling?" he said, not seeming to understand the word.

"Unwilling." I thought about how to explain the idea more clearly. "People don't want to acknowledge that there is a problem in the first place." Pierre nodded.

For several blocks I talked with Pierre about poverty, housing, food insecurity, and mass incarceration, how all of these things were tied to a legacy of slavery and US apartheid.

"So I think part of why I'm interested in this kind of thing is because history is so important, because in this country we don't think about or talk about our history nearly enough," I said.

Pierre nodded again. "Yes, I think that is a big problem. You don't talk for real, about the real problems."

We kept making our way up Broadway until we turned right on Duane Street. In the middle of the block, Damaras stopped, smiled at us, and took a deep breath. Behind Damaras was the African Burial Ground National Monument, the site that contained the remains of 419 free and enslaved people of African descent, buried during the seventeenth and eighteenth centuries.

In 1697, New York City instituted "mortuary apartheid," which prohibited Black people from burying their loved ones in churchyards across lower Manhattan. The Black community, free and enslaved, was forced to bury its dead on a desolate piece of land outside the city limits. Historians estimate that this burial ground, in use from the mid-1690s to 1795, contained the remains of between ten thousand and twenty thousand free and enslaved Black people—the earliest and largest African burial ground in the country. At the end of the eighteenth century, the burial ground closed. And as the city grew, streets were paved, buildings were erected, and the burial ground was largely erased from public memory.

In 1990, the federal government prepared to erect a new $276 million, thirty-four-story office tower on this forgotten site. Per federal regulation, the government had to ascertain the archeological and environmental implications of moving forward with the project. A firm hired by the government found that the proposed building site had been the African Burial Ground but also suggested that any remains had likely been destroyed by two centuries of prior construction. The possibility that there might be any remains at all, however, compelled the government to keep looking. At first, thirty feet beneath the city streets, they found a few human bones. Then, dozens. And finally, they unearthed the intact skeletal remains of hundreds of men, women, and children that stretched across what once had been a six-acre burial ground. "Almost all of our country is a burial ground," Damaras observed as her arms swept across her body. "Go to any state in the country," she said, "and you will find the remains of people who have been here before we called this America."

After concerns were raised by Black community members about the care, or lack of care, taken during the process of excavation, the remains were ultimately transferred to the W. Montague Cobb Research Laboratory at Howard University, where they underwent extensive examination. What researchers learned was that nearly half of the remains were from children under the age of twelve. Damaras's brow furrowed, she tucked her lips inside her mouth, and she took in a deep breath, her eyes closing briefly as if she was trying to collect herself. "There are other historians in this company who talk about the children. I am way too emotional to do that," she said. Infant mortality rates in the colony were high, and infanticide—unclear if by the masters or the mothers—was a regular practice. "What I will tell you is that many enslaved children were not allowed to breastfeed," Damaras said. Some mothers were enlisted as wet nurses for white children; others were prevented from breastfeeding because they were expected to work without interruption. Damaras also told us about the damage that researchers found in the bodies of young people—including cases of osteoarthritis, a condition that normally doesn't affect people until they are beyond their fifties. But here they saw osteoarthritis in the remains of children as young as sixteen. Damaras's face, ever so briefly, became swollen with grief before she quickly recomposed herself.

Historian Christopher Moore—a descendent of Groot Manuel (or Big Manuel), who was one of the first eleven enslaved Africans brought to the city of New York—wrote that those burying their loved ones in the cemetery did their best to use traditional practices but were limited by stringent legal restrictions that dictated the lives and movements of Black people at that time. No more than twelve people were allowed to take part in funeral processions or graveside services at a given time. Burials could not take place at night, despite this being a standard element of many African burial practices. Black people who were enslaved needed a written pass to travel more than one mile away from their homes. The distance between their homes and the cemetery was often greater than one mile.

The harm done did not end after a person's funeral but continued after their death. It was not uncommon for local doctors and medical students to illegally exhume bodies from the cemetery to use them for dissections and experiments.

In 2003, after time at the lab at Howard University, the remains from the African Burial

Ground were returned to New York City in a grand ceremony. Each of the 419 sets of remains was placed in its own hand-carved coffin made in Ghana. The coffins were split between seven crypts. Each crypt—along with nearly eight thousand handwritten letters "from the living to the African ancestors"—was lowered into the ground and marked with seven burial mounds. The site was designated a National Historic Landmark in 1993, and in 2006 it was designated a National Monument by President George W. Bush.

The discovery of the African Burial Ground was central to New York having to more honestly account for its history—not sidestepping its slave-holding past—and, according to a 1993 article in the magazine *Archaeology,* "challenged the popular belief that there was no slavery in colonial New York." I looked at the burial mounds behind Damaras, observing the way they rose and fell like waves. I thought of all that lay beneath the layers of grass and soil and stone—the history, the stories. If it were not for the federal law mandating assessment prior to construction, this burial ground might have been forgotten beneath the pavement, lost under the shadow of skyscrapers. I couldn't help but wonder how many more buried, forgotten memorials there were across the country.

"I'd like to end my tour here," Damaras said. "Thank you for being uncomfortable with me."

She looked at each of us and clasped her hands together, lifting and dropping them between each word to create the effect of punctuating her remarks. "If there's anything I can leave you with, question everything. Myself, everything you read, everything you hear. Fact-check, fact-check, fact-check." She pulled her hands apart and swept them across each other. "Don't believe anything if it makes you comfortable."

Before leaving to catch my train, I asked Damaras if there was anywhere else in the city that I should visit.

"Central Park," she said. "Central Park was built on Seneca Village, which was a neighborhood for free Black people [in the nineteenth century]. That was their settlement. That was their territory," she told me. "I don't think a lot of people know that. So you go to Central Park—it's one of the most visited places in the United States of America—and people don't know they're sitting on the remains."

A few weeks later, I made my way to the corner of West 85th and Central Park West. The air was biting, and the sky was a lustrous sheet of winter grey. Steam billowed out of an open manhole surrounded by striped orange-and-white barricades. Red double-decker buses made wide left turns, and yellow taxis sped around them. On one side of the street were residential apartments listed at three to four million dollars, and on the other side was an Upper West Side entrance to Central Park. I turned into the park and ascended the asphalt walkway toward the park's interior. Two blue jays chased each other around one of the trees, dipping and whizzing between its barren branches, hiding from each other on opposite sides of the large trunk. Sparrows searched for food in the dry and frigid soil. An intermittent procession of people walked their dogs along the intersecting paths—collies, retrievers, pugs, and poodles all stretching themselves to the very ends of their leashes. Parents pushed bundled newborns in strollers, and cyclists sped down the park's main road, their bodies whistling through the wind.

I walked up to a three-sided kiosk, which told me I was standing at what was once the center of Seneca Village, an independent Black community that existed from 1825 to 1857. By 1855, the village had around 225 residents, two-thirds of whom were Black; about a third were Irish immigrants, and a small group was of German descent. Evidence based on church records suggests the community lived together peacefully, with Black and white families attending baptisms together, being buried alongside one another in the same cemetery, and intermarrying. The historical significance of Seneca Village was not simply that the Black people living there were free, or even that the community eventually became peacefully integrated; it was also that many of the Black residents owned property. Owning property gave them stability, some measure of economic security, and, as per the law passed at the 1821 Constitutional Convention, the right to vote.

The village was built after a white couple, John and Elizabeth Whitehead, who owned a significant portion of land in the area, divided their estate into smaller pieces of land and sold them as two hundred separate lots. Black New Yorkers, eager to escape the density of the city and the racism that undergirded their daily lives, jumped at the opportunity to purchase small parcels of land and build a community. The Whiteheads' first sale was to a twenty-five-year-old Black shoe shiner named Andrew Williams, who purchased three plots of land for $125. That same day, Epiphany Davis, a trustee of the African Methodist Episcopal Zion Church, purchased a dozen plots for $578. Over the next decade and beyond, Black families built homes, gardens, churches, and a school. By the 1850s, they had created a thriving community that extended from what is now 82nd Street to 89th Street and from Central Park West to Seventh Avenue. The families moving into this village knew that landownership was the gateway to electoral and political power. In 1850, there were seventy-one Black people who owned property in New York City, and one in five lived in Seneca Village.

But by the mid-1850s, as the city expanded farther and farther north, the land the village sat on became increasingly valuable. According to public historian Cynthia Copeland, wealthy New Yorkers who had traveled to Europe and seen places like the Champs-Élysées in Paris and Kensington Gardens in London believed New York should have something similar. For many, the land was valuable, but the people living on it were not. A July 1856 article in the *New-York Daily Times*, which would later become the *New York Times*, referred to the settlement as "Nigger Village." So in 1855, Mayor Fernando Wood, the same mayor who would later push for New York City to secede from the Union, used the city's power of eminent domain to make the village city property, clearing out all of the village residents, along with over a thousand other people who had settled in Central Park, including farmers and squatters. Though many residents initially resisted the order, unwilling to give up land and homes they had spent years building for what they considered paltry compensation, the people of Seneca Village were removed by force in the fall of 1857. Another *New-York Daily Times* article from about a decade later described the scene: "The supremacy of law was upheld by the policemen's bludgeons, and with many broken heads and en-sanguined eyes. Then commenced the laborers of the Park engineers and surveyors."

There are no photographs of Seneca Village. So much of what historians imagine is based on conjecture gleaned from small pieces of evidence discovered over the years. I looked around and saw two playgrounds within a hundred-yard radius of the kiosk. A young girl was flinging her legs into the sky on a swing to my left, shouting for her father to watch her soar back and forth. I thought of the families almost two centuries ago who had begun building a life on this land, and how abruptly and callously it had been taken away from them. Fifty feet from where I stood was where one of Seneca Village's churches once sat. I closed my eyes and imagined the songs echoing from a building that had been torn down and replaced by oak trees and rolling hills. I thought about the homes that had been scattered across this stretch of land, and I turned around to look at the apartments that cost millions of dollars. I walked farther into the park for a few minutes until I came across the Great Lawn, a fifty-five-acre clearing where, in the sum-mers, people picnicked, played baseball, watched concerts, threw Frisbees. I thought about how this space only existed because several generations ago hundreds of Black people were violently forced from their homes.

I walked through the park back to the street, teeming with the familiar sounds of the city. I had walked across this city so many times before, but now its untold history was unraveling all around me. Every corner cast a shadow of what it had once been. New York was unique in that, like Damaras had shared, it presented iteself to me as a place ahead of its time. The pretense of cultural pluralism told a story that was only half true. New York economically benefited from slavery, and the physical history of enslavement—the blood, the bodies, and the buildings constructed by them—was deeply entrenched in the soil of this city.

In May of 2019, a new museum opened on Liberty Island that put forward a new interpretation of the Statue of Liberty's origin—that it "was also intended, in part, to celebrate the abolition of slavery in the United States."

After going through airport-like security at the harbor's terminal, I boarded the ferry, and it rumbled its way to the island where the monument has sat for more than 130 years. It had been two decades since had I visited the Statue of Liberty, and as the ferry approached Liberty Island, I was struck by the sheer scale of it. What I quickly discovered was that no plastic replica or photograph can prepare you for how enormous the statue is—the largest in the world at the time when it was built. The details, too, were more intricate than I had remembered: the creases of her robe as it drapes over her shoulder and the folds of her sleeve as it slides down her outstretched arm; the small parts and waves in her hair; the texture of the muscles in her arms. How the crown sits like a half-sun atop her head, rays reaching into the sky. Similarly, I had never noticed the torch's golden flame, at least not as I did now. It was an image that felt at once so familiar and yet so profoundly new.

For most of my life the Statue of Liberty was one of a number of pieces of American iconography that seemed to memorialize an idea that had never materialized. It is a feeling I suspect many Black Americans experience with respect to pieces of history that commemorate an ideal of US history. What is the Declaration of Independence but a parchment of half-truths and contradictions? What is a monument to the American Revolution if it doesn't say who was kept in chains after it ended? The Statue of Liberty is an extension of a tradition that seems to embody the contradictions in America's promise, and a reminder that its promises have not always been extended to us. As the narrator in James Baldwin's 1960 short story "This Morning, This Evening, So Soon" puts it, "I would never know what this statue meant to others, she had always been an ugly joke for me."

The commonly held narrative that the statue welcomes new immigrants to America's shores was never part of its original meaning. And the idea that the statue was meant to celebrate the promise of America is only part of the story.

The man who conceived of the Statue of Liberty, Édouard René de Laboulaye, was a French law professor who was an expert on the US Constitution, as well as an ardent abolitionist. After the Civil War ended and slavery was abolished with the Thirteenth Amendment, Laboulaye proposed that France provide the United States with a gift that would both affirm their alliance and, according to the museum, lift up the cause of freedom that had manifested through emancipation. Given Laboulaye's hatred of slavery, many historians believe that the abolition of slavery was a motivating force for the project (though there is no record of him saying so explicitly). "One of the first meanings [of the statue] had to do with abolition, but it's a meaning that didn't stick," said historian and author of the book *The Statue of Liberty: A Transatlantic Story* Edward Berenson in a 2019 interview.

As Laboulaye shared his idea with friends in

France, one that he hoped might give strength to the movement for democracy back in France, he piqued the interest of sculptor Frédéric-Auguste Bartholdi, who in 1871 visited the United States, making his way from coast to coast to discuss the potential project with US leaders, including former Union general and then US president Ulysses S. Grant. In an early model of the Statue of Liberty, then known as "Liberty Enlightening the World," she was in a similar position except that in her left hand she clutched a pair of broken shackles—believed to symbolize the abolition of slavery—rather than the tablet we know today. By the time the final version of the statue emerged on US soil in 1886, the shackles were no longer in Lady Liberty's hand but had become small pieces of broken chains, less conspicuously, at her feet and partially hidden beneath her robe.

In the museum, I watched a short film outlining the statue's history. Within the first minute, the film made an explicit connection between the conception of the statue and Laboulaye's abolitionism. Farther inside the museum a number of exhibits outlined the inconsistencies of what the monument represented. The museum stated directly that for many groups—Black people, women, Chinese immigrants, and a host of others—the statue's torch of liberty did not glow for them. There was an excerpt from an 1886 editorial in the Black newspaper the *Cleveland Gazette* that read, "Shove the Bartholdi statue, torch and all, into the ocean until the 'liberty' of this country [exists for the] colored man."

I had never heard that there might be a relationship between the statue and emancipation, and I could not remember ever seeing the chains in photos or replicas of the statue. I found a park ranger who I thought might be able to help explain how the National Park Service communicated this history to its visitors.

I wanted to confirm whether or not Laboulaye had *explicitly* stated that the statue was in celebration of abolition. Choosing his words carefully, the ranger reminded me that while Laboulaye was known to everyone as a fervent abolitionist, there was a legitimate reason for the statue to have been presented in a broader, less ideological context: While Laboulaye was tasked with raising money to fund the construction of the statue, his partners in the United States were raising money to fund the construction of the pedestal. Centering the story of the statue on emancipation only a few years after slavery had been abolished in the United States, the ranger suggested, would have made fundraising significantly more difficult. Centering the story instead on France and the United States' strong friendship made for a more compelling pitch to those with money, many of whom opposed Black freedom.

Some historians believe that there is not enough evidence to make such a claim, but historian Alan Kraut, who is the chair of the committee of historians that oversees the exhibits, seemed to agree with the ranger, stating, "There is no question that feelings between North and South were severely strained in the 1870s and 1880s and the ranger was correct that a very explicit connection between the Statue and the outcome of the Civil War would have made fundraising hard in the South. However, there is little doubt that Laboulaye saw the gift as an extension of his own abolitionist sentiments. He was the president of the French anti-slavery society."

In the end, Laboulaye went with a broader, less confrontational design.

I thanked the ranger for our brief exchange and made my way back outside, toward the statue. Dozens of languages commingled in the island's crisp afternoon air. I walked to the edge of the water in front of the statue and looked up. I could see the small specks of people moving around the pedestal, providing me with a new sense of scale for the size of the statue. But from this angle, I couldn't see the statue's feet, and couldn't see the chains beside them. As I looked around the perimeter, I actually couldn't see any place from which someone would be able to see the chains. They weren't only partially hidden beneath her robe, it seemed they were fully hidden from anyone who wasn't viewing the statue from a helicopter. I looked at the tablet in Lady Liberty's left hand and considered, for a moment, how different the statue would have been, in both design and symbolism, if there were broken shackles in that hand instead.

There were only a few ferries left back to Manhattan before the park would close, so I made my way to the dock and boarded the next one, taking a seat on the boat's second level near a window. As the ferry pulled away, I peered through the glass and took one last look at the statue before it began shrinking into a distant silhouette of itself. My eyes moved to Lady Liberty's feet, and I thought I could see the faint contours of broken chains. But I might also have imagined seeing them because I finally knew they were there.

"One slave is too much"

GORÉE ISLAND

On a mild autumn morning in downtown Dakar, Senegal, I met Momar Niang, who would accompany me to Gorée Island as a translator. More than a decade ago I had come to this island and toured the famous residence that sat at its edge. Memory, for me, is often a home where the furniture has been rearranged one too many times. Years after my initial visit, I remember less about the texture of the walls in this faded-pink house and more about how the tightness of its small rooms hugged my body. I remember little of what color the sky was that day, but I remember the sound of the ocean washing over the rocks at the island's rocky perimeter. I do not remember specifically what the guide said about the people kept in these rooms, but I remember how his words poured concrete into my chest.

Momar was educated at Cheikh Anta Diop University in Dakar and is now a journalist living on the outskirts of the city. Tall and thin, he glided as he walked, his pace unhurried, his chin tilted up just so—a match for his easy smile and patient temperament. He was not bald, but he kept his hair cut close to his scalp, and a thin mustache sat above his lips. English was his third language—as it is for many people in Dakar who count the local Wolof and French as the primary means of communication—and he spoke with a fluency that was in contrast to my bumbling, inelegant French.

I studied French in school for many years, but a decade of using the language sparingly had rendered it unfamiliar; it met my tongue awkwardly. The French spoken in Senegal carries the crown of Wolof on every syllable. Sentences are a carousel of language, the words wrapping around one another before drifting apart again. It took a while to reacquaint myself with the intimacy of the language's movements, the memory of how my mouth was meant to curl and bend in ways English did not require.

Downtown Dakar was bustling and vibrant. Sauntering bodies jostled at the edges of dusty street corners while cars swept between one another, coiling the road in a garland of exhaust. Minibuses teeming with passengers swerved around corners with alacrity and precision, their exteriors bursting with color, the blues, yellows, oranges, and reds bleeding together as they accelerated by. People crossed the street with purpose, moving between the taxis and minibuses they presumed would stop for them. The smell of baguettes and roasted nuts snuck through the exhaust, letting my body know that the apple I had eaten for breakfast was not enough. Every sound, every smell, was a layer of fog lifting itself to reveal a memory I had forgotten was there.

As we walked through downtown, Momar, who was thirty-nine, said, "I've never been to the slave house before." His voice was coated with the texture of cigarette smoke. I turned my head toward him as we stopped on the curb of the street before crossing. "I guess it was shameful for me," he added.

To get to Gorée Island we took a ferry from the edge of Dakar across a small slice of Atlantic Ocean. The traffic circles near the harbor spun in an unceasing cycle, the cars' sharp horns an orchestra of vibrant noise. When we arrived at the docking station, we found a room of tourists, vendors, and schoolchildren bringing the cavernous space to life.

There were no seats left in the room, so Momar and I stood in a corner toward the back. I returned our conversation to what he had said before, that he had felt too ashamed to go to the Maison des Esclaves, or House of Slaves.

"I don't know exactly why," he said, his voice searching. "Maybe I was intimidated by the fact of seeing chains, and the rustling of chains. It's a very sad history. And not visiting for me is maybe to try to forget the story."

More people streamed into the room, and Momar posited a counterfactual. "Sometimes I will ask myself a question: I could be now an American...my ancestors, I could be part of those who had been taken away." I thought of how a family, separated by an ocean, would have the arc of their lineages forever changed.

"[It's] a problem of fate or destiny," Momar added. "I'm also seeing that we have a link with Black Americans and they come from Africa. And if you see a Black American and his ancestors had the misfortune to be captured by the slave master, here in Africa, we should not say that we were lucky. No, we were not lucky. It's a tragedy. It's a real tragedy."

Even though Momar had thus far been unable to bring himself to visit the House of Slaves, he told me that he knew he and his country must forcefully confront the story it tells. "We should not shy away from it. We have to study this story. This is a part of our collective memory. And also to introduce all the coming generations to this story in a very unbiased way. What I mean is, we have to talk about the responsibility of the colonizers, those who [came] to take slaves and brought them to the Americas and Brazil, et cetera. But also it is the responsibility of Africans."

I asked Momar how the history of the slave trade was taught in Senegalese schools. He said the topic was not discussed in as much depth as it needed to be. "We have to identify in the curriculum somehow, some special classes dedicated to slavery. And that it should be done at the primary stage and not waiting to when you are in high school, because it's very important. And I think if you are introduced to the story earlier, this is the best way." Otherwise, he said, people fail to understand the historical realities that shaped the history and trajectory of the country.

When the ferry arrived, everyone moved briskly through the door leading to the dock. At the edge of the dock, the ferry rose and fell in the water. It was a medium-sized white vessel with two levels that looked as if it might hold about two hundred people, as long as half of those people were willing to stand. A cloth awning stretched tightly over the top of the boat as the ship moved with steady force over the water, the engine's unremitting hum vibrating under our feet.

It took about fifteen minutes to cross over from the mainland to the island. Stepping off the boat, I encountered a landscape of startling beauty. The homes on the island were arranged in uneven rows of weathered pastels. Yellow peeling into green. Orange washing into pink. Blue flaking off to reveal the eggshell underneath. Green vines climbed the sides of the buildings' stone walls, and each of the houses' rooftops was a coronet of red shingles. Clothes dangled from lines of laundry, a necklace of wet garments stringing the houses together. Behind the homes, a cluster of lush trees ascended a hill toward the highest point of the island. Palm trees on the water's edge whipped themselves into a gentle frenzy, and along the island's waterfront stood a stretch of restaurants serving poulet yassa, thiébou yapp, and mafé poisson. In striking contrast to the busy city just three kilometers behind us, no cars are allowed on the small island. The sound of the ocean was the backdrop for all conversations.

From an aerial view, Gorée Island looks like a small hook. The Portuguese arrived on the island as early as the 1440s, and set up a trading post there not long after. Its position just off the west coast of the Senegambia region made it a place of strategic importance for trade, and a place where European ships could restock supplies before leaving the continent. European powers spent two centuries fighting for control of Gorée, which was occupied in succession by the Portuguese, Dutch, British, and French. As the island's colonizers changed, so did its name. The Senegalese called the island Ber. The Portuguese called it Ila de Palma. The Dutch changed its name to Goede Reede, meaning "good port." The French, who officially took charge of the territory in 1677 and who would largely maintain control until Senegalese independence in 1960, amended it to Île de Gorée.

The island was a site of the slave trade from the sixteenth century, when it was under Portuguese control and slaves were part of its economy, until 1848, when, under French control, France abolished slavery in all of its colonies. For decades Gorée Island was thought of as the central point of departure for enslaved people leaving West Africa and headed to the New World. It was also a place from which captured Africans could not easily escape, as the small body of land was surrounded by water. So sweeping was its global reputation that in 1978 the United Nations Educational, Scientific, and Cultural Organization (UNESCO) named Gorée a World Heritage Site. In the more than forty years since it received that designation, it has become an even more popular site of interest for tourists visiting the region and of pilgrimage for those attempting to reckon with the history of chattel slavery.

In 1981, Michel Rocard, who would later become the French prime minister, visited the House of Slaves, and after being shown the place where the bodies were said to be held before their final departure, he said, "It is not easy for a white man, in all honesty, to visit this Slave House without feeling ill at ease."

Renowned activist Angela Davis visited the island in 1990, writing in the House of Slaves guest book, "To return home; to relive the profound suffering of my ancestors; to know that humanity's worst crimes were committed at this site. It must never happen again."

Pope John Paul II visited the island in 1992 and went on to ask forgiveness for the role Christians had played in maintaining and perpetuating the slave trade.

The island has been visited by US presidents Bill Clinton, George W. Bush, and Barack Obama. On his 2013 visit with his family, President Obama wrote in the site's guest book, "We are grateful for the opportunity to learn more about the painful history of the slave trade, and to help remind us of the need to remain vigilant on behalf of the rights of all humankind."

As Momar and I stepped from the dock onto the island, we and anyone else who looked even vaguely like a foreigner were inundated with people offering to take us on a tour of the island. We were stopped by a man who told us that we needed to go to a small building on our left to pay a tax for the island, which left us confused because there were groups of people walking by who were not being stopped and directed that way. Not wanting to make a big deal of it, we went to the small station to our left, where we paid a woman a small tax of 500 CFA francs, the equivalent of a little less than a dollar. At this station, we asked one of the men near us if he knew where the House of Slaves was located. The man nodded and said he would bring us there. What we did not realize was that he had now taken on the role of our guide.

Sam was tall with dark skin and transition-lens glasses that gave him an enigmatic air. He wore a long white boubou with gold trim and a pair of blue shoes coated in a thin layer of dust. Sam did not speak much English, so Momar translated as we discussed the history and aesthetics of the island.

I told Sam that we didn't necessarily need the "full tour" of the island, much of which entailed bringing us to different artists and vendors who would attempt to sell us their work. While their art was often beautiful, I had come here for a specific reason; I hoped Sam might simply show us where the House of Slaves was. He did little to hide his disappointment but signaled for us to follow him.

When we arrived at the House of Slaves, the first thing I saw was a pair of staircases.

The symmetrical curves of both staircases were bordered by faded pink half walls that served as handrails. Open to the elements, the stone was worn from years of weather and thousands of grazing hands. Stone columns at the top of the staircases held up the roof while behind sat a row of white French doors, their shutters open like an invitation. The house was undergoing renovations when we visited, and the workers continued their construction while visitors made their way through the rest of the structure. Sawdust spilled between the cracks of wood-paneled ceilings, golden flecks dancing downward in soft spirals. Wheelbarrows full of wet concrete cackled over the cobbled stones; the percussion of hammers hitting nails reverberated in the air.

The House of Slaves was once the residence of a woman named Anna Colas Pépin. Pépin was what was then known as a *signare,* a term used to describe a wealthy African or mixed-race French-African woman, often the wife of a European man—an alliance that ushered *signares* into a higher social class than Africans. *Signares,* including Pépin, often owned and traded enslaved people themselves.

In 1960, when Senegal became independent of France, President Léopold Sédar Senghor encouraged Boubacar Joseph Ndiaye, who lived on the island, to begin research on the house and its relationship to the slave trade. Ndiaye renamed the residence the Maison des Esclaves, or House of Slaves, and served as its curator from 1962 until his death in 2009. Historian Deborah Mack writes that it was Ndiaye who came up with the concept of the Door of No Return, which serves as the centerpiece of Gorée's story.

The Door of No Return is a famous symbol of the slave trade, appearing at historical sites across the western coast of Africa. The story goes that it was through these doors, looking out onto the Atlantic, that millions of enslaved Africans walked as they boarded ships that would bring them into bondage on the other side of the ocean.

Momar, Sam, and I were not alone in the house. The other groups of people spoke softly to one another in a range of different languages, their respective guides gesturing to different elements of the house. Directly across from me, I saw the Door of No Return opened toward the sea.

My toes reached out over the door's edge as the breeze from the ocean swept in and tickled my ears. The air tasted of salt and sun while the blue-green water of the Atlantic glittered in the midday light. Small flecks of mist jumped from the rocks and kissed my cheeks. Seagulls traced the shore-line with their shadows, their bodies hovering just above the water. I watched as dozens of them lifted their beaks, rose, tucked their wings, and plunged their bodies into the ocean, then rose back out of the water, some with small fish wriggling in their mouths. The thrum of the ferry's engine pulsed in the distance, with a smattering of smaller fishing boats circling the island in search of a place to cast their nets. Beneath me, low tide washed over the rocks on the shore, the stones' once-sharp edges rounded by the centuries-long kiss of salt water. I stood and looked at these rocks, at this shoreline, losing track of time staring into the ocean. I eventually stepped back from the door, my own shadow evaporating into the wall as my body moved away from the light.

On either side of the door were two narrow rooms where, Sam said, enslaved people were held before being forced onto slave ships. As I did in the old prison cell at Angola, I extended my arms between the walls. Here, my elbow touched one wall while the fingers at the end of my opposite arm grazed the other side. The stone wall was both dirty and wet, leaving my fingertips marked with a thin layer of black grime. I placed the heels of my feet at the base of the wall at one end of the room and walked until my toes hit the wall on the other side: I counted six steps. Though it was the middle of the day, the chamber was bathed in darkness, but for the light that crept in from two long, thin openings in the exterior wall. The wind cut through those small gaps and pierced the air inside.

Outside the rooms, Sam pointed to a small opening in a wall beneath a set of stairs with CELLULE DES RECALCITRANTS written over the top of it. This is where they kept the slaves who resisted, Momar translated for me. It was too dark to tell what it looked like. I turned on my phone's flashlight, bent down, and scooted inside. The stone seemed to almost absorb the light, so it still felt dark inside the shallow cavern. I waited for my eyes to adjust to the darkness. They did not. I hugged my knees close to my chest as I sat inside. The joints in my knees and ankles cracked. Dirt fell from the wall where I touched it. It was impossible to feel as if the walls weren't closing in on me. I thought of people being held here, how they might barely have been able to see their hands in front of their faces. How they would have been able to taste the salt water that hung in the air without seeing any of the ocean. I thought of all the times I had heard "But why didn't they fight back?" when slavery was discussed in my classes. I thought of the bell at plantations like the Whitney, which had been rung to tell the enslaved people to gather round and watch one of their loved ones being lashed until they bled. I thought of the rooms in Angola's Red Hat cell block, how the smallness of those spaces had closed in on me. The cramped cavern might have been where the lessons on first resistance had taken place in a person's earliest days of enslavement. Where spirits and bodies had been broken.

I found Eloi Coly, the curator and site manager of the House of Slaves, behind a desk covered with stacks of books, newspapers, notepads, and a small Senegalese flag near a telephone at the desk's corner. The walls of the room were pink, like the rest of the house, the paint's worn coat peeling to reveal the grey-white concrete underneath. Around us were photographs of famous visitors who had made their way here, many of them capturing Eloi shaking their hands or guiding them around the house. Eloi had a large frame and wore a gold-green boubou with a pattern of red stripes intersecting with one another. He was bald with thick glasses, the small streaks of sun gleaming off his head and reflecting from his eyes. Slices of light peeked into the room, sneaking past a thin blue curtain. Momar took a seat in the corner of the room, and Sam waved goodbye and went on his way.

Eloi began his career at one of the biggest high schools in Dakar as a cultural advisor, and in the mid-1980s he became assistant curator of the House of Slaves. After the 2009 passing of his longtime supervisor, Boubacar Joseph Ndiaye,

Eloi became the curator. As of our conversation, he had been working at the site for about thirty-five years, making the House of Slaves and Gorée Island the center of his life. Even though he has the option to live in Dakar, as many of the people who work on the island do, he instead has chosen to live next door to the house.

Living in such proximity to the house allows Eloi to fully live his commitment to ensure that this site is a place where people are made to confront the history of the transatlantic slave trade. "I believe that it's very important to keep the memory," he said to me directly in English, preferring not to use Momar. "How to keep this memory and how to teach what's happened. How to talk more about all of the violations of human rights."

Eloi told me that the island was not originally a place Europeans intended to use to capture and sell enslaved Africans. As I had read, Gorée was coveted by European nations because of its strategic value as a trading post for the alleged trove of resources in West Africa. "The purpose was not to find slaves," he said. "The purpose was discovery.

"Many of the other European nations came to Gorée Island to fight each other, just so they could occupy the place," he told me. It wasn't until the inception of slavery in the Americas, Eloi said, that the purpose of Gorée Island changed. "After

the discovery of America, because of the development of sugarcane plantations, cotton, coffee, rice
cultivation, they forced the [Native Americans] to
work for them. And it was because the Natives
died in great number that they turned to Africa,
and the purpose was to replace these Natives with
Africans."

As slavery became central to the economic prosperity of the United States, increasing numbers of
Africans were imported from the Senegambia region. I thought back to something Yvonne Holden
had told me during my tour of the Whitney
Plantation, how many of the enslaved people in
southern Louisiana were from the Senegambia
region and how they possessed specific knowledge
about cultivating rice and indigo seeds. It was
not impossible, I thought, that someone who had
passed through a door on Gorée Island would
have ended up on the Whitney Plantation.

As the desire for enslaved people increased, Europeans had to justify the human plunder. In order
to rationalize taking a person from their home,
separating them from their family, and shipping
them across an ocean to work in a system of intergenerational bondage, Eloi said, these Europeans
could not see these Africans as people. "They considered Black Africans not as human beings but
as a simple merchandise. If they consider Africans
as merchandise, that is because they understand

the necessity to dehumanize Africans in order to work for the acceptance by all the Europeans. The necessity to use Africans because Africans are not human beings."

Eloi continued, noting that this heinous industry required partnerships with leaders of certain African tribal groups. "During the sixteenth century, Africans used only arrows, not firearms. So the Europeans came with firearms, alcohol, and iron they [would] give to the African tribes living in and along the coast." Eloi said that during the African tribal wars various factions fought one another. The white Europeans were more than happy to give guns to these different groups. They cared less about who was fighting than about the payment they received in exchange: humans, the prisoners of war who had been captured from other tribes. "The only currency that was accepted by Europeans," Eloi said, his voice punctuating each word, "was slaves." This created a cycle in which certain tribes were encouraged to capture even more prisoners of war, in order to sell those prisoners to the Europeans for more guns and other goods.

Eloi wanted to make clear, however, that this was not necessarily a widespread practice. "Not all Africans were involved in the slave trade," he said. Many, he told me, organized themselves to resist the Europeans and fought to maintain sovereignty and control over their land and their people. He also rejected the idea that Africans were as culpable as their European counterparts. "It was the Europeans who organized this," he said. "[Africans] didn't know what the final destination was."

Eloi sees himself as part of a movement that is not only helping the world to reckon with the history of the slave trade but also helping Senegal present a history that does not begin with slavery and colonization. Eloi wants the public discourse to account for the continent's extensive history, a history that began before Western exploitation. "In Senegal, we are rewriting the history on Senegal from the origin until now. But it is something very difficult. They told us that Black is nothing." His voice hovered over the final word. "They try to forget that things start in Africa," he said. "The slave trade or colonization was not the starting point of Africa."

This forgetting, Eloi said, has deleteriously affected the collective self-esteem of African peoples. He noted that Senegal, along with other West African countries, has to make sure that it teaches a history that highlights who Black people were before slavery and who they are in spite of it. "We have to use education to deconstruct, in order to reconstruct," he said. "Africans have to know that the starting point was Africa."

When I first arrived in Senegal in 2009, I was told that millions of people passed through the Door of No Return on their way to the New World—a story that hundreds of thousands of visitors to Gorée have been told for decades and one promoted by the House of Slaves' original curator, Boubacar Joseph Ndiaye. The claim did not end with Ndiaye; it was an assertion supported by the United Nations agency UNESCO, which at the time of this writing still states on its World Heritage listing for Gorée Island that "[f]rom the 15th to the 19th century, it was the largest slave-trading centre on the African coast."

After additional research, however, it has become clear that these numbers were deeply inaccurate. Scholars now estimate that it was closer to 33,000 enslaved people who passed through Gorée. To be sure, 33,000 people is an extraordinary number, but it is not consistent with the millions originally said to have passed through the House of Slaves alone. The island of Gorée hosted a mélange of people, including domestic enslaved people, captured enslaved people meant for transit to the New World, free Africans, *signares,* slave traders, and soldiers. It was not singularly used as a mechanism of the slave trade.

Louis Nelson, an architectural historian and vice provost at the University of Virginia who has spent time working at Gorée, would later tell me,

"In our assessment of that building, we found one chamber that was likely the holding cell for human beings would have held maybe fifteen or twenty people at a max," though the story often told on the island was that some of them held hundreds. Nelson had been part of an international team of researchers who conducted research on the island and studied the House of Slaves and its history in partnership with local curators. "There also were pens, so there were dedicated buildings on Gorée for the containment of large numbers of people. And then lastly, those people are going to be marched in coffles down to the docks. So that Door of No Return that you stood in, that Barack Obama stood in, and that the pope stood in"—he paused briefly—"that door probably never really led to ships." His voice dropped an octave. More likely, he said, "that was the place where waste was thrown into the sea."

I brought the numbers up with Eloi, who paused, looking, it seemed, for the right words. "You know that in this small island of Gorée, the slave house where we are is not the only one. During the full period of slavery there were more than twenty houses like this. But this one belonged to the Senegalese state, who purchased this house to better know exactly what's happened during the slave trade. That's why, today, the slave house crystallizes all of the slave trade." He looked at me, head down, eyes peering over his glasses. "It's a *symbol* of the slave trade."

I could not tell if Eloi was intentionally side-stepping or if he had not fully understood because of the language barrier. I asked Eloi again, about the discrepancy in numbers from scholars and the story that had long been told at the House of Slaves.

"The number of slaves is not important when you talk about memory," he said. "When we talk about memory, we have to stand in the principles. One slave is too much."

There are scholars who agree with Eloi. When considering the story of Gorée Island, historical anthropologist François Richard finds it helpful to use a term coined by the renowned sociologist Pierre Bourdieu, calling Gorée a site of "sincere fiction." According to Richard, the statistical controversy of Gorée Island cannot and should not undermine its place as a site of memory and reckoning. Richard told the *Washington Post* that he believes "turning the question of international slavery into a statistical exercise is not the most useful way to think about it, and sadly that legacy has clouded academic debates more than it has helped."

I continued to try to get clarification. "So, you see the slave house as a symbol of something that was a much broader phenomenon. It is a place where we can remember and reckon with and learn about and think about the history of slavery?"

"Yes," Eloi said with a sigh that fell somewhere between frustration and relief.

Eloi's point could apply to historical sites across the world. The physical place, the land people come and stand upon, is an entry point to a much broader history, of which any single location is but one piece. Eloi believes that every country in West Africa should have a gathering place like this one to memorialize history. He described it as "a place of remembrance."

I couldn't help but think about whether that symbolism of Gorée was undermined by the inaccuracies that undergirded it. There were still people on Gorée sharing information with tourists as if the data was unimpeachable. In truth, this data has been disputed by scholars for years now. How could this place be a symbol of history but fail to ensure the history that it conveyed was factual?

Nelson told me later, "Eloi bears a responsibility, socially and culturally, to affirm the legacy of the position he inherited. And to simply dispense with or unseat a legacy that the nation looks to is not done easily." His language was deliberate, long silences punctuating every few words. "He was given this story and given the responsibility of shepherding and stewarding this very important site for national identity, national consciousness. And to completely invert that would be a very difficult thing to do."

Nelson also said that it is important for European and American scholars to be careful and consider whether there is a responsibility to be deferential to local interpretations. To come into a place one doesn't have any familial or cultural connection to, and upend the story it has told for decades, is likely to be more harmful than helpful. The story of Gorée, Nelson said, is not as simple as which empirical evidence is "correct" or "incorrect." There are a range of ethical, cultural, and social factors to consider when interpreting the historical significance of a site like the House of Slaves.

"I think one has to tread very carefully in the dissemination of that alternative interpretation, because to do so I think actually bears the ethical responsibility of relationship building," Nelson said. "If you're going to purport to tell the history of a place, you need to have relationships of trust in that place. I just think that that's a fundamental operational commitment."

Historian Ana Lucia Araujo told me that the story of the House of Slaves could be traced back to the original curator, Boubacar Joseph Ndiaye. Ndiaye, she noted, sought to fill a gap in the world's collective memory when there was little social will or physical infrastructure to catalyze this memory.

Ndiaye, she said, started playing the role of witness. "We do not have anybody who witnessed the Atlantic slave trade among us anymore," she told me after I had returned from my trip, whereas something like the Holocaust had victims who were, and still are, able to tell us this story.

It is not necessarily that Araujo thinks Ndiaye was willfully untruthful. In the 1960s, when this story began to emerge, there was little evidence to undergird or corroborate any of the claims. The story took on a life of its own, independent of empirics. Araujo likes to think of Ndiaye as a sort of griot, a person who used the power of storytelling to force people to confront a larger history many had forgotten, or were willing to ignore. "He would guide people, and generated this kind of emotion," she said. The problem was, this story—embedded within a larger social, cultural, and political project—became the official narrative repeated across the world. Soon, the story Ndiaye told was being supported by official bodies like UNESCO, lending ostensible validation to the story even when there wasn't evidence to support the numbers it purported.

"This is the problem of the memory of slavery, that we have all these gaps," Araujo said. "And you need to fill those gaps with something."

It isn't only Senegal that struggles with what reckoning looks like, Araujo reminded me. When

Araujo first came to the US from Brazil, she was struck by how the homes of presidents like Washington and Jefferson were privately owned and operated rather than being run by the National Park Service. From her perspective, this makes it difficult for the US to tell a cohesive story about its past, as each place can situate itself in the past in its own way. "In other words, they can tell the story they want," she said. "And I think that from this point of view, we have no grounds to judge what is being done elsewhere."

Eloi had been to the United States on a number of occasions and recalled a particular trip he took that was sponsored by the National Trust for Historic Preservation. This trip included a tour through different historical sites in the South. The experience, he recounted, helped him better understand the connection between West Africans and Black people in the Southern United States. "A part of the African heritage combined with what they found overseas. And that is what gives us African American culture."

Eloi said that he also visited several plantations while he was there. I asked him what had stayed with him following his visit. He was struck by what he referred to as the "continuation of the dehumanization of Africans." He said, "The problem that they have in the plantations is that they continue to tell more about the owner of the property, but they didn't focus on what has happened to the slaves. That is why it is difficult in the plantations to interest African Americans."

I told him about the Whitney Plantation's attempt to turn that narrative on its head. He was familiar with their work, he said, and hoped to come to the United States to visit the Whitney and the National Museum of African American History and Culture in Washington, DC. He hopes Gorée Island will be able to partner with plantations like the Whitney in order to provide visitors with both the point of origin and the destination of the transatlantic slave trade, helping them to understand how this happened, and why we cannot let it ever happen again. Eloi believes this work is essential in combatting the dominant narratives that have shaped our world's understanding of what slavery was.

He leaned back in his chair and crossed him arms. "History is written by the perpetrators," he said. And his goal is to be a part of writing something that challenges that.

Momar and I decided to get some lunch before leaving on the last ferry of the day. We walked through a series of narrow alleyways, pebbles crunching under our feet. On a street near the northern tip of the island, Momar stopped me and pointed to a sign that read RUE DE BOUFFLERS. "This road is named after [Stanislas de] Boufflers," Momar said. Boufflers was the French colonial governor of Senegal in the late eighteenth century.

"And there is currently a debate among civil society, which is directed around the fact that we should rename the streets of Dakar because all the streets are named after some French personalities, who were here during colonization." Momar transitioned from an observational tone to an assertive one. "It's time to give to our streets the name of our heroes, because we *do* have heroes in Africa."

As Momar spoke, a little boy, who could have been only five or six, rounded the corner, chasing the call of his mother several paces ahead of him. Momar nodded in the boy's direction. "It's time to change, and the change should begin [with] the symbols, because the young boy will soon ask, 'Who is Boufflers?'"

As I watched that little boy turn the corner, and as I listened to Momar, I thought of how at that moment there might be little Black boys just like this one in New Orleans, running down a street named after Robert E. Lee. How there might have been little Black girls in Mississippi running down roads named after Nathan Bedford Forrest. How there might have been Black children in Georgia wandering down streets named after Jefferson

Davis. I thought about the parallels between the debate in Senegal over the remnants of colonialism and the debate in the United States over the remnants of slavery.

"It's like the conversation that we're having in the US about the Confederate monuments," I said to Momar. "The monuments are statues of people who fought the war for the South to keep slavery, but they're up all over. People say, 'Why are these statues up of people who were fighting to keep slavery? That doesn't make any sense.' So people are trying to get them taken down now. That's our version."

"It's very similar," he said, nodding. He told me about a controversy that had played out at a university in Ghana the year before, surrounding a statue of Mahatma Gandhi, who—he paused and laughed in anticipation of the euphemism he was about to use—"talked badly" about Black people. "And you know the students came one day to put down the statue, and there is a whole lot of fuss in the university and some people were against it. You know, 'This guy's, like, he's a racist and we have to take it off.'"*

---

* "Kaffirs are as a rule uncivilized," wrote Gandhi in 1908, using a derogatory word for Black South Africans. (Joseph Lelyveld, *Great Soul: Mahatma Gandhi and His Struggle with India* [New York: Vintage Books, 2021], 54.) His biographer Ramachandra Guha

He continued: "We even are saying the same thing in Senegal because our ancient capital city is in Saint-Louis, and in the very middle of the city you've got a statue of Governor [Louis] Faidherbe, and people are saying, 'No, this is not good. We are now independent since 1960.'" Saint-Louis, as was common for many parts of the French colonial project, was named after the French king Louis IX. Momar believes these names, these symbols, and these statues hang like a weight around his country's neck. "We have to take all this"—he stretched his arms wide and looked up at the street sign again—"all that is supposed to symbolize the French domination. They should be separated."

As we rode the ferry back to Dakar, a smoky dusk was settling over the city's skyline. An endless swathe of construction projects shot dirt and cement powder up toward the clouds, knitting the horizon in threads of orange and brown. Water lapped against the front of the boat as it pushed forward, the small white waves it made moving outward before disappearing into the endless blue.

says that Gandhi was indeed racist in his early life but contends that he outgrew those views as he got older.

I had one more day in Senegal and wanted to go back to Gorée. Momar agreed to accompany me again, and as we waited for the ferry to arrive early the next morning, the day's new light softened everything it touched. I asked Momar what his impression of Gorée Island had been yesterday.

He took a deep breath and leaned forward in his chair, placing his elbows on his thighs. "Yes, quite a discovery," he said. "I was very struck by the place, and how the walls are wet, and how the rooms are small and tiny. And I was just searching myself, at the place of those who have suffered." He looked to his left and his right as if to mime what he had done in the house yesterday. "I was putting myself back in the seventeenth century. I was trying to imagine on how we can treat the human being like this, and how we can pack so many people in such small places. And all around it's like I can feel the pain myself."

Momar had been cautious, it seemed—taking something in and then stepping back as if to avoid psychological and sensory overload.

In the docking station, a baby near us cooed in discomfort. Her mother cradled the new child, readjusting her arms and bouncing her gently. Momar told me that he kept thinking of the children ensnared in slavery's grip. He said he couldn't imagine the speed with which illness would have spread, or the fear that these children would have felt. He became quiet again and stared at a spot ahead of us on the floor. We waited for the ferry to arrive.

We walked through a series of alleyways and past homes that signaled we were leaving the tourist-centered part of the island. The school we were visiting sat at the eastern edge of the island, and I marveled at its backdrop, how the ocean water caught and held the light when the sun was at its peak, how you could not tell the difference between where the ocean ended and the sky began. Founded in 1977 by the newly independent country's first president, Léopold Sédar Senghor, and named after the acclaimed Senegalese author and feminist Mariama Bâ, the Maison d'Education Mariama Bâ, with an all-female student population, is one of the top boarding schools in Senegal. Around us the sound of schoolchildren transitioning between classes consumed the air, their sandals shuffling along the sandy floors, desks being dragged across classrooms, backpacks zipping and being flung over shoulders.

Hasan Kane is the school's history teacher. He met us in a lush courtyard, wearing an orange-and-yellow plaid short-sleeved shirt tucked into a pair of dark brown khakis. His voice was soft and his eyes were wide, and light gleamed off the top of his dark scalp. Hasan exuded a calmness we hope for in anyone teaching young people, his voice holding space for both patience and conviction. He led us into an empty classroom on the second floor, where we sat around the desk at the front. Hasan spoke English well, but I still had trouble capturing the specific nuances of what he was attempting to say in his third language. I told him to communicate in whatever language best allowed him to express his sentiments, and if it was French, Momar would simply translate for me. Hasan began our conversation in English, then switched to French, with Momar intermittently pausing him in order to effectively translate.

Hasan said he was constantly attempting to find a balance: helping his students understand the heinous implications of slavery without letting them fall into a state of paralysis. It was important that this history be taught, he thought, but the end result could not be young people thinking of themselves or their ancestors solely as oppressed, exploited people who could never escape the legacy of Western subjugation. He wanted his students to understand it, but he did not want them to be defined by it. "It's important to go beyond this view between victims and perpetrators," he said, adding that tackling this history would help students understand the implications of slavery in the present day.

Echoing Eloi, Hasan emphasized a central part of his pedagogy: teaching his students that Africa's history did not begin with slavery. "You must," he said, "present how Africa was before slavery, and how it is during slavery, and how it is after slavery."

Hasan continued: "If you want to understand the economic situation in Africa, you have to understand what happened during slavery and how slavery has got a huge impact, because slavery has deprived us of the first input for development, which is the human force. We have to understand how colonization impacted negatively on our situation, and also how slavery deprived Africa of its workforce."

Part of what Hasan teaches his students is that we cannot understand slavery and colonialism as two separate historical phenomena. They are inextricably linked pieces of history. Slavery took a toll on West Africa's population; millions of people were stripped from their homelands and sent across the ocean to serve in intergenerational bondage. The profound harm continued during colonialism, with much of the continent stripped of its natural resources instead of its people. Hasan reflected, "In both situations, in slavery and colonization, what you have is a system of plunder.

First, in slavery, we have a plunder of human beings. Africa had been ripped of its people. And colonization is a plunder of natural resources. We have been exploited by the colonizers. On both systems, what you have is a plunder system."

In Hasan's voice, I could hear the echoes of Walter Rodney, the Guyanese historian and political activist who wrote, in his 1972 book *How Europe Underdeveloped Africa,* "[E]very African has a responsibility to understand the system and work for its overthrow." What Hasan was doing was providing his students with the guidance to understand the history of their country so they might build something better.

There is a phrase that Hasan believed captured the essence of the entanglement of capitalism, colonialism, and slavery: "White sugar means Black misery." He said, "If Europe is what it is nowadays, it's because of the blood and the efforts of Africans who have been taken to America to work on plantations and generate profits. It favored the industrial development of Europe, since part of Europe's development was made possible by the fact that we [sent] to America slaves who worked hard to create development. That's the root of Europe's current development."

I was curious to hear what he thought of reparations—what might it mean for his people to be compensated for the lives stolen and resources plundered? Hasan took in a deep breath and tucked his lips into his mouth before speaking. "It's still a debate here, and opinions are diverse," he said in English, not using Momar to translate this time.

Hasan emphasized that the question was not whether his country *deserved* reparations but, not unlike the debate in the United States, "What are we going to repair?" Hasan was not opposed to figuring out the logistics of financial compensation, but he emphasized the need for a sort of moral compensation. "Some people prefer a sense of memory," he said. "Once you get money, you say, 'Okay. Now you received money. We repaired everything. Don't talk about it anymore.'" That is not the outcome Hasan wants. What he wants is an apology for what happened, and then to have that apology, that reckoning, inform how economic, cultural, and political decisions are made moving forward.

Hasan noted that the question of compensation is complicated. When we begin to excavate the intricate web of people and processes that constituted the slave trade, there is a vast range of individuals whom one might deem responsible for its expansion and perpetuation.

"For example, kings who were selling prisoners to the slave nations. This is also a question that we should bear in mind," he said. "The first

Europeans who came, they did not know the interior, and they collaborated with kingdoms that
were near the coast. They gave them weapons and
some means, and they go inside the country, deep
in the country, to take slaves, to capture people
and bring them to the coast, and sold them as
slaves to European boats."

I asked Hasan how he communicated this history
to his students, and he told me that you must teach
the entire history, not just part of it. "When you
say before children that millions of Black people
have been sold as slaves, naturally the reaction of
these children is to say, 'Who sold them?' That's
why it's important. You cannot bypass this aspect
of the history . . . That's why it's important that we
clarify all the responsibilities."

Given this, I was curious how Hasan weighed
the question of responsibility. While there may
have been multiple parties participating, did he
think each party was equally culpable? Hasan was
quick to answer: "The idea came from Europe,
and Europe in that sense is more responsible than
Africans." Still, he said, it doesn't mean that it
should be a part of history that is glossed over. It
has to be addressed.

Not all students in Senegal have teachers like
Hasan, and not all students attend schools like
Mariama Bâ. At many schools across the country,
history is still sometimes taught in ways that center

Europeans and that fail to account for the longer, richer histories of African people. Hasan said it is important that the country develop a curriculum so students can develop a holistic understanding of what slavery and colonialism did to their country and their continent. This, he said, is essential, because knowing their history helps them to more effectively identify the lies the world tells about Africa. It equips students with an intellectual and historical tool kit, so they won't accept and internalize the idea that Africa has no history, that Africa's poverty is its own fault, that Africa would be better off if it were under European control. "If they know that the arguments are false," he said, "they will know that all the rest also is false."

I was struck by the parallels between how Ibrahima Seck, the director of research at the Whitney Plantation, spoke about the role of history and how Hasan was speaking about it now. They had similar conceptions as to how teaching history, a full history, would shape how students navigated the world. They were acutely aware that this knowledge gave their students new eyes, a new sense of freedom and understanding—the ability to know the lie, so they could not be lied to anymore. I told Hasan that what he was telling me made me think of my trip to the Whitney Plantation in Louisiana, and his eyes got wide. He asked me if I knew Ibrahima Seck.

I told him I had indeed met Seck and that I had spoken to him when I went there in those months before coming to Gorée.

Hasan smiled. That's my best friend, he told me. He and Seck used to teach together at a high school in Dakar.

The wind howled off the shore and we all smiled together as the sun moved higher into the midday sky.

After my conversation with Hasan, I asked him if I might be able to speak with some students. We made our way up a flight of stairs to another class-room, where he introduced us to a group of seven young women who were studying between classes. The room was filled with natural light and a dozen wooden desks, some with brown plastic chairs attached to them and others attached to a small wooden bench. Each of the girls was wearing the uniform required of students—navy-blue dresses with white oxford blouses underneath. Four of the girls wore head wraps that covered their hair, others had their hair showing, with thin braids stretching across their scalps. I introduced myself to the girls, who ranged in age from sixteen to eighteen, using the French that still tripped off my tongue. The girls, whose names I have changed here, chuckled, and one of them, Fatou, told me that I should speak English. The rest of them nodded. I smiled, feeling both gratitude and a slight embarrassment at my uneven first impression. I began by asking them how they had been taught about slavery throughout their school experience.

"I think we learned [about] slavery in fourth grade," Aida said, adjusting the black head wrap near the bottom of her neck. "We were told that Europeans came here, in Africa, first to discover the world and to make people Christians. But then when they came, they discovered our resources and they found out—" She corrected herself. "Or they believed," she said, extending the last word's final syllable, "that we didn't have a culture." The other girls both nodded their heads in agreement and shook their heads at the absurdity of the sentiment. "And they brought us to America so that we could cultivate lands and do work for them."

Aida said that one of the most brutal aspects she remembers learning about was how captured Africans were transported from one side of the Atlantic to the other. She described the way she learned how little people were fed over the weeks and months of travel, how unfathomably small the area was where people's bodies were chained, and how disease was rampant. She remembered one lesson in particular describing that if enslaved Africans died or became too sick to be useful, "they were put in the sea." Her face wilted. "They didn't respect us at all."

Another girl, Corine, chimed in from a few desks over, a white scarf covering her hair and falling back over her shoulders. "They were looking at another woman like they were looking at an animal." Her brow furrowed and her cheeks tightened. "I don't understand how you can come to one country, and you see the people are different from you, then you start saying that 'these people don't have culture,' 'I need to colonize them,' or 'I need to be beyond them,' 'I need to exploit them.'" She paused and shook her head. "They are just humans."

Corine discussed how centuries of European colonization and exploitation could not be disentangled from the literary and philosophical texts that provided implicit justification for the way European colonizers had approached Africa and African people. "Like Hegel," she said. The idea that "'Africa is a tabula rasa'—I don't understand that."

When she mentioned Hegel, the early-nineteenth-century philosopher, the other girls in the classroom rolled their eyes and began mumbling to one another in French, their voices hissing with disdain. Clearly Hegel had been a topic of discussion before.

Corine was right that the famous philosopher thought little of Africa and African people. He wrote that African history, whatever there was of it, contributed nothing to global development and world history. In his work, he wrote of the inferiority of Africans and how they did not possess the capacity to be seen as fully human but instead existed as static subordinate entities. "From these various traits it is manifest that want of self-control distinguishes the character of the Negroes. This condition is capable of no development or culture, and as we see them at this day, such have they always been. The only essential connection that has existed and continued between the Negroes and the Europeans is that of slavery."

He wrote how this supposed inferiority led to their position within the slave-trading hierarchy. "*Negroes,* uninterested and lacking in interest, in a state of undisturbed naivety, are to be regarded as a nation of children. They are sold and allow themselves to be sold without any reflection as to the rights or wrongs of it."

Meanwhile, he thought that the white race represented the best of what humanity had to offer. "It is in the *Caucasian* race," he wrote, "that spirit first reaches absolute unity with itself. It is here that it first enters into complete opposition to naturality, apprehends itself in its absolute independence, disengages from the dispersive vacillation between one extreme and the other, achieves self-determination, self-development, and so brings forth world history."

Hegel's racism is part of a much longer, insidious strain of philosophy that for centuries reified racist ideas and practices. Indeed, perhaps the central tension of the Enlightenment is that many of these European thinkers were espousing liberalism, rationalism, and human progress while providing the kindling for slavery and colonialism.

A prime example is Immanuel Kant, who wrote, "In the hot countries the human being matures earlier in all ways but does not reach the perfection of the temperate zones. Humanity exists in its greatest perfection in the white race. The yellow Indians have a smaller amount of Talent. The Negroes are lower and the lowest are a part of the American peoples." Enslavers in the United States would go on to use these Enlightenment-era rationalizations to justify the perpetuation of slavery.

Corine expressed concern that the history of slavery and colonization might hang over her country, giving them a sense of inferiority that they wouldn't be able to shake off. She said it "should just be something that we should forget, because if we don't, we won't move anymore."

Seated next to her, Fatou, with round cheeks and narrow eyes, had a different perspective. To her mind, it was essential to understand how slavery and colonization shaped what contemporary society looked like. She said that if you look around, it's clear how Western influence and mindsets dictate how things operate in her own country. "So I don't see that. We can't forget it," she said. "Because even if it's not the same slavery or colonization, it is still here."

"Can I say something?" Aida asked. She wanted to point out the distinction between forgiveness and forgetting. "We shouldn't forget slavery, but we can forgive." The implications of forgetting, she said, would be detrimental to future generations, who wouldn't have the historical grounding to understand why racial prejudice and inequality are pervasive throughout the world. "They won't ever understand if we forgot slavery," she said. "But if they know it, maybe they would know that it is because people were not really open-minded and that there was a time where we were not accepted as we were."

Fatou brought up that she believes colonization has affected how people in Senegal, and people throughout Africa, think of themselves. "Africans always have the mind, the conclusion of, 'Europeans are better than us,'" she said. "It's like a complex."

The girls went back and forth about the toll the remnants of colonization had taken on their country. The unemployment rate is too high. The infrastructure is too old. The schools are too under-resourced. They told me that so many of the most talented young people from Senegal go on to universities around the world, and then don't come back. They say it comes from the fact that they don't have the same job opportunities back in Senegal, but also because people have internalized the idea that they are more valuable and more important if they live and work in Europe or America. "Africans don't believe in Africa," Fatou said.

I told the girls some more about why I was here, and how I had spent the previous day at the House of Slaves. I was curious, with this famous historical site just a few minutes down the road, if they had visited the house and, if they had, what they thought of the experience.

"We don't feel good," said Khady, who had previously been quiet and sitting at the front of the room. "Because, it makes us remember what our ancestors lived and felt at this time. And it makes us sad." She paused. "A point of sadness in our hearts."

A few days later, I had arrived back home in the US, and one afternoon I found myself scrolling through the photos I had taken during my trip to Gorée. In one photograph, small children chased a soccer ball around a field of sand, clouds of dust rising behind swift ankles. A group of women in colorful garments sat on benches under baobab trees, whose thick trunks and infinite branches stretched like a canopy across the courtyard. Stray cats curled around the benches, dragging their backs along the splintered, uneven wood.

I found another photograph I had taken of the Door of No Return from the opposite end of the House of Slaves. In the photo, the stone, arched corridor narrows as your eyes move closer to the door. Upon first glance, you cannot tell that the door opens out over the ocean; it is instead simply a burst of light erupting from the wall. What I like about this photo is that the sun's vibrant glow draws your attention to the door while simultaneously obscuring what's behind it. Almost as if it were saying, "Look at me, but don't look past me."

That door could no longer be what I had first imagined, but perhaps it did not need to be. Around 33,000 people were sent from Gorée Island to the New World. Perhaps it matters less whether they did so by walking through a door in this house or if they were marched down to a dock and made to board from there. Perhaps it matters less that millions of people were not sent into bondage from this island but that people from this island were sent into bondage at all. When I stood in the room in the House of Slaves that sat adjacent to the ocean, when I opened my arms and touched its wet stone walls, did it matter exactly how many people had once been held in that room? Or was it more important that the room pushed me into a space of reflection on what the origins of slavery meant? When I bent down and crawled inside that small space where I had been told enslaved people who resisted were held, when the darkness of that hole washed over me, did it matter whether enslaved people had actually been held there or did it matter that my sense of what bondage meant for millions of people had been irreversibly heightened? Can a place that misstates a certain set of facts still be a site of memory for a larger truth?

The words of Dr. Araujo sank into me: "This is the problem of the memory of slavery, that we have all these gaps." The gaps. Gaps that have to be filled. Gaps that David Thorson spoke of at Monticello when he said, "I think that history is the story of the past, using all the available facts, and that nostalgia is a fantasy about the past using no facts, and somewhere in between is memory."

There are the gaps that Monticello is attempting to fill by making clear that the story of Thomas Jefferson cannot be told without the story of the Hemings family. A reminder that we cannot read what Jefferson wrote about the United States in his Declaration of Independence while ignoring what he wrote about enslaved people in his *Notes on the State of Virginia*.

There are the gaps that serve as a catalyst for the Whitney Plantation's commitment to a story that not enough plantations are willing to tell. It is a place that has refused to accept that a plantation should be a site of weddings and not a site of reckoning, a place that centers on the story of the enslaved, because enslaved people are at the center of the story.

There are the gaps that Angola prison tiptoes around even though there are eighteen thousand acres of evidence under its feet, a place where thousands of Black men still dig plows into the soft earth of its fields.

There are the gaps that Blandford Cemetery fills with fiction, and flags from an army who fought a war to keep millions of people in chains. It is a place less interested in what truth looks like than in avoiding how such truth might implicate their loved ones buried in the soil.

There are the gaps that the Galveston community uses to transform grief into a song, a place that commemorates freedom by reminding us of all that it took to get there, a place that reminds us how precious freedom is and how tightly we must hold on to it.

There are the gaps that New York City has long swept under its skyscrapers and kept hidden from the beams of its northern lights, a place where the echo of its past runs from Wall Street to Central Park, and where the story of contemporary cosmopolitanism veils a darker history.

There are the gaps that sit at the edge of Gorée Island, a place attempting to tell a story that some feel has been forgotten, grappling with the tension that exists at the nexus of fact and truth, a place that still holds the ghosts of thousands and remains a symbol for the plight of millions.

There are the gaps that exist inside me, a Black man in America unable to trace my roots past a certain point in history. Whose lineage beyond the plantations where my ancestors were held remains obscured by the smog of displacement. They are the gaps that I am trying to understand, the gaps I am trying to fill.

"I lived it"

EPILOGUE

MY GRANDFATHER'S GRANDFATHER WAS ENSLAVED. They shared a name, a lineage, and the hard soil of Mississippi. *My grandfather's grandfather was enslaved.* I thought about how I felt pulled closer to the center of the concentric circle of history. *My grandfather's grandfather was enslaved.* I said it out loud and let it idle on the edges of my lips. My family told me my grandfather's grandfather was born into slavery, and I never knew until I asked.

In my work as a writer and researcher, I have spent thousands of hours in conversation with people I thought might be able to give me a better sense of the past, and people who have shared with me how the past has come to shape the world we currently live in. I have spent thousands of hours immersed in books that attempt to outline the history of the United States and that have helped me make sense of all that I see around me. I have traveled across the country—and across the ocean—visiting the historical sites that tell the story of how we got here. Still, each passing year I have become acutely aware that the past not only is housed in museums, memorials, monuments, and cemeteries but lives in our lineage. I realized that, in an effort to dig into the archives that explain the history of this country, I had forgotten that the best primary sources are often sitting right next to us.

My mother's father and my father's mother are nearly a decade apart in age. Both of their spouses have passed away, though each of them still wears their wedding ring—a well-worn golden band that wraps around their finger like a prayer. Their lives are tethered together by their children's love, their shared grandchildren's admiration, and their great-grandchildren's unrehearsed laughter. They are tethered together too, by growing up in an era, in a region, in a country, that for much of their lives told them they were nothing. Their stories are both remarkable and ordinary. Their memories, just like those I have explored in this book, are at once powerful, nuanced, incomplete, and so poignant. Their stories led to mine.

As we walked through the National Museum of African American History and Culture

Epilogue

(NMAAHC), I pushed my grandfather in a wheel-chair he had reluctantly agreed to sit in. His cane lay across his lap and he held a map of the museum in his hand. He is a proud man who also knows that his knees aren't what they once were—that years of high school and college football acceler-ated the deterioration of his aging joints. As we moved through the museum, my grandmother's gait was steady and unhurried. She walked behind us and moved ahead of us with an effortless in-dependence, following only the pulsations of her own curiosity.

I had been to the museum once before on a brief visit and was struck by a single institu-tion's remarkable ability to capture so much of Black America's complex relationship with this country—both tumultuous and inspiring, both violent and virtuous—and how so many of the exhibits complicated various accounts of US history that are misrepresented in our broader social discourse. There are certainly other muse-ums dedicated to documenting the history and contributions of Black life peppered throughout different cities across the country, animated by the local flavor that makes each of them unique. What makes the NMAAHC different is its am-bition. This museum recognizes that Blackness is not peripheral to the American project; it is the foundation upon which the country was built.

We walked past a statue of Thomas Jefferson, standing before a tower of bricks, each bearing the name of a person Jefferson enslaved, including his own children. We walked past a scarlet Ku Klux Klan robe, the satin-red color leaping from the garment and gleaming under the spotlight elevated above it, radiating as if the cloth had been glazed in fire. We walked past a sepia-toned photograph of four men dangling from a single tree. The coiled rope wrapped around the tree's branches, its pale brown fibers braided tightly together, the hangman's knot sitting above each limp man's neck.

In the far corner of the museum, on the floor overhanging Jefferson's statue, was a small room dedicated to Emmett Till. Till, as many know, was a fourteen-year-old boy from Chicago who was visiting his family in Money, Mississippi, in 1955 when he was brutally murdered by two white men. It is not simply that he was murdered but also that he was kidnapped, beaten, shot in the head, his neck tied to a large metal cotton gin fan, and his body thrown in the Tallahatchie River. Carolyn Bryant, a white woman, said Till had whistled at her, grabbed her, and made lewd comments to her in the grocery store where she worked as a cashier. Six decades later, however, Carolyn admitted that she had lied about the incident. Emmett had never touched her or said anything explicit.

Epilogue

We approached Emmett's casket, its bronze hue radiating under the museum lights. It sat open, exposing us to a photograph of what Emmett's mother, who insisted on an open-casket funeral, had chosen to show: what white supremacy had done to her son. I had seen images of it before, and did not need to listen to anything other than the soft buzzing light above us to know of Mamie Till Mobley's unceasing sobs. My grandfather looked at the casket, his eyes moving unhurriedly across its frame. "He was killed in the next town over from where your grandmother and I lived. Only a few miles away," he said without looking up.

While I knew vaguely about how the smoke of slavery and Jim Crow had billowed over their lives, I did not know the specific shapes of their silhouettes. I did not know how either of them had walked through this burning country without turning into ash.

The year my grandfather was born, a gallon of gas was twenty cents and a loaf of bread was nine. Slavery had ended six decades ago, and twelve years later everyone would forget. The year my grandfather was born, he had eight siblings and two parents and a grandfather born into bondage he tried to bury. The year my grandfather was born, millions of Americans were unemployed and over a thousand

banks shut down. The Great Depression had taken a deep breath, and the US didn't exhale for years. The year my grandfather was born, twenty-one people were lynched and no one heard a sound. The trees died and the soil turned over and the leaves baptized all that was left behind. The year my grandfather was born, there were full trains leaving Mississippi, and only empty ones coming back.

When I sit down with my grandfather he is eighty-nine years old. Born in Monticello, Mississippi, he has a voice, rich and sonorous, that still sings of the Deep South. His booming laugh is a room full of memories. He is tall, though not as tall as he once was; shoulders that were once broad and muscular are now sunken with time. He has a broad nose and narrow eyes and soft creases in the skin around his mouth. He keeps his hair neatly cut, about half an inch long, grey-black strands fading into white. When I was a boy I would stare at his eyebrows—thick, dark shadows anchoring his face, the way their curves evoked inquisition, how one raised brow could act as both invitation and warning. His presence, even as his body has begun the process of shrinking into itself, is distinguished and imbued with authority. He was professorial before I knew the word, distinguished before I could pronounce it correctly. It would not be right to say I feared him, but I did feel my spine straighten in his presence. He grew up in Mississippi and came back to the state of his birth when everyone told him he should stay away.

We sat in his living room in New Orleans, in a home just around the corner from where my mother—his daughter—and my father live. His body folded into his old reclining chair, while I sat adjacent to him on the cream leather couch I had known for so long. The strain of decades on his body was evident. Thick, bulging veins braided themselves down the sides of his legs. The ceiling fan whirred overhead, metronomically slicing the light above us.

My grandfather grew up in a state where people were lynched, and buried before the sun rose the next morning. It was a small rural dot of under a thousand people where every person knew the contours of their neighbors' lives. Lynching was not something he had to hear about in the news or read in a textbook. In 1930s Mississippi, it saturated the air; its possibility was the humidity that clung to his skin. The town was about two-thirds white and a third Black, said my grandfather, and he remembers the separation between the two beginning as early as such a thing was possible.

As he began speaking, his voice, low and mellifluous like a cello, transported me back into the sense of comfort and safety I had known as a child.

"I can tell you the thing that affected me most was that as I got old enough to go to school, you could not go to school if you were Black—'colored,' they called us then—until you were six. And you had to start in the pre-primer and primer, meaning you were eight years old getting into first grade. Which means that if you followed all the way through their program, passing each year, you would finish tenth grade at eighteen," he told me, rocking back and forth in his chair. "And that was all the education they had for Blacks in the county...You would finish tenth grade at eighteen and be ready to work on the farm. And if you were industrious, they would hire you to clean the courthouse."

My grandfather was a bookish child, and many people, Black and white alike, took notice. He told me that a couple of the white women in town "learned that I was an avid reader, and they started leaving the *Saturday Evening Post* and *Time* magazine and all kinds of books and magazines like that on their back porch."

While my grandfather shared this anecdote with me as a source of pride, emblematic of his young intellect and industrious dedication to learning in spite of limited resources, I found myself unsettled by the way he described the terms of the transaction. It felt like he had been the recipient of a condescending act of charity. The image of my eleven-year-old grandfather trotting to the back of someone's home and tossing the used newspapers and magazines he found into a paper bag left me with a sinking feeling in my gut. This is the puzzle of poverty, the conundrum of second-class citizenship—how does one take someone's charity and turn it into something more just? Was my expectation that my grandfather shouldn't have taken advantage of such an offer? Shouldn't I praise his ingenuity and unabated commitment to literacy rather than grumble over the manner in which it had transpired?

My grandfather's story is also one that reflects how, in 1940s Mississippi, the trajectory of a child's life was subject, above all else, to the arbitrary whims of good fortune. My grandfather was only able to avoid the fate of work as a farmhand or of mopping the courthouse because his principal had taken a liking to him and didn't want to see his precocious young pupil subjected to a destiny that he, and so many other young Black Mississippi children, did not deserve.

Because there was no high school for Black children in his county, the principal of his grade school, along with my grandfather's older sister, who had been a guiding force for his education throughout his life, conspired to send him to a school in a different county twenty miles away. Because there was no way of traveling forty miles round-trip every day in 1945, my grandfather lived in the town of his new high school, Brookhaven, in the home of a woman who rented to students in similar circumstances.

Over the course of our conversation, he shared some of the indignities he experienced throughout his childhood. He recalled one afternoon when he headed to the cotton gin to sell seeds from the cotton his family grew on the few acres they had been able to claim as their own. The white store employee did not see a child with burgeoning intellect but a young boy he sought to make his minstrel. As my grandfather recounted the story, the veins snaking across his temple rose like a river cresting from his skin.

"The fella said, 'I'll give you your sample if you dance.' And I said, 'I can't dance.'" But the employee didn't take kindly to what he perceived as my grandfather's "uppity" attitude. "He got a whip or something," my grandfather recalled. The employee must have known, as he prepared to exert revenge on the slender boy, that he could do so without suffering any consequences. "But another guy stopped him," said my grandfather.

For so much of my life my grandfather existed as a paragon of strength and fortitude. His once-domineering physique and deep voice made it impossible to imagine that he was ever on the receiving end of another man's intimidation. In my childhood imagination he was a mountain that no storm could erode. And yet here was this story of my grandfather, an anecdote that transformed him from the mythos of my memory into a small and fragile boy—a boy being told to perform under the thinly veiled threat of violence in a state where boys like him could so easily be disappeared into the night. Emmett Till's life had been taken because of an alleged whistle and a lie; surely it was not inconceivable that my grandfather's life could have been taken for explicitly refusing to do what a white man asked him to. It was eight decades after emancipation, but this was still Mississippi.

The longer I sat with my grandfather, the more he shared. His mind moved from one anecdote to the next, processing memories out loud as he unearthed them from places he had not visited for many years. When he was a boy, "night riders"—white supremacist vigilantes—would make their way through the town on horseback, attempting to frighten the Black families into paralyzing submission. "My mother would make us go in the back and not come out to the front, and I think she would walk out there sometimes, and say, 'We're not doing anything, we're just trying to live.'"

My grandfather said that they avoided any direct assaults from the men, but he could hear them shouting into the night as they rode through the community. I asked what sort of things they said.

"They would really intimidate some people," he told me. "Yell at them and call them 'niggers,' and [tell them] 'Stay away from downtown.' All kinds of stuff."

I pictured my grandfather and his siblings in the back room of a small Mississippi home holding their breath, waiting for the sound of horses to clamor off into the distance, then standing on their tiptoes to look over the windowsill, watching the shadows of these men and their stallions fade into the night.

I asked my grandfather how all of this had made him feel. He responded by saying that because his mother and father both worked for white people who liked them, he always believed everything would be fine. "If you had some white people that would vouch for you," you would be okay, he said, "as long as you stayed in your boundaries." He said he always thought they would be safe because his family "stayed in our place."

I was surprised to hear my grandfather say this; history is laden with examples of Black families who did exactly as they were supposed to and still found family members hanging from a tree or at the bottom of a river. I can understand, however, why the twelve-year-old version of my grandfather would believe this. It makes sense to cling to a rationale that will make you feel as if you still have some semblance of control. It is something we all do and often the only thing we can do to continue to move through the world without being paralyzed by fear. Still, I was surprised that he had held on to such a notion for so long—long after he had left Mississippi and the lynching ropes of the early twentieth century had disintegrated into the soil. But time does not always create the emotional distance we might hope. Such recollections remain in the marrow of our bones.

When my grandfather was about sixteen, a Black man in Brookhaven—the town to which he had moved to attend high school—told the police about a white man who was selling liquor on the black market. While Prohibition ended nationally upon the signing of the Twenty-First Amendment in 1933, Mississippi continued to enforce it until 1966.

"He was one of the members of the Klan," my grandfather said of the white man selling the alcohol. "He was arrested based on the testimony of this Black guy, and so they came after this Black guy, the night riders." He paused. "I can't know if they were 'Klansmen' or not, but they all did the same thing," He took a deep breath and looked forward, staring at a blank wall. "The night riders, henchmen, whatever you wanna call them, came and got him, and hung him on a tree and cut off his penis and put it in his mouth."

I had never heard this story before. And I had

never heard my grandfather describe something so gruesome.

"I stayed out of downtown at night, and I made sure when I went downtown that I stayed where people could see me," he said.

I looked at my grandfather as he said this and wondered if he still harbored any anger from these moments. I asked him if there would ever be an America in which white Americans were not actively working to keep themselves positioned atop the racial hierarchy.

He thought for a moment and then said, "Some of them will never give it up."

The year my grandmother was born, the Florida Panhandle was burning hot with white terror. Black children were taught to keep their eyes down, their mouths shut, and to make it home before the sun dissolved behind the trees. The year my grandmother was born, the country was on the cusp of entering a war being fought across two oceans. Black men would be sent to fight for freedom and come back to a land where they didn't have their own. The year my grandmother was born, she was held in her mother's arms and had no way of knowing how soon that embrace would disappear and never return, how soon her mother's face would become something she couldn't remember. The year my grandmother was born, there were laws that wrapped themselves around the necks of everyone she knew, and no one knew if they would let go.

When I sit down with my grandmother she is seventy-nine years old. Born in Quincy, Florida, in 1939, she has luminous silver-white hair that curls generously around her head, each hoary ringlet bouncing as she steps from one room to the next. Her voice is the front porch of a home with everyone you love waiting inside. She speaks with the gentle conviction of someone who has experienced several lifetimes in one, each word becoming a lesson unto itself. Her oval-shaped glasses magnify the kindness in her eyes, and she moves about the world with the purpose and energy of a person decades younger than she is. As a child I saw her as an emblem of tenderness, with full recognition that such tenderness was never to be mistaken for docility. My grandmother is unassuming, but she is not meek. She is calm, but she is not silent. She loves her family with unmatched vigor, and all of us know that anything we have done was only possible because of her. Sometimes I watch her cradle my daughter and I think of all my grandmother has done over four generations to make the life she holds in her hands possible.

During the earliest parts of my childhood, my mother's parents lived only a few hours away in Mississippi before retiring and moving to New Orleans in a house around the corner from ours. My father's parents, meanwhile, lived in West Palm Beach, Florida—a fourteen-hour-drive that we typically did once a year.

My grandmother told me her father passed away when she was a year old and her mother when she was three. "Tuberculosis and other things," she said when I asked her about the causes of their deaths. She had fifteen brothers and sisters, though many of them were older—some with children of their own older than she—and had moved away before she had ever had the opportunity to know them. After her parents died, she and eight of her siblings moved fifty miles away from Quincy, to live with their grandfather on a sharecropper's farm in Lamont, Florida.

Born in 1870, her grandfather came into the world just five years after the abolition of slavery, but from what my grandmother says, the context in which he grew up didn't feel that different from slavery. He was raised on the land that only five years earlier may have been a plantation. I asked my grandmother if she knew many of the details of his life, which plantation he was on, who the owners had been, what freedom felt like in a family of children born on both sides of emancipation. I had opened a box and wanted to pull everything out, but there were so many things my grandmother couldn't recall. "My memory doesn't let me say all the things that I would love to know about him myself," she said.

It became clear that my grandmother was carrying some of the same regret that I was attempting to stave off in my conversation with her. With each question I asked her about him, it became clear to her that there were so many questions she had not asked herself, and was too young to even know that these were questions that might be worth asking. Given that, I asked her directly, hypothetically, if she had the chance, what she might have wanted to know from him.

"Mmmmm," she said, closing her eyes and leaning back in her chair.

"I would want to know, how did it feel?" she said. "How was he treated? Because he became such a strong and respected person where we lived in the country. What motivated him to not run away? Not to be so angry? Because he was a very gentle man. He was not hostile. He was respected."

She continued: "How did he relate to living in those conditions? Because I know how bad it was when *we* came along...I know how I felt living in the segregated sections...going through that period of time. How did he manage? No public schools to go to...how did he learn? Because he could read and write—he really got some good education. Was he just that smart? Did he just really want to know and he just picked up every book he could get his hands on and read? How did that come about? I would like to know that. I would like to know more about his parents...He never talked about his mother or dad."

There was a longing in her voice I had not heard before. The gentle pang of guilt over all she realized she did not know.

My grandmother's life, like my grandfather's, was enveloped by the fog of segregation. One of her earliest memories was when she was about four years old and accompanying her grandfather on a Greyhound bus trip to visit his family in a town in another part of the state, watching him be forced to stand for much of the eight-hour-long ride. He held on to the small rail behind one of the seats and did his best not to stumble. There was an open seat available in the white section, but the bus driver had made it clear he would not allow him to sit there.

"My grandfather was an old man," she said. "And he had to stand up." She said of the bus, "It really wasn't designed for people to stand. It's designed for you to sit down. When the bus moved it would shake."

The explicit discrimination was not limited to the bus. Whenever the bus stopped at a bus station to drop passengers off, pick up new ones, and provide a chance for the current passengers to relieve themselves, what my grandmother and so many others found in the station were spaces built with little interest in accommodating their needs.

"Most times inside the bus station it was dirty, [but] the white side was well-kept. Again, the bathrooms [labeled 'Colored'] might not be working, they might be locked," she said. "It was like, 'Okay we don't exist.'"

She recalled what they would be told by the white bus station employees when they asked about using the restroom. The message was clear, even to a child: If you want to go outside and pee, it's all right, but you ain't gonna come inside the white side and use it.

"We knew [there] was so much segregation

wherever we went, not just that one situation, but it was just all around us everywhere we went. Grocery stores. Restaurants just weren't there; we didn't have restaurants. Even when your granddad and I got married—we drove from Tallahassee to West Palm Beach—unless you got off the highway and found yourself in a Colored town, you better pack your lunch because you cannot get nothing on the highway."

My grandmother shook her head and my small daughter, only a few weeks old, fidgeted and cooed on her lap.

It is not that any of these stories were new. I had been inundated with them my entire childhood. Documentaries of Freedom Riders captured on grainy black-and-white film. Photographs of Rosa Parks in every US history textbook I was assigned. Images of signs showing which public accommodations were for "White" people and which were for "Colored." It wasn't that the stories themselves were something I was unfamiliar with, it was that whenever I had encountered these stories, these images, I had not fully considered the way they might have affected my own family—perhaps because of the way we talk about certain episodes of US history. Black-and-white photographs and film footage can convince us that these episodes transpired in a distant past, untouched by our contemporary world.

Epilogue

Segregation shaped every aspect of my grand-mother's education. For a woman who would go on to become an educator, she said she is ashamed about so much of what she was taught, and so much of what she wasn't.

"All of the books that we got had been handed down from the white schools," she said. "The children had written their names in them, some of the pages are torn out. You might be reading a story and there might be three or four of the sheets of the article gone. So many things we didn't get."

Still, she said her teachers worked as hard as they could in order to provide their students with the best education possible given the circumstances, going as far as copying by hand what was in the textbooks in order for the students to have something to read in front of them.

In the midst of state-sanctioned segregation and only two generations removed from slavery, she had experienced much of the same whitewashing of US history that those of subsequent generations would.

"I didn't learn the truth about slavery until actually I got out of school and went to college, because all of that information was not available to us," she said. "I'm trying to recall…the passage—what do you call it?"

"The Middle Passage?" I responded.

"Middle Passage. That was not even in our

books. When we were in school, I didn't learn anything about the Middle Passage."

She spoke, regretfully, about the way she was taught to think about people on the African continent, how those caricatures specifically were designed to make them think of Africans as less than human, and how it contributed to making Black Americans feel as if slavery had somehow rescued them from the backwardness of their ancestral homeland.

"We just [were taught] that Africans were nasty, bad people," she said, a wave of shame rising in her eyes. "We didn't know anything good about them. They were monkeys. They referred to them as monkeys swinging on trees. They lived in the Congo and they were savages and all those kinds of things. But we didn't learn anything good about them."

She continued: "To me, in my mind, it was like another world, and everybody in Africa was bad. That's all I ever heard. Never knowing that we were part [of it], we came over, and we didn't come over on our own. How did we get here? I didn't learn that we were forced here. I didn't learn that."

She added, "You have a very deep fear…you stay in your place. You knew your place as a Black person—I'm using the word 'Black,' but we were called Negroes. You just knew there were things you could and could not do and you didn't have freedom. I didn't have a feeling of freedom that we could accomplish or achieve. It made you—I don't want to say less than a person, or less than a human..." She paused. "I used to have a really, really bad inferiority complex."

This fear extended out into every facet of my grandmother's life.

She told me how, because they lived in the rural South, they did not have many transportation options of their own, and as a result they walked almost everywhere, following the road, praying for safety.

"We weren't afraid as much of the animals that might attack us; we were afraid of what *people* would do if they saw us out walking. When we saw a car coming, we would run in the woods." When my grandmother and her siblings *were* spotted walking along the road, even if they weren't subjected to outright physical violence, they were often subjected to verbal and physical harassment. My grandmother told me about how white children—on their own school buses, heading to their own schools—would, upon seeing them, lower their windows and throw things at them, epithets sizzling from their lips.

"What kind of things did they throw?" I asked.

"Whatever they had. If they are eating an orange or apple or something, they'd just throw it out on us. If they had ice cream," she said, sighing, "they would throw that on us."

She remembers them calling out, "'Go home, nigger! You ain't got no business here.'"

My grandmother's fear was born out of the reality that threats were all around her. "Perry [Florida] was right down about thirty-some miles south of Lamont, and it was known for lynching." Her voice emphasized each of the sentence's final words. "A lot of people just got lost. They don't know where they went."

Her own grandfather, born just after slavery, had told her a story about a time when he was on the receiving end of a lynch mob's intimidation.

"I don't remember what he had done, but they took him out to string him up," she recalls. "They took him way out in the woods someplace, blindfolded him, took him out, called him nigger and all that kind of stuff and [said,] 'Today we're gonna kill you.' Again, I don't know what it was, I don't remember now, and he may have told us. They had the rope, getting ready to lynch him. He took the blindfold off, and they asked him, 'What is your last wish before you die?' He said, 'Let me pray. I just want to pray.' Whatever he said in his prayers or however God moved, when he opened his eyes and looked around, there was nobody there."

Epilogue

"They all left?" I asked, unprepared for the story to end this way.

"They all left," she said. "But then he had to figure out how to get from out in the woods where he was because they blindfolded him and he didn't know where he was. It took him a day to figure out how to get out of the woods."

It is difficult to know if this story is true or not, which is not to doubt the authenticity of my grandmother's reflection—such a thing might have very well happened, or it might be a story he told his grandchildren in an effort to engender a sense of caution to keep them safe. He may have thought, *I have seen it happen to others, and it could happen to me. It could happen to you. It could happen to any of us.*

Time collapsed in on us. I saw my grandmother sitting in front of me become the little girl she once had been. I imagined her walking home along that north Florida road, her ankles lightly dusted by the dirt that spit out from under her shoes. Heat rising from the splintered red earth beneath her feet. Wildflowers lining the sides of the road, their stems leaning over to kiss the clay. I saw her, books in hand, trying to avoid the eyes of the children who targeted her. My grandmother, who only wanted books that did not have the pages torn out of them, who only wanted to be able to use the restroom in a bus station without being expected to relieve herself outside like a dog, who only wanted to walk through the world without being consumed with fear that she might be disappeared into the night. I imagined the faces of those white children on the bus, their mouths full of violence, their jaws contorted with callousness when their lips opened, their adolescent brows raised in anticipation of her quiet surrender. I imagined how the laughter must have cascaded among them. Their bellies full of malice. I imagined how their heads jettisoned themselves from the side of the bus, how their small arms clawed over half-opened windows just to throw food at my grandmother in a spectacle of cruelty. These children were not born to hate this way. They had been taught. They had watched their parents and they had watched the world and this is what they had been shown.

As we finished our conversation, I asked my grandmother about her thoughts on our trip to the National Museum of African American History and Culture. "It was really depressing, very depressing to see that. I had a hard time, even now, trying to accept the fact that we can be so cruel to one another. It's just so inhumane. Looking at the slavery as it existed with the chains around your neck, hands all bound. You can't go to the bathroom. That was really real. So it was very, very depressing."

Epilogue

"What about the parts that were specific to segregation?" I asked.

"It just kind of made me go back to that time of life when I lived this. I kept saying, 'I lived this.' So it wasn't anything new for me. For some people, it's like, 'Oh, really?' No, it was for real, and I had lived it."

She continued: "I knew about when Emmett Till was killed and dragged. That was just horrible...We knew about the rioting, we knew about the fires, and all those kinds of things. So it was not anything surprising to me, because I lived it.

"It's surprising, even the younger generation today, they can't believe [it]," she said. "They can't see how we went through it. How did we allow somebody to treat us that way? And if I show movies in school, the kids would say, 'Nobody would do that to me. Nobody would do that to me.' 'No, I wouldn't have done that.' 'Why didn't y'all fight back?' I'm like, 'Hey, you hear about so many people who fought back. A lot of it is not in the textbooks, but a lot of people fought back, and they were killed. You never hear about them anymore.'"

Then, again, she said, "I lived it."

A silence settled between us, and I kept thinking about her refrain. *I lived it. I lived it. I lived it.* It echoed throughout the room and became the gravity around us. It crept into my ears and made a home in there. I watched the realization wash over her like a tide had risen around her body. There was so much I had not known about my grandmother's life until this moment. So many painful experiences that she still carried deep in the marrow of her bones. I thought of how easily these memories might have slipped away with her, had we not sat down—these stories might have remained grains of sand at the bottom of an hourglass. I thought about all of the ways the world today is at once so different, and not so different at all.

The exhibits at the museum were not abstractions for my grandparents; they were affirmations that what they had experienced was not of their imagination, and harrowing reminders that the scars of that era had not been self-inflicted. When my grandmother said, "I lived it," what I heard was *This museum is a mirror.* When my grandmother said, "I lived it," what I heard was *My memories are an exhibit of their own.* When my grandmother said, "I lived it," what I heard was *Always remember what this country did to us.* When my grandmother said, "I lived it," what I heard was *Don't let them tell you we didn't fight back.* When my grandmother said, "I lived it," what I heard was *I did not die. I have somehow made it here when so many did not. I escaped the jaws of a cruel thing and lived to tell this story.* When my grandmother said, "I lived it," what I heard was *I am still alive.*

Epilogue

My grandparents' stories are my inheritance; each one is an heirloom I carry. Each one is a monument to an era that still courses through my grandfather's veins. Each story is a memorial that still sits in my grandmother's bones. My grandparents' voices are a museum I am still learning how to visit, each conversation with them a new exhibit worthy of my time.

When I think about the history of slavery and racism in this country, I think about how quick we are to espouse notions of progress without accounting for its uncertain and serpentine path. I think of how decades of racial violence have shaped everything we see, but sometimes I find myself forgetting its impact on those right beside me. I forget that many of the men and women who spat on the Little Rock Nine are still alive. I forget that so many of the people who threw rocks at Dr. King are still voting in our elections. I forget that, but for the arbitrary nature of circumstance, what happened to Emmett Till could have happened to my grandfather. That the children who threw food at my grandmother and called her a nigger are likely bouncing their own great-grandchildren on their laps. That the people who lynched a man in my grandfather's town may have had children who inherited their parents' hatred. That the woman who stood alongside the Obamas to officially open the National Museum of African American History and Culture was the daughter of a man born into slavery. My grandfather's grandfather was born into slavery, while my grandmother's grandfather was born at its edge. We tell ourselves that the most nefarious displays of racial violence happened long ago, when they were in fact not so long ago at all. These images and videos that appall our twenty-first-century sensibilities are filled with people who are still among us. There are people still alive today who knew and held and loved people who were born into slavery.

I do not misunderstand the language of progress. Though I realize that I do not yet have all the words to discuss a crime that is still unfolding. But I do know that spending the day with my grandparents in a museum documenting the systemic and interpersonal violence they witnessed—the hand that beat them and the laws that said it was okay—reminded me that in the long arc of the universe, even the most explicit manifestations of racism happened a short time ago.

The history of slavery is the history of the United States. It was not peripheral to our founding; it was central to it. It is not irrelevant to our contemporary society; it created it. This history is in our soil, it is in our policies, and it must, too, be in our memories.

Across the United States, and abroad, there are places whose histories are inextricably tied to the story of human bondage. Many of these places directly confront and reflect on their relationship to that history; many of these places do not. But in order for our country to collectively move forward, it is not enough to have a patchwork of places that are honest about this history while being surrounded by other spaces that undermine it. It must be a collective endeavor to learn and confront the story of slavery and how it has shaped the world we live in today.

We can learn this history from the scholars who have unearthed generations of evidence of all that slavery was; from the voices of the enslaved in the stories and narratives they left behind; from the public historians who have committed themselves to giving society language to make sense of what's in front of them; from the descendants of those who were held in chains and the stories that have been passed down through their families across time; from the museums that reject the temptation of mythology and that prioritize telling an honest and holistic story of how this country came to be; from the teachers who have pushed back against centuries of lies and who have created classrooms for their students where truth is centered; by standing on the land where it happened—by remembering that land, by marking that land, by not allowing what happened there to be forgotten; by listening to our own families, by sitting down and having conversations with our elders and getting insight into all that they've seen.

At some point it is no longer a question of whether we *can* learn this history but whether we have the collective will to reckon with it.

ABOUT THIS PROJECT

The most difficult decision involving this book was the question of which locations to include in its pages. There are thousands of places I could have visited, as the story of slavery is etched into every corner of this country and far beyond. There are dozens of places I visited that did not make it into the book, though each visit informed the way I wrote about the places you find here. I am mindful that someone else's experience visiting one of the sites depicted in this book might be different from my own. As such, this book is not at all meant to be the definitive account of any of these sites but a reflection of my own experiences, concerns, and questions at each place at a specific period in time.

As a graduate student I was trained largely by sociologists, and part of what that discipline demands is an engagement and interrogation of one's *positionality* relative to the subject matter one is studying. So I am mindful that my experience at each of these places, and my conversations with all of the people who appear in these pages, are tied to various parts of my identity: being Black, being born and raised in the South, being a straight cisgendered man, and, at the time this book was being written and reported, being a doctoral student at an Ivy League university. Each of these realities creates dynamics that shape and alter the ways strangers, scholars, tour guides, and museum officials interact with me, and it is likely that someone with a different racial, geographic, or educational background would have experiences at each of these places that are different from my own. There were many occasions throughout the book, especially when I was in an environment in which there were no other Black people present, when I wondered how a tour or conversation might have been different if I was not Black. Would the tour have been exactly the same if everyone on it was white? Would different language have been used? Different framing? What things may have been included or excluded as a result of my presence?

I also want to make a note about sourcing. In the book, I included interviews with formerly enslaved people that were collected as part of the Federal Writers' Project. I did so because I believe there is value in hearing directly from the voices of enslaved people themselves as they recount what it was like to live in bondage. I included these narratives with full recognition that these texts have their own limitations. As the Library of Congress notes, "Some informants, mistaking the interviewer for a government representative who might somehow assist them in their economic plight, replied to questions with flattery and calculated exaggeration in an effort to curry the interviewer's favor." They go on: "It is uncertain, then, whether the former slaves reported their experience under slavery accurately and truthfully. Two other major questions surrounding the use of the slave narratives concern, first, whether the interviewers were able to elicit candid responses from their informants and, second, whether what the informants said was accurately recorded."

What's more, historians continue to have questions about how the race of the predominantly white interviewers may have shaped the informants' responses, as well as how accurately the interviewers transcribed the conversation.

Ultimately, I decided to use these narratives because I believe they remain a valuable resource to begin to understand the perspective of enslaved people. Scholar Saidiya V. Hartman may have put it best:

> [H]ow does one use these sources? At best with the awareness that a totalizing of history cannot be reconstructed from these interested, selective, and fragmentary accounts and with

an acknowledgment of the interventionist role of the interpreter, the equally interested labor of historical revision, and the impossibility of reconstituting the past free from the disfigurements of present concerns. With all these provisos issued, these narratives nonetheless remain an important source for understanding the everyday experience of slavery and its aftermath...I read these documents with the hope of gaining a glimpse of black life during slavery and the postbellum period while remaining aware of the impossibility of fully reconstituting the experience of the enslaved.

Much of what shaped my desire to write this book was my experience as a high school teacher in Prince George's County, Maryland, right outside Washington, DC. Though I was an English teacher, history informed both the way I approached the texts that we read and how I made sense of the social realities of my students' lives. It was as a teacher that I first began to fully account for the way the history of this country shaped the landscape of my students' communities, from slavery to Jim Crow apartheid to mass criminalization and beyond. I have come to realize that those conversations with my students, now a decade ago, about how we might begin to understand our

About This Project

lives in relation to the world around us were some of the earliest sparks of this book. I tried to write the sort of book that I would have wanted to teach them. I hope I made them proud.

ACKNOWLEDGMENTS

This book, first and foremost, is only possible because of the public historians, the guides, the descendants, the activists, the curators, and the educators who work so hard to keep the memory of slavery alive. They were enormously generous with their time, and I learned so much by having the opportunity to listen, observe, and ask questions about their work.

My editor, Vanessa Mobley, pored over every page, every line, and every word with the rigor and intentionality a writer can only dream of. Neither of us could have anticipated that we would be editing this book during a global pandemic, but even in such adverse circumstances, Vanessa's indefatigable work ethic and keen eye helped make this book the best version of itself. We spent countless hours together on Zoom, going over what worked, what didn't, and where I needed to push the work a bit further. At each turn she made the book stronger, and she made the writing clearer.

My agent, Alia Hanna Habib, is a tireless advocate for my work and has ensured at every step of this process, from proposal to publication, that the integrity of the book comes first. She is also one of my favorite people in the world to simply talk about books with. I feel lucky to have her, and the entire Gernert Company team, in my corner.

I owe an enormous amount to the historians who have spent their lives thinking, writing, and researching about slavery. The research component of this book, during which I had the privilege of getting lost in their work, could have gone on forever. In particular, I would like to thank Annette Gordon-Reed, Daina Ramey Berry, Leslie Harris, Walter Johnson, and Kevin Levin for reading a draft of this book and coming together (over Zoom) for a manuscript seminar I will never forget. They provided the most generative feedback and made the book more robust, more nuanced, and more precise.

I'm grateful to Elizabeth Acevedo, Safia Elhillo, Eve L. Ewing, Sarah Kay, Vann R. Newkirk II, Ben Weber, and Talmon Smith, who each read sections of—and sometimes all of—this manuscript at various stages of the writing process. Their insights, questions, comments, and generosity were invaluable.

Thank you to my phenomenal fact-checker Naomi Sharp, who helped me catch, clarify, and correct things that tightened and strengthened this project. And thank you to my research assistant,

Acknowledgments

De'Sean Weber, who has helped keep this book, and my life, in order.

Thank you to Michael Taeckens and Whitney Peeling, as well as Lena Little, Pamela Brown, Craig Young, and everyone else at Little, Brown who have worked so hard to get this book into the hands of readers.

Thank you to New America, the Emerson Collective, and the Art for Justice Fund for the resources, the space, and the time you provided me to complete this project.

I am grateful to my colleagues at *The Atlantic,* Harvard University, and Cave Canem, who over the years have made me a more thoughtful writer and a better person.

To my parents, Sheryl and Clint Jr.: you have supported me in everything I do. I love you both so much. To my siblings, Jess and Tal: I'm lucky to count you as both friends and family. Auntie Allison, thank you for a lifetime of always being in my corner.

To my grandparents, William and Frances: thank you for sitting down and telling me your stories. It is remarkable to think about how much you have seen this world change over the course of your respective lives, and it is also remarkable to think about the ways it hasn't changed as much as it should have. Seeing you with your great-grandchildren—my children—is one of my greatest joys. I wish your spouses, Leatrice and Clint Sr., could have met them. I'm grateful for the legacy they left.

To my kids: you are with me in everything I do and in everything I see. You each make my life so much fuller, and that feeling grows more every day.

Ariel, what can I possibly say? Thank you for your love, your support, your belief, your laughter, your kindness. Thank you for being the first person to read this manuscript and provide feedback on it. Your brilliance made this book better; your love makes my life richer.

NOTES

AUTHOR'S NOTE

Page xiii. **This list:** This list is based on the map of Indigenous territories at Native-Land.ca and was made in consultation with historians and Indigenous scholars.

"The whole city is a memorial to slavery"
PROLOGUE

Page 4. **Take 'Em Down NOLA:** "Take 'Em Down NOLA Take [']Em Down Action Public Statement," Statements, Take 'Em Down NOLA website, September 28, 2016, http://takeem-downnola.org/updates.

Page 8. **As historian Walter Johnson has said:** Marc Parry, "How Should We Memorialize Slavery?," Chronicle Review, *Chronicle of Higher Education,* August 29, 2017.

"There's a difference between history and nostalgia"
MONTICELLO PLANTATION

Page 12 **At any given time at Monticello:** "Slavery at Monticello," The Jefferson Monticello website, accessed August 12, 2018, https://www.monticello.org/slavery/.

Notes

Page 18. **"who left Monticello for lives of freedom":** Lucia Stanton, *"Those Who Labor for My Happiness": Slavery at Thomas Jefferson's Monticello* (Charlottesville: Univ. of Virginia Press, 2012), 106.

Page 19. **There were the Gillettes:** "Paradox of Liberty: Enslaved Families of Monticello," The Jefferson Monticello website, accessed October 23, 2020, https://www.monticello.org/slavery-at-monticello/enslaved-families-monticello.

Page 19. **How David Hern:** "Paradox of Liberty: Enslaved Families of Monticello," https://www.monticello.org/slavery-at-monticello/enslaved-families-monticello.

Page 21. **"those are only the interstate sales":** Walter Johnson, *Soul by Soul: Life Inside the Antebellum Slave Market* (Cambridge, MA: Harvard Univ. Press, 2001), 19.

Page 21. **separated from their families:** Edward Bonekemper in "The Myth of the Lost Cause: Revealing the Truth About the Civil War," posted by The Film Archive, November 10, 2018, YouTube video, 1:57:23 (Bonekemper at 15:51), https://www.youtube.com/watch?v=EbEjmEyHf8U.

Page 24. **"judgement of the great day":** Henry Bibb, *Narrative of the Life and Adventures of Henry Bibb, An American Slave, Written by Himself* (Madison: Univ. of Wisconsin Press, 2001), 202–3.

Page 24. **Though Jefferson was acutely aware:** Stanton, *"Those Who Labor for My Happiness."*

Page 24. **"where it can be done reasonably":** Stanton, *"Those Who Labor for My Happiness,"* 67.

Page 25. **He separated children as young as thirteen:** Lucia Stanton, "The Enslaved Family at Monticello: Management and Response" (speech given at Omohundro Institute of Early American History and Culture [OIEAHC] Conference, Glasgow, Scotland, July 2001).

Page 25. **"a child raised every 2 years":** Stanton, *"Those Who Labor for My Happiness."*

Page 25. **"must not be resorted to but in extremities":** Stanton, *"Those Who Labor for My Happiness,"* 65.

Page 26. **"over fidelity to the master":** Stanton, *"Those Who Labor for My Happiness,"* 65.

Notes

Page 26. **"presence of his old companions":** "James Hubbard," The Jefferson Monticello website, accessed August 20, 2018, https://www.monticello.org/site/research -and-collections/james-hubbard.

Page 26. **before they found water:** Annette Gordon-Reed, *The Hemingses of Monticello: An American Family* (New York: W. W. Norton, 2008), 113.

Page 31. **"undepraved by such circumstances":** Thomas Jefferson, *Notes on the State of Virginia* (Boston: Wells and Lilly, 1829), 169–70.

Page 31. **"The torment of mind":** "From Thomas Jefferson to Nicholas Lewis, 29 July 1787," Founders Online, National Archives, https://founders.archives.gov/documents/Jefferson/ 01-11-02-0564.

Page 32. **"famous statement to the contrary":** Winthrop D. Jordan, *White over Black: American Attitudes Toward the Negro, 1550– 1812* (Chapel Hill: Univ. of North Carolina Press, 2012), 453.

Page 32. **"indelible lines of distinction between them":** Jordan, *White over Black,* 522.

Page 32. **letter written to his friend Jared Sparks:** "From Thomas Jefferson to Jared Sparks, 4 February 1824," Founders Online, National Archives, https://founders.archives.gov/ documents/Jefferson/98-01-02-4020.

Page 33. **"St. Domingo is become independant":** "From Thomas Jefferson to Jared Sparks, 4 February 1824," https://founders.archives.gov/documents/Jefferson/98 -01-02-4020.

Page 33. **an 1814 letter to Edward Coles:** "Thomas Jefferson to Edward Coles, 25 August 1814," Founders Online, National Archives, https://founders.archives.gov/?q =%22I%20have%20seen%20no%20proposition%20so%20ex- pedient%22&s=1111311111&sa=&r=1&sr=.

Page 34. **enslaved population between 1774 and 1778:** William Cohen. "Thomas Jefferson and the Problem of Slavery," *Journal of American History* 53, no. 56 (1969): 503–26.

Page 34. **"Among North American slaves":** Michael Tadman,

"The Demographic Cost of Sugar: Debates on Slave Societies and Natural Increase in the Americas," *American Historical Review* 105, no. 5 (2000): 1533–75. Quoted in C. Vann Woodward, *American Counterpoint: Slavery and Racism in the North-South Dialogue* (New York: Oxford Univ. Press, 1983). 91.

Page 34. **"So far as history reveals":** C. Vann Woodward, *American Counterpoint: Slavery and Racism in the North-South Dialogue* (New York: Oxford Univ. Press, 1983). 91.

Page 34. **According to the National Archives:** Joan Brodsky Schur, "Eli Whitney's Patent for the Cotton Gin," Educator Resources, National Archives, last modified September 23, 2016, https://www.archives.gov/education/lessons/cotton-gin-patent.

Page 35. **one in three Southerners was an enslaved person:** Cohen, "Thomas Jefferson and the Problem of Slavery."

Page 36. **"like abandoning children":** Stanton, *"Those Who Labor for My Happiness,"* 57.

Page 39. **"are inferior to the whites":** Jefferson, *Notes on the State of Virginia,* 150.

Page 40. **"the senses only, not the imagination":** Jefferson, *Notes on the State of Virginia,* 147.

Page 42. **"mighty near white":** "Appendix H: Sally Hemings and Her Children," The Jefferson Monticello website, accessed October 23, 2020, https://www.monticello.org/thomas-jefferson/jefferson-slavery/thomas-jefferson-and-sally-hemings-a-brief-account/research-report-on-jefferson-and-hemings/appendix-h-sally-hemings-and-her-children/.

Page 43. **"Her name is SALLY":** Annette Gordon-Reed, *Thomas Jefferson and Sally Hemings: An American Controversy* (Charlottesville: Univ. of Virginia Press, 1997), 75.

Page 44. **did not believe the Jefferson-Hemings story:** Gordon-Reed, *The Hemingses of Monticello.*

Page 46. **"by a slave woman":** "Madison Hemings's Recollections Published as 'Life Among the Lowly' in the *Pike County Republican,*" Jefferson Quotes & Family Letters, The

Notes

Jefferson Monticello website, accessed October 23, 2020, http://tjrs.monticello.org/letter/1849.

Page 46. **"substitute for a wife":** Gordon-Reed, *The Hemingses of Monticello,* 87–88.

Page 54. **"must surely have been a fanatical abolitionist":** Gordon-Reed, *Thomas Jefferson and Sally Hemings,* 8.

Page 55. **"on the basis of no stated evidence":** Gordon-Reed, *Thomas Jefferson and Sally Hemings,* 11.

Page 56. **"My family doesn't need to prove themselves":** William Branigan, "A Branch on Jefferson's Tree?," *Washington Post,* January 3, 2000, https://www.washingtonpost.com/archive/local/2000/01/03/a-branch-on-jeffersons-tree/29c7aebb-830a-4d70-9c11-a66c375ab834/.

Page 57. **"seems to have taken things too far":** M. Andrew Holowchak and Vivienne Kelley, "Monticello Claims to Have Found Sally Hemings's Room. Is This True?," History News Network, Columbian College of Arts & Sciences, George Washington University, accessed November 2, 2018, https://historynewsnetwork.org/article/168841.

Page 61. **content from Slavery at Monticello:** Personal correspondence with the Thomas Jefferson Foundation.

Page 70. **"[T]he transition from colored guides":** Terry Tilman, *Memoirs of a Monticello Hostess,* collection of handwritten notes, Thomas Jefferson Foundation Archives, accessed May 19, 2019, folder 65, item 1, TJF Visitation 110–13.

"An open book, up under the sky"
THE WHITNEY PLANTATION

Page 77. **led this massive armed rebellion:** Daniel Rasmussen, *American Uprising: The Untold Story of America's Largest Slave Revolt* (New York: Harper Perennial, 2012).

Page 77. **On the German Coast of Louisiana:** Rasmussen, *American Uprising,* 17.

Page 78. **more than 80 percent of the soldiers:** Philippe R.

Girard, *The Slaves Who Defeated Napoleon* (Tuscaloosa: Univ. of Alabama Press, 2011), 343.

Page 78. **"the insurrection of St. Domingo":** "To James Madison from William C. C. Claiborne, 12 July 1804 (Abstract)," Founders Online, National Archives, https://founders.archives.gov/documents/Madison/02-07-02-0446.

Page 79. **"[F]or nearly seventy years":** David Brion Davis, *Inhuman Bondage: The Rise and Fall of Slavery in the New World* (New York: Oxford Univ. Press, 2008), 270.

Page 80. **The farther they marched:** Rasmussen, *American Uprising.*

Page 80. **"sitting on long poles":** Rasmussen, *American Uprising,* 148.

Page 81. **"Had not the most prompt and energetic measures":** Rasmussen, *American Uprising,* 148–49.

Page 82. **"the blessings of African slavery":** "Address of George Williamson, Commissioner from Louisiana, to the Texas Secession Convention," Causes of the Civil War website, last modified June 8, 2017, accessed October 23, 2020, http://www.civilwarcauses.org/gwill.htm.

Page 84. **Marcellin's widow, Marie Azélie Haydel:** Ibrahima Seck, *Bouki Fait Gombo: A History of the Slave Community of Habitation Haydel (Whitney Plantation) Louisiana, 1750–1860* (New Orleans: UNO Press, 2015), chap. 4.

Page 84. **When the Civil War ended:** US National Archives and Records Administration, *Records of the Field Offices for the State of Louisiana, Bureau of Refugees, Freeman, and Abandoned Lands, 1863–1872* (Washington, DC: US Congress and National Archives and Records Administration, 2004).

Page 84. **But much of the community:** Seck, *Bouki Fait Gombo.*

Page 84. **Poverty is common in Wallace:** United States Census Bureau, "Wallace Louisiana Decennial Census 2010: Race," table P8, accessed October 23, 2020, https://data.census.gov/cedsci/table?q=Wallace%20louisiana%20decennial%20census%202010&tid=DECENNIALSF12010.P8&hidePreview=false.

Page 85. **some of the highest cancer risks:** Antonia Juhasz,

"Louisiana's 'Cancer Alley' Is Getting Even More Toxic—but Residents Are Fighting Back," *Rolling Stone,* October 30, 2019.

Page 89. **"It's sort of like taking the frame off":** Mimi Read, "New Orleans Lawyer Transforms Whitney Plantation into Powerful Slavery Museum," NOLA.com, October 14, 2014.

Page 90. **"What is incarceration?":** Jessica Marie Johnson, "Time, Space, and Memory at Whitney Plantation," *Black Perspectives* (blog), African American Intellectual History Society, March 14, 2015.

Page 91. **under the age of twenty:** United States Census Bureau, *1860 Census: Population of the United States,* "Introduction," vii, xlviii, https://www2.census.gov/library/publications/decennial/1860/population/1860a-02.pdf.

Page 92. **"Children feed like pigs":** Francis Fedric, *Slave Life in Virginia and Kentucky; or, Fifty Years of Slavery in the Southern States of America,* Documenting the American South, Academic Affairs Library, University of North Carolina at Chapel Hill, 1999, 7–8, accessed October 23, 2020, https://docsouth.unc.edu/neh/fedric/fedric.html.

Page 92. **Children under ten were 51 percent:** Kenneth F. Kiple and Virginia H. Kiple, "Slave Child Mortality: Some Nutritional Answers to a Perennial Puzzle," *Journal of Social History* 10, no. 3 (1977): 284–309.

Page 92. **"Not one-fourth of the [slave] children":** Walter Johnson, *River of Dark Dreams: Slavery and Empire in the Cotton Kingdom* (Cambridge, MA: Harvard Univ. Press, 2013), 192.

Page 93. **beginning in 1929:** "Born in Slavery: Slave Narratives from the Federal Writers' Project, 1936 to 1938," Library of Congress, accessed March 4, 2019, https://www.loc.gov/collections/slave-narratives-from-the-federal-writers-project-1936-to-1938/articles-and-essays/introduction-to-the-wpa-slave-narratives/slave-narratives-from-slavery-to-the-great-depression/.

Page 96. **Enslaved Africans arrived:** David Eltis, Stephen Behrendt, David Richardson, and Herbert S. Klein, *The Trans-Atlantic Slave Trade: A Database on CD-ROM* (New York:

Cambridge Univ. Press, 1999); and Michael A. Gomez, *Black Crescent: The Experience and Legacy of African Muslims in America* (New York: Cambridge Univ. Press, 2005).

Page 97. **Much of the increase:** "Slavery in Louisiana," Whitney Plantation website, accessed March 7, 2019, http://whitney plantation.com/slavery-in-louisiana.html.

Page 99. **it was common:** Rasmussen, *American Uprising.*

Page 99. **Historian Walter Johnson aptly notes:** Walter Johnson, "To Remake the World: Slavery, Racial Capitalism, and Justice," *Boston Review,* February 20, 2018.

Page 102. **"The body trade was as elaborate":** Daina Ramey Berry, "Beyond the Slave Trade, the Cadaver Trade," *New York Times,* February 3, 2018.

Page 102. **According to James Roberts:** James Roberts, "The Narrative of James Roberts, a Soldier Under Gen. Washington in the Revolutionary War, and Under Gen. Jackson at the Battle of New Orleans, in the War of 1812: 'A Battle Which Cost Me a Limb, Some Blood, and Almost My Life,'" Documenting the American South, Academic Affairs Library, University of North Carolina at Chapel Hill, 2001, 26, accessed April 18, 2019, https://docsouth.unc.edu/neh/roberts/roberts.html.

Page 104. **"On the whole the plantations were":** Ulrich Bonnell Phillips, *American Negro Slavery: A Survey of the Supply, Employment and Control of Negro Labor as Determined by the Plantation Régime* (New York: D. Appleton, 1918), 343.

Page 105. **As historian Drew Gilpin Faust has written:** Drew Gilpin Faust, "The Scholar Who Shaped History," review of *The Problem of Slavery in the Age of Emancipation,* by David Brion Davis, *New York Review of Books,* March 20, 2014.

"I can't change what happened here"
ANGOLA PRISON

Page 130. **"Southerners constantly manipulated laws":** Thomas Aiello, email message to author, October 12, 2020.

Notes

Page 130. **So much so that in 1884:** Shane Bauer, *American Prison: A Reporter's Undercover Journey into the Business of Punishment* (New York: Penguin, 2018), 129.

Page 131. **As one man told:** Shane Bauer, "The Origins of Prison Slavery," *Slate*, October 2, 2018.

Page 131. **"to establish the supremacy of the white race":** Hon. Thomas J. Semmes, chairman of the Committee on the Judiciary, in *Official Journal of the Proceedings of the Constitutional Convention of the State of Louisiana, Held in New Orleans, Tuesday, February 8, 1898, and Calendar, by Authority* (New Orleans: H. J. Hearsey, 1898), 374.

Page 132. **than their white counterparts:** Jenny Jarvie, "In Louisiana, a Fight to End Jim Crow–Era Jury Law Is on the Ballot," *Los Angeles Times*, September 12, 2018.

Page 132. **Innocence Project:** Richard Davis, Meredith Angelson, Jee Park, Innocence Project New Orleans, and Counsel for *Amicus Curiae, Brief for Amicus Curiae Innocence Project New Orleans in Support of Thedrick Edwards,* Thedrick Edwards v. Darrel Vannoy, Warden, US Court of Appeals for the Fifth Circuit, No. 19-5807, p. 3, https://www.supremecourt.gov/DocketPDF/19/19-5807/148364/20200722123734456_Edwards%20v%20Vannoy%20No%20195807%20IPNO%20Amicus%20FINAL.pdf.

Page 136. **In his book *Slaves of the State*:** Dennis Childs, *Slaves of the State: Black Incarceration from the Chain Gang to the Penitentiary* (Minneapolis: Univ. of Minnesota Press, 2015), chap. 3, Kindle.

Page 139. **"well managed prisons in the country":** Childs, *Slaves of the State.*

Page 142. **The plantation produced:** Edward E. Baptist, *The Half Has Never Been Told: Slavery and the Making of American Capitalism* (New York: Basic Books, 2016), 360; and Bauer, "The Origins of Prison Slavery."

Page 152. **"forgotten, distorted, skimmed over":** W. E. B. Du Bois, *Black Reconstruction in America: An Essay Toward a History of the Part Which Black Folk Played in the Attempt to Reconstruct Democracy in America, 1860–1880* (New York: Oxford Univ. Press, 2007), 585.

Notes

Page 155. **lived with his family:** Louisiana Works Progress Administration, *History and Description of the Angola State Prison Farms in 1901* (New Orleans: Daily States, 1901), 8.

Page 155. **"only home he had known in a long time":** Childs, *Slaves of the State,* 117.

Page 156. **"I saw a big farm":** Liam Kennedy, "'Today They Kill with the Chair Instead of the Tree': Forgetting and Remembering Slavery at a Plantation Prison," *Theoretical Criminology* 21, no. 2 (2017): 142–43.

Page 156. **A poem from Mark King:** Kennedy, "'Today They Kill with the Chair,'" 143.

Page 157. **In 1998, Chuck Unger:** Kennedy, "'Today They Kill with the Chair,'" 143.

Page 157. **Incarcerated activist and writer Mumia Abu-Jamal:** Childs, *Slaves of the State,* 97.

Page 157. **"images of Southern slavery":** Kennedy, "'Today They Kill with the Chair,'" 142.

Page 157. **"involuntary servitude and slavery":** "Strike Breaks Out at Angola Prison as Momentum Builds for National Prison Strike," It's Going Down website, May 10, 2018, https://itsgoingdown.org/strike-breaks-out-at-angola -prison-as-momentum-builds-for-national-prison-strike/.

Page 160. **"There was a toilet in the cell":** Albert Woodfox, *Solitary* (New York: Grove Press, 2019), loc 715, Kindle.

Page 160. **In his memoir:** Billy W. Sinclair and Jodie Sinclair, *A Life in the Balance: The Billy Wayne Sinclair Story* (New York: Arcade, 2012), 51.

Page 162. **He was sentenced to death:** Gilbert King, *The Execution of Willie Francis: Race, Murder, and the Search for Justice in the American South* (New York: Basic Books, 2008).

Page 163. **"Everybody was watching me":** Willie Francis (as told to Samuel Montgomery), "My Trip to the Chair," in *Demands of the Dead: Executions, Storytelling, and Activism in the United States,* ed. Katy Ryan (Iowa City: Univ. of Iowa Press, 2012), 40.

Page 164. **but it did torture him:** King, *The Execution of Willie Francis.*

Page 164. **"The best way I can describe it is":** Francis, "My Trip to the Chair," in *Demands of the Dead*, 41.

Page 165. **a year later, on May 9, 1947:** King, *The Execution of Willie Francis.*

Page 165. **"I know how it felt":** Francis, "My Trip to the Chair," in *Demands of the Dead*, 33.

Page 165. **"Boy, you sure feel funny":** Francis, "My Trip to the Chair," in *Demands of the Dead*, 36.

Page 166. **The average person:** Deborah Fins, *Death Row U.S.A.: Spring 2020* (New York: NAACP Legal Defense and Educational Fund 2020), 50, https://www.naacpldf.org/wp-content/uploads/DRUSASpring2020.pdf.

Page 166. **an estimated one out of every twenty-five people:** Samuel R. Gross, Barbara O'Brien, Chen Hu, and Edward H. Kennedy, "Rate of False Conviction of Criminal Defendants Who Are Sentenced to Death," *PNAS* 111, no. 20 (2014): 7230–35.

Page 167. **"slightly cooler than their beds":** *Ball, Code, and Magee v. LeBlanc, Cain, Norwood, and the Louisiana Dept. of Public Safety and Corrections*, Civil Action No. 13.368, Statement of Claim, June 10, 2013, https://www.clearinghouse.net/chDocs/public/PC-LA-0014-0001.pdf.

Page 168. **air-conditioning to many other prisoners:** Michael Kunzelman, "Court Overturns Heat-Index Limit on Louisiana's Death Row," Associated Press, February 1, 2018.

Page 168. **physical and mental harm:** The Marshall Project, "Marcus Hamilton v Warden of Angola," July 21, 2017, https://www.themarshallproject.org/documents/3899095-Marcus-Hamilton-v-Warden-of-Angola.

Page 169. **"with the electric chair":** James Ridgeway and Jean Casella, "Wilbert Rideau on Solitary Confinement: 'The Zenith in Human Cruelty,'" *Solitary Watch*, December 18, 2010.

Page 169. **no matter the distance they were going:** Marshall Project, "Marcus Hamilton v Warden of Angola," https://www.themarshallproject.org/documents/3899095-Marcus-Hamilton-v-Warden-of-Angola.

Notes

Page 169. **Since May 15, 2017:** Julia O'Donoghue, "Louisiana Tests Relaxed Restrictions on Death Row Inmates," NOLA.com, October 26, 2017.

"I don't know if it's true or not, but I like it"
BLANDFORD CEMETERY

Page 192. **In an August 1869 letter:** Robert E. Lee, *Republican Vindicator,* September 3, 1869.

Page 193. **"a moral & political evil":** "Letter from Robert E. Lee to Mary Randolph Custis Lee (December 27, 1856)," *Encyclopedia Virginia,* Virginia Humanities, last modified February 1, 2018, https://www.encyclopedia virginia.org/Letter_from_Robert_E_Lee_to_Mary_Randolph _Custis_Lee_December_27_1856.

Page 194. **According to historian Elizabeth Brown Pryor:** Adam Serwer, "The Myth of the Kindly General Lee," *The Atlantic,* June 4, 2017.

Page 194. **A testimony from one of the people:** John W. Blassingame, *Slave Testimony: Two Centuries of Letters, Speeches, Interviews, and Autobiographies* (Baton Rouge: Louisiana State Univ. Press, 1977), 467.

Page 197. **"Few would succeed in getting to the rear safe":** Kevin M. Levin, *Remembering the Battle of the Crater: War as Murder* (Lexington: Univ. Press of Kentucky, 2012), 27–31.

Page 197. **Levin outlines how soldiers described in detail:** Levin, *Remembering the Battle of the Crater,* 28–29.

Page 198. **"with the capture of a single hero":** Levin, *Remembering the Battle of the Crater,* 31.

Page 199. **"opposed to any system of laws":** "Gen. Rosecrans and Gen. R. E. Lee," copy of text of letter dated August 26, 1868, and published in the *Staunton Spectator,* September 08, 1868, p. 2, col. 2, Virginia Center for Digital History, accessed September 28, 2020.

Page 199. **"with *nauseating* flatteries of the late Robert**

E. Lee": David W. Blight, *Race and Reunion: The Civil War in American Memory* (Cambridge, MA: Belknap Press, 2002), 270.

Page 199. **W. E. B. Du Bois wrote in a 1928 essay:** W. E. B. Du Bois, "No Excuses for a Racist Murderer: W.E.B. DuBois on the Legacy of Robert E. Lee," 1928 essay reprinted in *In These Times,* August 22, 2017.

Page 201. ***Smithsonian*'s investigation found:** Brian Palmer and Seth Freed Wessler, "The Cost of the Confederacy," *Smithsonian,* December 2018.

Page 201. **the United Daughters of the Confederacy:** Allen G. Breed, "Women's Group Behind Rebel Memorials Quietly Battles On." Associated Press, August 10, 2018.

Page 205. **Confederate soldiers prepared to enter battle:** Steven H. Cornelius, *Music of the Civil War Era,* American Music Through History series (Westport, CT: Greenwood Press, 2004).

Page 205. **while wearing Confederate-inspired uniforms:** Kevin M. Levin, Workshop Seminar, May 15, 2020.

Page 208. **Confederate and Union soldiers:** Blight, *Race and Reunion.*

Page 209. **"[I]mpartial history will record":** Richard A. Pryor, *Essays and Addresses* (New York: Neale Publishing, 1912), 76.

Page 210. **former Confederate president Jefferson Davis:** David W. Blight, "Forgetting Why We Remember," *New York Times,* May 29, 2011.

Page 210. **According to the official website:** "Blandford Cemetery," City of Petersburg website, accessed August 14, 2019, https://www.petersburgva.gov/303/Blandford-Cemetery.

Page 210. **Blight describes what happened next:** Blight, "Forgetting Why We Remember."

Page 216. **in public places across the country:** "Whose Heritage? Public Symbols of the Confederacy," Southern Poverty Law Center, February 1, 2019, https://www.splcenter.org/20190201/whose-heritage-public-symbols-confederacy.

Notes

Page 218. **The UDC alone is responsible:** Peter Galuszka, "The Women Who Erected Confederate Statues Are Stunningly Silent," *Washington Post,* October 13, 2017.

Page 218. **Frederick Douglass wrote in 1870:** *New National Era,* December 1, 1870, *Chronicling America: Historic American Newspapers,* Library of Congress, Washington, D.C., https://chroniclingamerica.loc.gov/lccn/sn84026753/1870-12-01/ed-1/seq-3/.

Page 219. **In 1871, he spoke with great fervor:** https://www.loc.gov/exhibits/civil-war-in-america/ext/cw0211.html.

Page 219. **In 1931, W. E. B. Du Bois attacked the decision:** W. E. B. Du Bois, "The Perfect Vacation," *The Crisis,* August 1931, 279.

Page 220. **twenty-three Confederate holidays and observances:** "Whose Heritage? Public Symbols of the Confederacy," https://www.splcenter.org/20190201/whose-heritage-public-symbols-confederacy.

Page 220. **On February 22, 1896, thirty-five years after:** Blight, *Race and Reunion,* 257.

Page 221. **In *Marse Chan: A Tale of Old Virginia*:** Thomas Nelson Page, *Marse Chan: A Tale of Old Virginia* (New York: Charles Scribner's Sons, 1908), 13–14.

Page 225. **His 1886 obituary read:** Kevin M. Levin, "Happy Richard Poplar Day," *Civil War Memory* (blog), September 18, 2010, quoting obituary in the *Petersburg Index-Appeal,* May 23, 1886, http://cwmemory.com/2010/09/18/happy-richard-poplar-day/.

Page 225. **But as Levin notes:** Kevin M. Levin, *Searching for Black Confederates: The Civil War's Most Persistent Myth* (Chapel Hill: Univ. of North Carolina Press, 2019), chap. 1, Kindle.

Page 225. **Poplar's 1886 obituary suggests:** *Petersburg Index-Appeal,* May 23, 1886, http://www.petersburgexpress.com/POW.html.

Page 226. **There is no evidence to support this:** Levin, *Searching for Black Confederates.*

Notes

Page 226. **This story was a response:** Levin, *Searching for Black Confederates*.

Page 227. **"if not to protect our property":** Bruce Levine, *Confederate Emancipation: Southern Plans to Free and Arm Slaves During the Civil War* (New York: Oxford Univ. Press, 2006), 55.

Page 227. **"our whole theory of slavery is wrong":** Letter from Howell Cobb to James A. Seddon (January 8, 1865) in *The War of the Rebellion: A Compilation of the Official Records of the Union and Confederate Armies* (Washington, DC.: Government Printing Office, 1900), series 4, vol. 3, 1,009–1,010, https://www.encyclopediavirginia.org/Letter_from_Howell_Cobb_to_James_A_Seddon_January_8_1865.

Page 227. **The war had effectively already been lost:** "1865, March 13: Confederacy Approves Black Soldiers," This Day in History, History.com, last modified March 11, 2020, https://www.history.com/this-day-in-history/confederacy-approves-black-soldiers.

Page 228. **before he was inaugurated:** Edward H. Bonekemper III, *The Myth of the Lost Cause: Why the South Fought the Civil War and Why the North Won* (Washington, DC: Regnery History, 2015), 258.

Page 229. **"subverted to work out our ruin":** "A Declaration of the Immediate Causes Which Induce and Justify the Secession of the State of Mississippi from the Federal Union," Lillian Goldman Library, Yale Law School, accessed August 5, 2019, https://catalog.hathitrust.org/Record/010446488/Cite.

Page 230. **"destructive of its beliefs and safety":** "Confederate States of America—Declaration of the Immediate Causes Which Induce and Justify the Secession of South Carolina from the Federal Union," Lillian Goldman Library, Yale Law School, accessed August 5, 2019, https://www.atlantahistorycenter.com/assets/documents/SCarolina-Secession-p1-13.pdf.

Page 230. **"same *necessity and determination to preserve African slavery*":** "Address of George Williamson, Commissioner from Louisiana to the Texas Secession Convention,"

Notes

Causes of the Civil War, accessed August 5, 2019, http://www.civil warcauses.org/gwill.htm.

Page 231. **"be rendered beneficial or tolerable":** "Texas: A Declaration of the Causes Which Impel the State of Texas to Secede from the Federal Union," American Battlefield Trust, accessed August 5, 2019, https://www.loc.gov/resource/rbpe.34604300/?sp=1&st=text.

Page 231. ***"growing out of property in slaves":*** Remarks by John C. McGehee, president of the convention. *Journal of the Proceedings of the Convention of the People of Florida, Begun and Held at the Capitol in the City of Tallassee [sic] on Thursday, January 3, A. D. 1861* (Tallahassee: Office of the Floridian and Journal, printed by Dyke & Carlisle, 1861), 8, https://catalog.hathitrust.org/Record/010943337.

Page 231. **"lust of half-civilized Africans":** Letter from Stephen F. Hale (Alabama state commissioner) to Governor Beriah Magoffin of Kentucky, December 27, 1860, https://docsouth.unc.edu/imls/smithwr/smith.html.

Page 232. ***"Southern slaveholding States":*** "Virginia: The Secession Ordinance. An Ordinance to Repeal the Ratification of the Constitution of the United States of America by the State of Virginia, and to Resume All the Rights and Powers Granted Under Said Constitution," American Battlefield Trust, accessed August 21, 2019, https://catalog.archives.gov/id/598395.

Page 232. **If these primary sources were not enough:** "Constitution of the Confederate States; March 11, 1861," Lillian Goldman Law Library, Yale Law School, accessed August 6, 2019, http://avalon.law.yale.edu/19th_century/csa_csa.asp.

Page 233. **"It has been a conviction of pressing necessity":** "Cornerstone Speech," American Battlefield Trust, accessed August 6, 2019, https://www.battlefields.org/learn/primary-sources/cornerstone-speech.

Page 234 **Crittenden said the following:** Bonekemper, *The Myth of the Lost Cause,* 45.

Page 235. **"by land, navigable rivers, or by the sea":** George Ticknor Curtis, *Constitutional History of the United States from Their*

Declaration of Independence to the Close of the Civil War, Vol. 2, ed. Joseph Culbertson Clayton (New York: Harper & Bros., 1896), 526, https://avalon.law.yale.edu/19th_century/critten.asp.

Page 235. **if no American ever owned a slave:** Jefferson Davis, *The Rise and Fall of the Confederate Government* (New York: Thomas Yoseloff, 1958), 79–80.

Page 235. **"the immediate cause":** Kevin M. Levin, "Alexander Stephens Reinforces the Cornerstone," *Civil War Memory* (blog), January 23, 2013, http://www.adena.com/adena/usa/cw/cw223.htm.

Page 238. **"the history and legacy of these heroes":** "What Is the Sons of Confederate Veterans?" Sons of Confederate Veterans website, accessed August 17, 2019, https://scv.org/what-is-the-scv/.

Page 239. **a mechanism to propagate hate:** Heidi Beirich, "Furling the Flag," *Intelligence Report,* Southern Poverty Law Center, October 27, 2015, https://www.splcenter.org/fighting-hate/intelligence-report/2015/furling-flag.

Page 240. **who spoke out against racism:** "Here's Why the Confederate Monuments in New Orleans Must Come Down," Southern Poverty Law Center, January 13, 2016, https://www.splcenter.org/fighting-hate/intelligence-report/2003/neo-confederates-scv-purges-moderates.

Page 240. **recent amicus brief:** "Here's Why the Confederate Monuments in New Orleans Must Come Down," https://www.splcenter.org/sites/default/files/new_tedn_amicus_brief_doc._31-1_filed_1.11.16_copy.pdf.

Page 242. **"and his 'Invisible' but victorious army":** Thomas Upton Sission, "Address of Greeting from Sons of Veterans," "Minutes of the Nineteenth Annual Meeting and Reunion of the United Confederate Veterans Held at Memphis, Tenn. On Tuesday, Wednesday, and Thursday, June 8th, 9th, and 10th, 1909," New Orleans: United Confederate Veterans, 74, https://books.google.com/books?id=Js UTAAAAYAAJ&dq=%22Great+and+trying+times+always+produce+great+leaders%22&source=gbs_navlinks_s_s.

Notes

Page 242. **"for their abhorrent and reprehensible purposes":** "Statement from the President General," United Daughters of the Confederacy website, December 1, 2018, accessed September 29, 2020, https://hqudc.org/.

Page 242. **As historian Karen L. Cox remarks:** Karen L. Cox, *Dixie's Daughters: The United Daughters of the Confederacy and the Preservation of Confederate Culture* (Gainesville: Univ. Press of Florida, 2003), 1.

Page 243. **Heidi Christensen, former president of the Seattle:** Kali Holloway, "Seven Things the United Daughters of the Confederacy Might Not Want You to Know About Them," *Salon*, October 6, 2018.

Page 243. **In 1914, Laura Martin Rose:** Laura M. Rose, *The Ku Klux Klan; or, Invisible Empire* (London, UK: Forgotten Books, 2012), 14.

Page 244. **In the opening pages of the book:** Rose, *The Ku Klux Klan*, 3.

Page 244. **As Cox notes:** Karen L. Cox, "The Confederacy's 'Living Monuments,'" *New York Times*, October 6, 2017.

Page 245. **As historian Eric Foner notes:** Eric Foner, "Our Lincoln," *The Nation*, January 8, 2009.

Page 246. **"superior position assigned to the white race":** Editors, "Mr. Lincoln and Negro Equality," *New York Times*, December 28, 1860.

Page 247. **Frederick Douglass scathed Lincoln:** Frederick Douglass, *The Collected Works of Frederick Douglass: Autobiographies, 50+ Speeches, Articles & Letters: The Future of the Colored Race, Reconstruction, My Bondage and Freedom, Self-Made Men, The Color Line, The Church and Prejudice*...(New York: Musaicum Books, 2018), 180.

Page 247. **According to Lincoln, white racism was so deeply entrenched:** Foner, "Our Lincoln."

Page 248. **"existing permanently half-slave and half-free":** Eric Foner, "Abraham Lincoln, Colonization, and the Rights of Black Americans," in *Slavery's Ghost: The Problem of Freedom in the Age of Emancipation*, by Richard Follett, Eric Foner, and Walter Johnson (Baltimore: Johns Hopkins Univ. Press, 2011), 37.

Notes

Page 248. **A few days before his assassination:** Foner, "Our Lincoln."

Page 255. **business relationships with them:** Ta-Nehisi Coates, "Small Truth Papering Over a Big Lie," *The Atlantic*, August 9, 2010, https://www.theatlantic.com/national/archive/2010/08/small-truth-papering-over-a-big-lie/61136/.

Page 255. **"to the level of the white race":** James Oliver Horton, "Confronting Slavery and Revealing the 'Lost Cause,'" National Park Service, last modified March 10, 2017, accessed June 15, 2019, https://www.nps.gov/articles/confronting-slavery-and-revealing-the-lost-cause.htm.

Page 255. **The *Louisville Daily Courier* warned non-slaveholding Southerners:** Horton, "Confronting Slavery and Revealing the 'Lost Cause.'"

Page 256. **"put on an equality with a white person":** Horton, "Confronting Slavery and Revealing the 'Lost Cause.'"

Page 257. **In his book *The Peculiar Institution*:** Kenneth M. Stampp, *The Peculiar Institution: Slavery in the Ante-Bellum South* (New York: Vintage, 1956), 33.

Page 257. **Or as historian Charles Dew said:** Edward L. Ayers and Carolyn R. Martin, eds., *America on the Eve of the Civil War* (Charlottesville: Univ. of Virginia Press, 2011), 51–52.

Page 259. **"the supremacy of the Caucasian race":** Della Hasselle, "Lusher Charter School Considers Changing Confederate History-Based Name Amid Petitions, Protests," NOLA.com, June 25, 2020.

Page 261. **"great-great-grandparents were monsters":** Campbell Robertson, "Flag Supporters React with a Mix of Compromise, Caution, and Outright Defiance," *New York Times*, June 23, 2015.

"Our Independence Day"
GALVESTON ISLAND

Page 263. **"either there or elsewhere":** "Texas Remembers

Notes

Juneteenth," Texas State Library and Archives Commission, June 19, 2020, https://www.tsl.texas.gov/ref/abouttx/juneteenth.html.

Page 265. **"Just like that we was free":** Ira Berlin, Marc Favreau, and Steven F. Miller, ed., *Remember Slavery: African Americans Talk About Their Personal Experiences of Slavery and Emancipation* (New York: New Press, 2000), 266; and Elizabeth H. Turner, "Juneteenth: Emancipation and Memory," in *Lone Star Pasts: Memory and History in Texas,* ed. Gregg Cantrell and Elizabeth H. Turner (College Station: Texas A&M Univ. Press, 2007), 143–75.

Page 275. **Scholar Imani Perry:** Imani Perry, *May We Forever Stand: A History of the Black National Anthem* (Chapel Hill: Univ. of North Carolina Press, 2018), 7, 12, Kindle.

Page 277. **about 3.5 million:** United States Census Bureau, "Texas Population: Race," American Community Survey five-year estimates, 2018, https://data.census.gov/cedsci/table?q=texas%20population%20race&t=Race%20and%20Ethnicity&tid=ACSDT5Y2018.B02001&hidePreview=false.

Page 277 (footnote). **Black Texans represented:** "Texas Profile," Prison Policy Initiative website, https://www.prisonpolicy.org/profiles/TX.html.

Page 277 (footnote). **more than 20 percent:** United States Census Bureau, "Poverty Status in the Past 12 Months," American Community Survey 5-year estimates, 2018, https://data.census.gov/cedsci/table?q=race%20texas%20poverty&tid=ACSST5Y2018.S1701&hidePreview=false.

Page 277 (footnote). **The infant mortality rate:** "Infant Mortality Rate by Race," in *2019 Healthy Texas Mothers and Babies Data Book,* B-2, Texas Department of State Health Services website, https://www.dshs.texas.gov/healthytexasbabies/Documents/HTMB-Data-Book-2019-20200206.pdf.

Page 277 (footnote). **The high school graduation rate:** "Public High School Graduation Rates," in *The Condition of Education,* National Center for Education Statistics website, last modified May 2020, https://nces.ed.gov/programs/coe/indicator_coi.asp.

Notes

Page 280. **"I refuse to take this oath":** James L. Haley, *Sam Houston* (Norman: Univ. of Oklahoma Press, 2015), 390–91.

Page 283. **"they can own their own memories":** Turner, "Juneteenth," in *Lone Star Pasts,* 158.

Page 284. **In 1941, the *Houston Informer*:** Turner, "Juneteenth," in *Lone Star Pasts,* 162.

Page 285. **As one Juneteenth celebrant put it:** William H. Wiggins Jr., *O Freedom: Afro-American Emancipation Celebrations* (Knoxville: Univ. of Tennessee Press, 1990), xvii.

Page 287. **"sells us like you sell a hoss":** "Mintie Maria Miller, Galveston, Texas: Image 90," *Federal Writers' Project: Slave Narrative Project, Vol. 16, Texas, Part 3, Lewis-Ryles,* 1936, manuscript/mixed material, https://www.loc.gov/resource/mesn.163/?sp=90.

Page 287. **"tore de meat off one dem field hands":** "[Josephine Ryles] Image 285," *Federal Writers' Project: Slave Narrative Project, Vol. 16, Texas, Part 3, Lewis-Ryles,* 1936, manuscript/mixed material, https://www.loc.gov/resource/mesn.163/?sp=284.

Page 287. **"work no more 'less us git pay for it":** "William Mathews, Galveston, Texas: Image 73; Image 75," *Federal Writers' Project: Slave Narrative Project, Vol. 16, Texas, Part 3, Lewis-Ryles,* 1936, manuscript/mixed material, https://www.loc.gov/resource/mesn.163/?sp=72&st=text.

Page 288. **"till he makes another crop or two":** "Tempie Cummins, Jasper, Texas: Image 270," *Federal Writers' Project: Slave Narrative Project, Vol. 16, Texas, Part 1, Adams-Duhon,* 1936, manuscript/mixed material, https://www.loc.gov/resource/mesn.161/?sp=271.

Page 289. **As historian W. Caleb McDaniel has said:** W. Caleb McDaniel, "Historian: No, the Civil War Didn't Erase Slavery's Harm," *Houston Chronicle,* July 12, 2019.

Page 289. **The former Confederate mayor of Galveston:** Turner, "Juneteenth" in *Lone Star Pasts.*

Page 289. **even those who did hear about it:** Turner, "Juneteenth," in *Lone Star Pasts.* Nancy Cohen-Lack, "A Struggle for Sovereignty: National Consolidation, Emancipation, and Free Labor in Texas, 1865," *Journal of Southern History,* 58, no. 1 (February, 1992), https://www.jstor.org/stable/2210475?origin=crossref&seq=1#metadata_info_tab_contents.

Page 290. **Making matters even more difficult:** Turner, "Juneteenth," in *Lone Star Pasts*, 146–47.

Page 290. **Further, freedpeople were barred:** Turner, "Juneteenth," in *Lone Star Pasts*, 143–75; and Barry A. Crouch, *The Freedmen's Bureau and Black Texans* (Austin: Univ. of Texas Press, 1999).

Page 290. **A woman named Susan Merritt of Rusk County, Texas:** Turner, "Juneteenth," in *Lone Star Pasts*, 147; and Ron C. Tyler and Lawrence R. Murphy, ed., *The Slave Narratives of Texas* (Austin, TX: Encino Press, 1974), 121.

Page 291. **"man read the paper telling us we were free":** Turner, "Juneteenth," in *Lone Star Pasts*, 147.

Page 291. **As Felix Haywood said:** Turner, "Juneteenth," in *Lone Star Pasts*, 148; and Tyler and Murphy, *The Slave Narratives of Texas*, 114.

Page 291. **In 1863, when the Emancipation Proclamation was signed:** Board of Governors of the Federal Reserve System, "Distribution of Household Wealth in the U.S. since 1989," https://www.federalreserve.gov/releases/z1/dataviz/dfa/distribute/table/.

Page 296. **"This Fourth July is *yours*, not *mine*":** Frederick Douglass, *Oration, Delivered in Corinthian Hall, Rochester, by Frederick Douglass, July 5th 1852, Published by Request* (Rochester: Printed by Lee, Mann & Co., American Building, 1852), 15, http://www.lib.rochester.edu/IN/RBSCP/Frederick_Douglass/ATTACHMENTS/Douglass_Fifth_of_July_Speech.pdf.

Page 307. **Texas, the home of one in ten public school students in the country:** https://tea.texas.gov/sites/default/files/enroll_2019-20.pdf.

Page 308. **In 2015, the State Board of Education:** Laura Isensee, "Why Calling Slaves 'Workers' Is More Than an Editing Error," Houston Public Media News 88.7, NPR, October 23, 2015.

Notes

Page 308. **A textbook that had been used at the school:** Annabelle Timsit and Annalisa Merelli, "For 10 Years, Students in Texas Have Used a History Textbook That Says Not All Slaves Were Unhappy," *Quartz*, May 11, 2018.

Page 308. **"central role":** https://www.npr.org/2018/11/16/668557179/texas-students-will-soon-learn-slavery-played-a-central-role-in-the-civil-war.

"We were the good guys, right?"
NEW YORK CITY

Page 314. **Summarizing the work of historian David Blight:** Ta-Nehisi Coates, "Slavery Made America," *The Atlantic*, June 24, 2014.

Page 316. **"*Racism* is first and foremost":** Barbara E. Fields and Karen J. Fields, *Racecraft: The Soul of Inequality in American Life* (Brooklyn, NY: Verso, 2014), 17.

Page 317. **It's likely that some of the wood:** Ira Berlin and Leslie M. Harris, "Uncovering, Discovering, and Recovering: Digging in New York's Slave Past Beyond the African Burial Ground," in *Slavery in New York*, ed. Ira Berlin and Leslie M. Harris (New York: New Press, 2005), 1–28.

Page 319. **The Dutch, however, did scramble to defend themselves:** "The Dutch and the Native Americans," *Atlantic World Home*, Library of Congress, accessed October 18, 2020, http://international.loc.gov/intldl/awkbhtml/kb-1/kb-1-2-4.html.

Page 320. **"a bulwark against the people":** W. J. Sidis, *The Tribes and the States* (unpublished manuscript, ca. 1935), chap. 7, http://www.mortenbrask.com/wp-content/uploads/The-tribes-and-the-states-SIDIS.pdf.

Page 320. **Peter Stuyvesant, director general of the colony:** Christopher Moore, "A World of Possibilities: Slavery and Freedom in Dutch New Amsterdam," in *Slavery in New York*, ed. Ira Berlin and Leslie Harris (New York: New Press, 2005), 51.

Notes

Page 322. **In February 1915, French wrote:** Freeman Henry Morris Murray, *Emancipation and the Freed in American Sculpture: A Study in Interpretation* (Washington, DC: published by the author, 1916), 214–15.

Page 322. **Historians generally estimate that:** Donald L. Fixico, "When Native Americans Were Slaughtered in the Name of 'Civilization,'" History Stories, History.com, March 2, 2018, last modified August 16, 2019, https://www.history.com/news/native-americans-genocide-united-states.

Page 323. **"the hordes of India":** Michael Richman, Daniel Chester French, and Metropolitan Museum of Art (New York), *Daniel Chester French, an American Sculptor* (New York: Preservation Press, 1983), 108.

Page 324. **During parts of the seventeenth and eighteenth centuries:** Berlin and Harris, "Uncovering, Discovering, and Recovering," in *Slavery in New York*, 1–28.

Page 324. **As the American Revolution began:** Eric Foner, *Gateway to Freedom: The Hidden History of America's Fugitive Slaves* (Oxford, UK: Oxford Univ. Press, 2015), 30.

Page 324. **In the early days of the Dutch settlement:** Berlin and Harris, "Uncovering, Discovering, and Recovering," in *Slavery in New York*, 1–28.

Page 324. **This land, however, was not given out of benevolence:** Berlin and Harris, "Uncovering, Discovering, and Recovering," in *Slavery in New York*, 1–28.

Page 325. **As Berlin and Harris write:** Berlin and Harris, "Uncovering, Discovering, and Recovering," in *Slavery in New York*, 9.

Page 326. **The British in New York became increasingly dependent:** Jill Lepore, "The Tightening Vise: Slavery and Freedom in British New York," in *Slavery in New York*, ed. Ira Berlin and Leslie Harris (New York: New Press, 2005), 61.

Page 326. **British Manhattan owned enslaved people:** David Brion Davis, *Inhuman Bondage: The Rise and Fall of Slavery in the New World* (New York: Oxford Univ. Press, 2008), 129, https://books.google.com/

books?id=cPn3N0CvKyAC&q=in+british+manhattan#v=snippet&q=in%20british%20manhattan&f=false.

Page 326. **According to historian Jill Lepore:** Lepore, "The Tightening Vise," in *Slavery in New York*, 62.

Page 326. **Berlin and Harris referred to New York:** Berlin and Harris, "Uncovering, Discovering, and Recovering," in *Slavery in New York*, 12.

Page 327. **to free the enslaved people they owned:** Lepore, "The Tightening Vise," in *Slavery in New York*, 81.

Page 327. **"Over one hundred and fifty accused witches":** Lepore, "The Tightening Vise," in *Slavery in New York*, 86.

Page 328. **less likely to plan a mass rebellion:** Lepore, "The Tightening Vise," in *Slavery in New York*, 87–88.

Page 328. **On the eve of the American Revolution:** Eric Foner, "Slavery and Freedom in New York City," Longreads.com, posted April 30, 2015, excerpt from *Gateway to Freedom: The Hidden History of the Underground Railroad* (New York: W. W. Norton, 2015), chap. 1.

Page 328. **On a visit to the colony one traveler complained:** Lepore, "The Tightening Vise," in *Slavery in New York*, 60.

Page 329. **The first and final thing an enslaved person did:** Lepore, "The Tightening Vise," in *Slavery in New York*, 75.

Page 332. **"Coromantee and Pawpaw peoples of Ghana":** "Mannahatta Park: New York's Municipal Slave Market," NYC Parks, https://www.nycgovparks.org/parks/mannahatta-park/highlights/19696.

Page 332. **"is what is on the marker":** Allison Meier, "Wall Street's 18th-Century Slave Market Finally Recognized with Historic Marker," *Hyperallergic,* July 3, 2015.

Page 333. **Moses Taylor, a nineteenth-century banker:** James C. Cobb, "Cleansing American Culture of Ties to Slavery Will Be Harder Than You Think," *Time,* March 30, 2016.

Page 334. **"plantation owners defaulted on the loans":** Makebra M. Anderson, "JPMorgan Chase & Co. Admits Link to Slavery," *St. Louis American,* February 2, 2005, last modified April 13, 2016.

Notes

Page 334. **By 1822, more than half of the goods shipped:** David Quigley, "Southern Slavery in a Free City: Economy, Politics, and Culture," in *Slavery in New York*, ed. Ira Berlin and Leslie Harris (New York: New Press, 2005), 269.

Page 334. **paraphrasing what Wood indeed proposed:** "Fernando Wood," National Park Service, accessed October 18, 2020, https://www.nps.gov/people/fernando-wood.htm.

Page 337. **In 1834, for example:** "Tappan Brothers," Mapping the African American Past (MAPP) website, accessed October 18, 2020, https://maap.columbia.edu/place/5.html.

Page 337. **According to Berlin, in his book:** Ira Berlin, *The Long Emancipation: The Demise of Slavery in the United States* (Cambridge, MA: Harvard Univ. Press, 2015), 134–35.

Page 339. **"suspicion of being a runaway":** Quigley, "Southern Slavery in a Free City," in *Slavery in New York*, 281.

Page 340. **As historian Manisha Sinha writes:** Manisha Sinha, "Black Abolitionism: The Assault on Southern Slavery and the Struggle for Racial Equality," in *Slavery in New York*, ed. Ira Berlin and Leslie Harris (New York: New Press, 2005), 241.

Page 340. **In its 1823 annual meeting, the ACS calculated:** Sinha, "Black Abolitionism," in *Slavery in New York*, 239–62.

Page 340. **In 1829, the New York arm of the ACS concluded:** Sinha, "Black Abolitionism," in *Slavery in New York*, 243.

Page 341. **At the New York State Constitutional Convention:** Patrick Rael, "The Long Death of Slavery," in *Slavery in New York*, ed. Ira Berlin and Leslie Harris (New York: New Press, 2005), 140.

Page 341. **As historian Patrick Rael writes:** Rael, "The Long Death of Slavery," in *Slavery in New York*, 143.

Page 344. **In 1697, New York City instituted:** Alondra Nelson, *The Social Life of DNA: Race, Reparations, and Reconciliation After the Genome* (Boston: Beacon Press, 2016), 44.

Page 345. **Historians estimate that this burial ground:** "African Burial Ground: History & Culture," National Park Service, last modified April 26, 2019, https://www.nps.gov/afbg/learn/historyculture/index.htm.

Notes

Page 345. **And finally, they unearthed the intact skeletal remains:** Christopher Moore, "New York's Seventeenth-Century African Burial Ground in History," National Park Service, last modified April 26, 2019, https://www.nps.gov/afbg/learn/historyculture/african-burial-ground-in-history.htm.

Page 346. **Infant mortality rates in the colony were high:** Lepore, "The Tightening Vise," in *Slavery in New York*, 57–90.

Page 347. **The distance between their homes and the cemetery:** Moore, "New York's Seventeenth-Century African Burial Ground," https://www.nps.gov/afbg/learn/historyculture/african-burial-ground-in-history.htm.

Page 347. **The harm done did not end after a person's funeral:** De Costa and Miller, "American Resurrection and the 1788 New York Doctors' Riot," 292–93.

Page 348. **Each crypt—along with nearly eight thousand handwritten letters:** Moore, "New York's Seventeenth-Century African Burial Ground," https://www.nps.gov/afbg/learn/historyculture/african-burial-ground-in-history.htm.

Page 348. **"no slavery in colonial New York":** Spencer P. M. Harrington, "Bones and Bureaucrats," *Archaeology*, March/April 1993 (online archive June 14, 2006).

Page 350. **Evidence based on church records suggests:** "The Lost Neighborhood Under New York's Central Park," produced by Ranjani Chakraborty and Melissa Hirsch, *Vox*, Missing Chapter, online video, 8:15, January 20, 2020.

Page 351. **That same day, Epiphany Davis:** Douglas Martin, "Before Park, Black Village; Students Look into a Community's History," *New York Times*, April 7, 1995.

Page 351. **In 1850, there were seventy-one Black people:** Martin, "Before Park, Black Village."

Page 352. **According to public historian Cynthia Copeland:** "The Lost Neighborhood Under New York's Central Park," *Vox* video.

Page 352. **A July 1856 article in the New-York Daily Times:** "The Present Look of Our Great Central Park," *New-York Daily Times*, July 9, 1856,

3, https://www.nytimes.com/1856/07/09/archives/newyork
-city-the-present-look-of-our-great-central-park-tired-of.html.

Page 352. **Another *New-York Daily Times* article:** Martin,
"Before Park, Black Village."

Page 354. **In May of 2019, a new museum opened:** "Imagining Liberty," Museum Management Program, National Park
Service, accessed October 18, 2020, https://www.nps.gov/
museum/exhibits/statue_liberty/imagining_liberty.html.

Page 356. **James Baldwin's 1960 short story:** James Baldwin,
"This Morning, This Evening, So Soon," *The Atlantic,* September 1960.

Page 356. **"One of the first meanings [of the statue]":** Gillian
Brockell, "The Statue of Liberty Was Created to Celebrate
Freed Slaves, Not Immigrants, Its New Museum Recounts,"
Washington Post, May 23, 2019.

Page 359. **"There is no question that feelings between":** Alan Kraut, email message to author, September
1, 2020.

"One slave is too much"
GORÉE ISLAND

Page 366. **Its position just off the west coast of
the Senegambia region:** "Gorée Island," Slavery and
Remembrance, The Colonial Williamsburg Foundation, accessed November 9, 2019, http://slaveryandremembrance.org
/articles/article/?id=A0110.

Page 367. **It was also a place from which captured Africans
could not easily escape:** "Goree: Senegal's Slave Island,"
BBC News, June 27, 2013.

Page 368. **"It is not easy for a white man":** "Goree: Senegal's
Slave Island," *BBC News.*

Page 370. **often owned and traded enslaved people themselves:** Joseph-Roger de Benoist and Abdoulaye Camara,
"Gorée dans l'histoire," in *Histoire de Gorée,* ed. Joseph-Roger de

Notes

Benoist and Abdoulaye Camara (Paris: Maisonneuve & Larose, 2003), 11–29.

Page 370. **In 1960, when Senegal became independent of France:** Deborah L. Mack, "When the Evidence Changes: Scholarship, Memory, and Public Culture at the House of Slaves, Gorée Island," *Exhibitionist* (Fall 2011): 40–45.

Page 371. **Historian Deborah Mack writes:** Mack, "When the Evidence Changes," 40–45.

Page 379. **it was an assertion supported by the United Nations:** "Island of Gorée," World Heritage List, UNESCO website, accessed October 25, 2020, https://whc.unesco.org/en/list/26/#:~:text=The%20 island%20of%20Gorée%20lies,centre%20on%20the%20Afri-can%20coast.

Page 379. **Scholars now estimate that it was closer to 33,000:** Max Fisher, "The Sincere Fiction of Goree Island, Africa's Best-Known Slave Trade Memorial," *Washington Post,* July 1, 2013.

Page 381. **When considering the story of Gorée Island:** Fisher, "The Sincere Fiction of Goree Island."

Page 381. **Richard told the *Washington Post*:** Fisher, "The Sincere Fiction of Goree Island."

Page 394. **Walter Rodney, the Guyanese historian:** Walter Rodney, *How Europe Underdeveloped Africa* (Brooklyn, NY: Verso, 2018), 34.

Page 401. **The only essential connection that has existed:** Darrel Moellendorf, "Racism and Rationality in Hegel's Philosophy of Subjective Spirit," *History of Political Thought* 13, no. 2 (1992): 243–55.

Page 401. **"*Negroes,* uninterested and lacking in interest":** Teshale Tibebu, *Hegel and the Third World: The Making of Eurocentrism in World History* (Syracuse, NY: Syracuse Univ. Press, 2011), 83.

Page 401. **"It is in the *Caucasian* race":** Tibebu, *Hegel and the Third World,* 272.

Page 402. **A prime example is Immanuel Kant:** Charles

Notes

W. Mills, "Kant's *Untermenschen*," in *Race and Racism in Modern Philosophy*, ed. Andrew Valls (Ithaca, NY: Cornell Univ. Press, 2005), 173.

"I lived it"
EPILOGUE

Page 412. **Emmett had never touched her:** Richard Pérez-Peña, "Woman Linked to 1955 Emmett Till Murder Tells Historian Her Claims Were False," *New York Times,* January 27, 2017.

ABOUT THIS PROJECT

Page 443. **As the Library of Congress notes:** "The Limitations of the Slave Narrative Collection," from *Born in Slavery: Slave Narratives from the Federal Writers' Project, 1936 to 1938* collection, Library of Congress, accessed October 15, 2020, https://www.loc.gov/collections/slave-narratives-from-the-federal-writers-project-1936-to-1938/articles-and-essays/introduction-to-the-wpa-slave-narratives/limitations-of-the-slave-narrative-collection/.

Page 443. **Scholar Saidiya V. Hartman may have put it best:** Saidiya V. Hartman, *Scenes of Subjection: Terror, Slavery, and Self-Making in Nineteenth-Century America* (New York: Oxford Univ. Press, 1997), 11. "The Limitations of the Slave Narrative Collection."

ABOUT THE AUTHOR

Clint Smith is a staff writer at *The Atlantic* and the author of *Counting Descent,* which won the 2017 Literary Award for Best Poetry Book from the Black Caucus of the American Library Association and was a finalist for an NAACP Image Award. Clint has received fellowships from New America, the Art for Justice Fund, Cave Canem, and the National Science Foundation. His writing has been published in *The New Yorker,* the *New York Times Magazine, Poetry* magazine, *The Paris Review,* and elsewhere. He received his BA in English from Davidson College and his PhD in Education from Harvard University.